WINTER SPORTS RECORDS

This edition published in 2012

Copyright © Carlton Books Limited 2012

Carlton Books Limited
20 Mortimer Street
London W1T 3JW

A CIP catalogue record for this book is available from the British Library

10 9 8 7 6 5 4 3 2 1

ISBN: 978-1-78097-166-7

Editor: Martin Corteel
Design Direction: Darren Jordan
Design: eMC Design
Picture Research: Paul Langan
Production: Rachel Burgess

Printed in Dubai

Above: Blair Morgan
powers his snowcross
bike to quarter-final
victory at the 2006
Winter X Games.

WINTER SPORTS RECORDS

CHRIS HAWKES

CARLTON

CONTENTS

Above: The call of the wild is at its loudest as Iditarod mushers drive forward their teams of dogs across the ice and frozen snow of Alaska.

INTRODUCTION

Welcome to the first edition of *Winter Sports Records*, a book that celebrates the finest achievements in the vast world of winter sports, from the fast-paced, adrenaline-fuelled action on the alpine slopes and bobsleigh tracks, to the grace and sheer athleticism found on figure-skating rinks, to the more sedate, strategic battles that occur in curling arenas around the world.

One of the marvels of mankind has been not only its endless capacity to adapt to the varied environments in which it finds itself, but then to take the most perfunctory of actions and turn it into a form of competition. Winter sports, perhaps more than any other of the vast array of sports practised by people around the globe, fall directly into this category. Take alpine skiing and dog-sled racing, for example: both, essentially, find their roots as a means of transport, an innovative way in which to get from A to B across a difficult terrain, and both of which now feature heavily on the winter sports calendar. In short, mankind's mantra over the centuries, a particularly refreshing one, has been, if there's an ice-covered slope, we shall race down it; if there's a frozen pond, we shall find a way of sliding across it – and from such a mantra hundreds of sports have been born.

The aims of this book were numerous: to represent as many of the vast number of winter sports as possible; to highlight as many of the incredible personal achievements of a manifold number of athletes as possible – feats that, too often perhaps, pass unnoticed in a world more familiar with football and Formula One; and to bring those achievements back to life in as innovative a way as possible to a new generation of readers.

Fortunately, that task was made much easier by the vast platform of statistics available in this digital age: databases recording the achievements of numerous athletes in various arenas are readily available to all who choose to delve into them – and without the considerable efforts of others, a book such as this would not be possible. I owe a huge debt of thanks to those who have put together websites on all the sports covered in this book.

I also owe a huge thank you to the number of individuals who have worked tirelessly behind the scenes to put a book such as this together: to my editor Martin Corteel, whose unflagging words of encouragement and cajolement continue to help me across the finishing line; to copy-editor Steve Dobel, whose assiduous eye to the finest of details ensures the copy in the book is as fine-tuned as it is possible to be; to Darren Jordan, whose creative flair helps lift the pages in this book; to Paul Langan, whose tireless search through archives to find the relevant photographs have helped bring the words contained in this book to life; and to Rachel Burgess, whose production skills ensure the work of others is brought together in as seamless a manner as possible.

My final thanks go to you, the reader. I hope the time you spend among the pages of this book is as enjoyable as it was to put them together.

Chris Hawkes
Savigny-le-Vieux, May 2012

Above: Stefan Gimpl flies high during his winning run in the 2007–08 FIS Snowboarding World Cup Big Air finals; it was the second of four World Cup victories for the Austrian.

Above: The United States' Lindsey Vonn, who won Winter Games gold medals in the downhill and Super-G at Vancouver 2010 is right on her edges as she skis to victory the March 2012 FIS Alpine Ski World Cup women's giant slalom event at Are, Sweden.

Chapter 1

SKIING

Alpine skiing sports (defined as sliding events in which competitors use skis with fixed- or free-heel bindings) include: downhill, giant slalom and Super-G skiing; ski jumping; cross-country skiing; and Nordic combined (a combination of ski jumping and cross-country skiing). All of these disciplines are governed by the International Ski Federation, which oversees skiing competitions at World Cups and World Championships, and are considered to be among the blue riband events at the Winter Olympic Games.

Below: Swiss downhiller Ambrosi Hoffman launches himself out of the gate at the start of a practice run at Wengen, Switzerland.

Men's Alpine Skiing: Olympic Games

Men's alpine skiing made its Winter Olympic Games debut at Garmisch-Partenkirchen, Germany, in 1936 with a combined event; downhill and slalom competitions were added in 1948; the giant slalom made its first appearance on the roster four years later, and the Super-G was contested for the first time at Calgary 1988.

Below: Kjetil André Aamodt is both the youngest and oldest Olympic Alpine skiing medallist.

THE MADMAN OF DOWNHILL

Born in Paris, but a resident of Val d'Isère from the age of six, Henri Oreiller earned a reputation as an audacious skier in his youth and, after becoming France's national champion, earned the nicknames "The Parisian of Val d'Isère" and, memorably, "The Madman of Downhill". His crowning moment came at the 1948 Winter Games in St-Moritz, Switzerland, when he stormed to the gold medal in the men's downhill (the first time the event had been staged) with an all-time record four-second winning margin. And the glory didn't end there; Oreiller also went on to pick up the combined title.

MOST MEDALS WON (OVERALL): TOP FIVE

Pos	Medals	Name (country)	G	S	B
1	8	Kjetil André Aamodt (Norway)	4	2	2
2	5	Alberto Tomba (Italy)	3	2	0
3	5	Lasse Kjus (Norway)	1	3	1
=	5	Bode Miller (USA)	1	3	1
5	4	Hermann Maier (Austria)	2	1	1
=	4	Benjamin Raich (Austria)	2	0	2
=	4	Stephan Eberharter (Austria)	1	2	1

THE WINTER GAMES' FIRST CHAMPION

Given his status as one of the pre-event favourites, Franz Pfnür would have been disappointed to find himself 4.4 seconds behind the leader following the downhill section of the men's combined event at Garmisch-Partenkirchen 1936 (in alpine skiing's first appearance at the Winter Games), albeit that his strongest discipline, the slalom (at which he was world champion in 1934), was still to come. And what a performance the 27-year-old German produced, clocking the fastest time in both runs (72.1 and 74.5 seconds) to storm to gold and etch his name in history as the Winter Games' first-ever alpine skiing champion.

Above: Henri Oreiller was the first Olympic downhill champion.

THE BLITZ FROM KITZ

Toni Sailer got his Winter Olympic career off to a spectacular start when he stormed to the gold medal in the first alpine skiing event at Cortina d'Ampezzo 1956, the men's giant slalom, with a winning margin of 6.2 seconds (the most dominant win in Olympic alpine skiing history) and picked up his second gold medal two days later, in the slalom, in equally dominant fashion (by a full four seconds). Four days later the 20-year-old Austrian, known as "The Blitz from Kitz", entered the third and final alpine skiing event, the downhill, oozing confidence, and continued his staggering dominance – he posted the fastest time (by 3.5 seconds) to become the first alpine skier in Winter Olympic Games history to complete a clean sweep of medals.

Right: Toni Sailer won a clean sweep of gold medals at the 1956 Games and did so by huge margins each time.

ON TOP OF THE OLYMPIC PILE

Perhaps the most versatile skier in history, Norway's Kjetil André Aamodt is the most decorated alpine skier in Winter Games history, with eight medals (four of them gold). He holds a host of other Winter Olympic alpine skiing records: he is both the youngest medallist (he was 20, at Albertville 1992) and the oldest (34, at Turin 2006); is the only skier to collect medals at four separate editions of the Games (in 1992, 1994, 2002 and 2006); and is the only male skier to make a successful defence of the Super-G title at the Games (he won gold in 2002 and 2006).

ALL THAT GLITTERS

Norway's Lasse Kjus (gold medallist in the men's combined at Lillehammer 1994) and the United States' Bode Miller (gold medallist in the men's super combined at Vancouver 2010) have both enjoyed golden moments at the Winter Games, but it hasn't always been the top spot on the podium for the duo. The pair share the record for the most silver medals won in competition at the Games: three – Kjus in the combined and downhill at Nagano 1988 and in the downhill at Salt Lake City 2002; and Miller in the giant slalom and slalom at Salt Lake City 2002 and in the Super-G at Vancouver 2010.

SLALOM SHOCK AT ST-MORITZ

While Henri Oreiller's domination of the men's downhill and combined events at the 1948 Winter Games at St-Moritz, did not come as a major surprise, Edi Reinalter's success in the men's slalom sent shockwaves of surprise through an ecstatic home crowd. The little-heralded Swiss skier produced a sensational second run (62.6 seconds) to overturn a 0.2-second deficit to France's James Couttet and become the Winter Games' first-ever men's slalom champion. It was the greatest moment of his career: perhaps knowing that his golden moment could never be beaten, Reinalter retired from the sport at the end of the year.

JUBILANT JOHNSON MAKES HISTORY

History was against Bill Johnson's bid for gold in the men's downhill at Sarajevo 1984: no American had ever won an alpine skiing gold medal at the Games, although two had won silver – Billy Kidd (1964) and Phil Mahre (1980), both in the slalom. But when race day arrived, the 23-year-old Californian, on a course perfectly suited to his gliding style, defied the odds in spectacular style, clocking 1:45.9 (0.27 seconds ahead of Switzerland's Peter Müller) to become not only the first American but also the first non-European to win the men's downhill at the Winter Games.

Right: "Wild" Bill Johnson shocked the skiing world with his 1984 downhill gold medal.

STEIN STRIKES GIANT SLALOM GOLD

Having been contested at the Alpine World Skiing Championships since 1950, the men's giant slalom was contested at the Winter Games for the first time at Oslo 1952. And although reigning world champion Zeno Colò of Italy was considered the firm favourite to claim the title, Norway's Stein Eriksen gave the home crowd cause for cheer when he clocked 2:25.0 to take the spoils – a full 1.9 seconds ahead of second-placed Christian Pravda of Austria and 4.1 seconds ahead of fourth-placed Colò – and become the first skier in history from a non-Alpine country to win a gold medal at the Winter Games.

FIRST SUPER-G CHAMPION

Having been contested as a World Cup event since 1983 and as part of the Alpine Skiing World Championships since 1987, the men's Super-G finally made its debut at the Winter Games at Calgary, Canada, in 1988, with reigning world champion Pirmin Zurbriggen (who had already stormed to success in the men's downhill) strongly tipped to win the gold medal. But while Zurbriggen disappointed to finish fifth, France's Frank Piccard (who had taken bronze in the men's downhill) struck gold, clocking 1:39.66 (a full 1.03 seconds ahead of Austria's Helmut Mayer) to become the first-ever Super-G champion at the Winter Games.

Above: Chiharu Igaya's slalom silver medal was a bigger surprise than Toni Sailer's gold at Cortina in 1956.

Left: Frank Piccard was France's first Alpine skiing Olympic gold medallist since the legendary Jean-Claude Killy in 1968.

IGAYA MAKES HISTORY

Although Austria's Toni Sailer grabbed the majority of the plaudits following his stunning victory in the men's slalom (to complete part two of his history-making sweep of the gold medals at Cortina d'Ampezzo 1956) by the breathtaking margin of four seconds, he wasn't the only competitor to carve his name in the record books. In finishing second, Japan's Chiharu Igaya (who had trained in the United States while a student at Dartmouth College) became the first, and to date only, Asian in history to pick up an alpine skiing medal at the Winter Games.

SMALLEST WINNING MARGIN

Given that he had only ever won six World Cup races in the Super-G over the previous six years, Markus Wasmeier's gold medal in the event at Lillehammer 1994 caused much surprise. But the 30-year-old German proved he was in the form of his life, when, six days later, he triumphed in the men's giant slalom as well, albeit by the slenderest of margins: his 0.02-second winning margin over second-placed Urs Kälin of Switzerland is the smallest ever in alpine skiing at the Winter Games.

MOST MEDALS WON (BY COUNTRY): TOP TEN

Pos	Medals	Country	G	S	B
1	61	Austria	20	18	23
2	31	Switzerland	8	12	11
3	25	Norway	9	9	7
4	24	France	11	7	6
5	15	Italy	8	6	1
=	15	USA	5	7	3
7	7	Germany	4	2	1
8	5	Sweden	1	0	4
9	3	Croatia	0	3	0
=	3	Liechtenstein	0	1	2

SPANISH SURPRISE

Everyone expected the men's slalom event at Sapporo 1972 to be a shootout between France's Jean-Noël Augert (the 1970 world slalom champion) and Italy's Gustav Thöni (considered the best technical skier in the world at the time). Augert (55.77 seconds) lay in second place after the first run, while Thöni (56.69) struggled to fifth. In first place was Spain's Francisco Fernández Ochoa (a skier with no significant international record), although few expected him to stay there after the second run. They were wrong: as Augert slipped to eighth and Thöni produced the fastest time in the second run to finish second, Ochoa held his nerve to become Spain's first, and to date only, gold medallist at the Winter Games.

Left: Francisco Fernández Ochoa is still Spain's only Winter Games gold medallist.

DOUBLE SILVER TROUBLE FOR THÖNI

If Italy's Gustav Thöni expected to put the disappointment of having to settle for a silver medal in the men's slalom at the 1972 Winter Games in Sapporo behind him at Innsbruck 1976 (despite the fact he had claimed men's giant slalom gold), he was wrong. Although the 24-year-old Italian managed to better the time of pre-race favourite Ingemar Stenmark of Sweden, he still finished 0.44 seconds behind compatriot Piero Gros to become the first man in history to win back-to-back silver medals in an alpine skiing event at the Winter Games.

TERRIFIC TOMBA

After Calgary 1988, Alpine skiing's 11th appearance at the Winter Games, the notion of defending an Olympic title had become the sport's version of the Holy Grail – no skier had managed to achieve the feat in the 42 events staged to date. But Italy's Alberto Tomba changed all that at Albertville 1992: the 1988 men's giant slalom champion produced the fastest time in both runs to see off the challenge of the event's 131 participants (a Winter Games record for any event) to become the first male alpine skier in history to make a successful defence of an Olympic crown.

GIANT FIELD

The men's giant slalom event at the 2010 Winter Games in Vancouver, Canada, in which Switzerland's Carlo Janka claimed the gold medal, was notable for another reason: the event featured competitors from 60 different countries – including from the Cayman Islands (Dow Travers) and Pakistan (Muhammad Abbas) for the first time in Winter Olympic competition – an all-time record in an event in the Winter Games.

MOST GOLD MEDALS WON (BY EVENT)

Event	No	Country
Downhill	7	Austria
Slalom	6	Austria
Giant slalom	4	Austria, Switzerland
Super-G	4	Norway
Combined	2	Austria, Norway, USA

Below: Alberto Tomba was Italy's skiing hero for more than a decade.

FIS Alpine Ski World Cup

The FIS Alpine Ski World Cup is a top international circuit of alpine skiing competitions staged annually. Competitors vie for points at each event during the season, at the end of which the overall World Cup trophy is awarded to the skier with the most points, and smaller trophies are awarded to those with the most points in each individual discipline.

Above: The first World Cup winner, Jean-Claude Killy remains France's finest Alpine skier.

KILLY A CUT ABOVE THE REST

The first FIS Alpine Ski World Cup was contested in 1967 and consisted of 17 races (11 in Europe and six in the United States) in slalom, giant slalom and downhill. France's Jean-Claude Killy dominated the championship, winning 12 of the races to become the inaugural champion. And the French star's domination continued the following year: he won six of the 20 races staged to become the first man in history to defend his overall FIS Alpine Ski World Cup title.

HAT-TRICK HERO THÖNI SETS NEW STANDARDS

The greatest technical skier of his generation, Gustav Thöni won the first-ever World Cup race he entered – the giant slalom at Val d'Isère in December 1969 – and went on to finish his rookie season an impressive third in the overall standings. The Italian was just getting started: the following season (1971), thanks to his domination of the slalom and giant slalom, he won the overall title for the first time. He repeated the feat the following year and in 1973 became the first skier in history to win three successive overall World Cup titles. A fourth success came in 1975.

FIVE OF THE BEST FOR GIRARDELLI

A skier who was born in Austria but famously switched his allegiance to Luxembourg following disagreements over the Austrian team's training methods, Marc Girardelli made his FIS Alpine Ski World Cup debut in 1980, secured his first podium the following year (in the slalom at Wengen) and was a regular contender (in slalom and giant slalom) from that moment on. He overcame a serious knee injury to collect his first overall World Cup title in 1985 (thanks to 11 race victories), defended it the following year and picked up the crown for the third time in 1989. A fourth title followed in 1991 to equal Gustav Thöni's record-breaking haul (before he garnered a history-making fifth title in 1993).

MOST INDIVIDUAL RACE WINS

Three men hold the record for the most World Cup race wins in the combined: Marc Girardelli (Luxembourg, between 1985 and 1996), Pirmin Zurbriggen (Switzerland, between 1982 and 1990), and Phil Mahre (USA, between 1979 and 1983) all achieved 11 victories.

Left: Gustavo Thöni used his technical brilliance to dominate slalom events in the early 1970s.

Left: Ingemar Stenmark knew he was the best in slalom events, so he rarely even entered downhills.

MOST WORLD CUP RACE WINS: TOP TEN

Pos	Wins	Name (country, span)	D	S-G	GS	S	C
1	86	Ingemar Stenmark (Sweden, 1973–89)	-	-	46	40	-
2	54	Hermann Maier (Austria, 1996–2009)	15	24	14	-	1
3	50	Alberto Tomba (Italy, 1986–98)	-	-	15	35	-
4	46	Marc Girardelli (Luxembourg, 1980–96)	3	9	7	16	11
5	40	Pirmin Zurbriggen (Switzerland, 1981–90)	10	10	7	2	11
6	35	Benjamin Raich (Austria, 1997–)	-	-	14	14	7
7	32	Bode Miller (USA, 1997–)	7	5	9	5	6
8	29	Stephan Eberharter (Austria, 1989–2004)	18	6	5	-	-
9	27	Phil Mahre (USA, 1975–84)	-	-	7	9	11
10	26	Franz Klammer (Austria, 1972–85)	25	-	-	-	1

THE BEST IN THE BUSINESS

Born in Lapland, Sweden, and a national competition winner by the age of eight, Ingemar Stenmark developed into the most dominant slalom and giant slalom skier of all time. And although he famously declined to compete in many downhill events, preferring to leave the dangers of the high-speed event to others of a more daring nature, his technical prowess saw him to three overall World Cup titles (in 1975, 1976 and 1977) and to a number of all-time records: the most wins (86); the most career podiums (155); the most race wins in a single season (13 in 1977 – a record he shares with Austria's Hermann Maier); the most World Cup titles in giant slalom (8) and slalom (8); and most race wins in both giant slalom (46) and slalom (40).

THE FRANZ KLAMMER EXPRESS

A downhill specialist remembered more for his bravery and raw speed than for any technical prowess or elegance, Austria's Franz Klammer first came to prominence in 1973, when, aged 19, he finished second in the men's downhill in front of his fellow countrymen at St Anton. His first race win came the following year, and in 1975 he won eight times to collect the first of five World Cup downhill titles (the others came in 1976, 1977, 1978 and 1983). By the time he retired in 1985, Klammer, by then known as "The Kaiser", held the all-time World Cup record for the most downhill victories (25).

THE HERMINATOR

A relative latecomer to the FIS Alpine World Cup scene (he was 23 years old when he claimed his first points, in 1996), Austria's Hermann Maier, known as "The Herminator", made a mockery of those who, because of his slight build as a youth, had dismissed his chances of ever developing into a top-class skier by becoming a double Olympic champion, a three-time world champion and a four-time overall World Cup winner (in 1998, 2000, 2001 and 2004). He established all-time World Cup records for: the most overall Super-G World Cup titles (five); the most career Super-G race wins (24); and shares the record, with Ingemar Stenmark, for the most race wins in a season (13 in 2001).

MR VERSATILITY

Generally accepted as the greatest American alpine skier of all time, Bode Miller first appeared on the FIS Alpine Ski World Cup scene as an 18-year-old in 1997. Renowned for his gung-ho, speed-at-all-costs approach, his first victory arrived in the giant slalom at Val d'Isère in December 2001, and his winning ways have continued ever since (with 33 World Cup race wins to date). One of seven men in World Cup history to have recorded at least one victory in each discipline he was able to race – Marc Girardelli (Luxembourg), Pirmin Zurbriggen (Switzerland), Kjetil André Aamodt, Jean-Claude Killy (France), Günther Mader (Austria) and Henri Duvillard (France) are the others – he is the only member of that elite group to have recorded at least five race wins in each category: downhill (8), slalom (5), giant slalom (9), Super-G (5) and combined (6).

Right: Few men have spent as long at the top of Alpine skiing as America's versatile superstar Bode Miller.

FIS Alpine World Ski Championships

Organized by the International Ski Federation (FIS), the first alpine skiing World Championships were held in 1931 and were staged on an annual basis until the outbreak of the Second World War. Between 1948 and 1982, the event was contested every second year, with the Winter Games acting as the World Championships in Olympic years. The competition has been staged in odd-numbered years since 1985.

MOST WORLD CHAMPIONSHIP MEDALS: TOP TEN

Pos	Medals	Name (country)	G	S	B
1	12	Kjetil André Aamodt (Norway)	5	4	3
2	11	Marc Girardelli (Luxembourg)	4	4	3
=	11	Lasse Kjus (Norway)	3	8	-
4	9	Pirmin Zurbriggen (Switzerland)	4	4	1
5	8	Anton Sailer (Austria)	7	1	-
=	8	Emile Allais (France)	4	4	-
7	7	Gustav Thöni (Italy)	5	2	-
=	7	Ingemar Stenmark (Sweden)	5	1	1
=	7	Rudolf Rominger (Switzerland)	4	1	2
=	7	David Zogg (Switzerland)	3	4	-
=	7	Benjamin Raich (Austria)	2	4	1

Right: Kjetil André Aamodt is used to winning medals at the biggest events.

MEDAL LEADER

An outstanding skier who enjoyed a headline-grabbing 16-year career on the international circuit (winning a record eight Olympic medals and recording 21 World Cup race wins), Kjetil André Aamodt picked up his first World Championship medal (a silver in the Super-G) at Saalbach 1991. It was the start of a glittering association with the event: his first gold medals arrived at Morioka 1993 (slalom and giant slalom), and by the time he competed in the event for the final time in 2005, he had collected an all-time championship record number of medals – 12 (five gold, four silver and three bronze).

SEELOS STRIKES HISTORIC DOUBLE GOLD

Remembered mostly in alpine skiing circles as the man who invented the parallel turn, Anton Seelos's job as a ski instructor meant he was barred from competing at the Winter Games. However, Seelos did get to taste glory in the World Championships, which were open to all-comers. At Innsbruck 1933, he won the slalom and combined events to become the first male skier in history to win two gold medals at a single World Championships. Later he also got to savour some Olympic success when he coached Christl Cranz to the gold medal in the women's combined at Garmisch-Partenkirchen 1936.

ALLAIS STORMS TO SENSATIONAL MEDAL SWEEP

Considered the first great French skier – and renowned founder of the Ecole Française de Ski (now the biggest ski school in the world) – Emile Allais first came to international prominence when he won two silver medals at the 1935 World Championships (in the downhill and the combined). He picked up a bronze medal in the men's combined at the 1936 Winter Games in Garmisch-Partenkirchen, Germany, but did even better at the following year's World Championships, winning the downhill, slalom and combined to become the first male skier in the competition's history to complete a clean sweep of the gold medals.

Right: Emile Allais set the benchmark for French skiing in the 1930s.

DOUBLE SLALOM JOY FOR ROMINGER

One of the early principal exponents of the Swiss Ski School and considered a specialist in each of the sport's disciplines, Rudolf Rominger first struck gold at the World Championships at Innsbruck, Austria, in 1936 when he won both the downhill and combined titles. He found himself on the top step of the podium for the third time in his career when he won the slalom event at the 1938 Championships at Engelberg, Austria, and made history the following year, in Zakopane, Poland, when he became the first man in World Championship history to make a successful defence of his slalom title.

CLASSY COLÒ MAKES DOWNHILL HISTORY

In the first 11 editions of the World Championships, no male skier had ever launched a successful defence of his downhill title; the closest to doing so was France's Emile Allais, who won the title in 1937 and finished runner-up the following year. So history was against Zeno Colò at Oslo 1952 (the Winter Games doubled as the World Championships that year) as he sought to defend the downhill title he had won at Aspen, Colorado, in 1950. But the Italian was the class act of the field, clocking 2:30.80 (1.2 seconds ahead of second-placed Othmar Schneider) to become not only Italy's first-ever gold medallist at the Winter Games but also the first man in World Championships history to win back-to-back downhill titles.

Right: Zeno Colò won double gold at Oslo in 1952.

THREE IN A ROW FOR STENMARK

Although he had been the pre-eminent performer in both slalom and giant slalom since the mid-1970s (he had been the World Cup season winner in both events in 1975, 1976 and 1977), it took time before Ingemar Stenmark enjoyed any success at the World Championships. That all changed at Garmisch-Partenkirchen 1978, when he stormed to gold in both the slalom and giant slalom. He defended both titles at the 1980 Winter Games (the event doubled as the World Championships that year) and, although he failed to defend his giant slalom title at Schladming, Austria, in 1982 (he finished second), the Swede won the slalom title to become the first, and to date only, male skier to record three successive wins in the event.

COUNTRY WITH MOST WORLD CHAMPIONSHIPS GOLD MEDALS

Austria (with 39 gold medals) leads the way, ahead of Switzerland (with 26). Austria also tops the list of silver medals won (with 39, compared to Switzerland's 29), while these alpine neighbours share the record for the most bronze medals won (32).

SKÄRDEL MAKES SUPER-G HISTORY

The Super-G was contested at the FIS Alpine World Ski Championships for the first time at Crans-Montana, Switzerland, in 1987 (with home favourite Pirmin Zurbriggen picking up the inaugural title). It wasn't until Sestriere 1997, however, that any skier made a successful defence of his title: 1996 champion Atle Skärdel of Norway (1:29.68) beat off the challenge of compatriot Lasse Kjus (1:29.89) to become the World Championships' first-ever back-to-back Super-G champion.

Right: Atle Skärdel led a Norwegian one–two in the Super-G at the 1997 World Championships.

Women's Alpine Skiing: Olympic Games

Women's alpine skiing first featured at the Winter Olympics (with a combined event) at the 1936 Games in Garmisch-Partenkirchen. Separate downhill and slalom events were added to the programme at St-Moritz 1948, the giant slalom was added four years later at Oslo 1952, and the Super-G became part of the roster at Calgary 1988 to complete the modern complement of five disciplines.

MOST MEDALS WON (OVERALL): TOP FIVE

Pos	Medals	Name (country, span)	G	S	B
1	6	Janica Kostelic (Croatia, 1998–2006)	4	2	0
=	6	Anja Pärson (Sweden, 2002–10)	1	1	4
3	5	Vreni Schneider (Switzerland, 1988–94)	3	1	1
=	5	Katja Seizinger (Germany, 1992–98)	3	0	2
5	4	Deborah Compagnoni (Italy, 1992–98)	3	1	0
=	4	Hanni Wenzel (Liechtenstein, 1976–80)	2	1	1

Right: Janica Kostelic came within 0.05 of a second from making it four Winter Olympics gold medals at Salt Lake City in 2002.

THE SNOW QUEEN OF CROATIA

Janica Kostelic made her Winter Games debut, aged 16, at Nagano 1998 (with a best finish of eighth in the combined). She won her first World Cup event the following year, but then suffered a serious knee injury that kept her out of action until late 2000. The Croatian rebounded in style, winning the overall World Cup title in 2001 (the first of three occasions). At Salt Lake City the following year she became the first female alpine skier in history to win three gold medals (in the combined, slalom and giant slalom) at a single Winter Games, and she also picked up silver in the Super-G. Her Olympic haul did not end there: in addition to a second successive Super-G silver medal, she defended her combined title at Turin 2006 to become the only woman in alpine skiing history to win four gold medals at the Winter Games. Her overall haul of six medals is also a record (shared with Sweden's Anja Pärson).

CLASS ACT OF THE FIELD

If Andrea Mead had caused a stir when she first competed at the Winter Games as a 15-year-old at St-Moritz in 1948 (finishing an impressive eighth in the slalom), she sent shockwaves through the sport four years later. The American, now 19, stormed to victory in the giant slalom (the first time the event had been contested at the Games) by an imposing 2.2-second margin over Dagmar Rom and then, six days later, repeated her dominance in the slalom to become the first alpine skier (of either sex) in history to win two gold medals at a single Winter Games.

SENSATIONAL SEIZINGER MAKES HISTORY

A former world junior champion and considered Germany's greatest-ever alpine skier, Katja Seizinger was arguably the strongest favourite in Olympic history to win the women's downhill title at Lillehammer 1994 (she had, after all, led the World Cup standings in the discipline since 1992). And the 21-year-old star did not disappoint: going off third, she clocked an impressive 1:35.93 – no one came close to beating it, and Seizinger had won her first Olympic title. She was at it again in Nagano four years later: running first on this occasion, she posted a time of 1:28.89 and, again, no one could match it. In the process, she had become the first, and to date only, female alpine skier in history to defend her Winter Olympic downhill title.

Right: Katja Seizinger, the first woman to retain her Olympic downhill title.

CRANZ STORMS TO GOLD

The outstanding favourite to win the inaugural women's alpine skiing title at Garmisch-Partenkirchen in 1936, having won the combined event at the 1934 and 1935 World Championships, Christl Cranz's chances of claiming the gold medal seemingly lay in tatters after a crash in the downhill section left her in sixth place and a massive 19 seconds behind the leader. But the 21-year-old German proved her class in the two slalom runs, recording a total time that was 11.3 seconds faster than that of her nearest rival (compatriot Käthe Grasegger) to become the Olympic Games' first female alpine skiing champion.

Right: Christl Cranz won the first Winter Olympics women's alpine skiing gold medal.

WOLF UPSETS THE FORMBOOK

If the bookmakers were to be believed, the inaugural women's Super-G competition at the Winter Games in Calgary in 1988, was set to be a three-way shootout for the gold medal between Switzerland's Maria Walliser (the overall World Cup champion in 1986 and 1987), her compatriot Michela Figini (the Super-G World Cup leader going into the event) and Germany's Marina Kiehl (who had won women's downhill gold three days earlier). Instead, 23-year-old Austrian Sigrid Wolf stole the show, posting a time of 1:19.03 (a full second ahead of second-placed Figini) to become the first-ever winner of the women's Super-G at the Winter Games.

TRIPLE SUCCESS FOR COMPAGNONI

Deborah Compagnoni secured her first World Cup podium in 1991, won her first victory the following year and soon became the pre-eminent skier of her generation in the technical events. She won her first Olympic gold medal at the 1992 Games in Albertville, France (in the Super-G), won a second at Lillehammer, Norway, two years later (in the giant slalom) and made history at Nagano 1998 when she completed a successful defence of her giant slalom title. In doing so, the 27-year-old Italian became the first woman in alpine skiing history to win gold medals at three separate editions of the Winter Games.

Above: Deborah Comagnoni was the first woman to win a gold medal at three Winter Games.

FRASER BECOMES FIRST SLALOM CHAMPION

The daughter of German and Norwegian immigrants, who was learned to ski on the slopes of Washington state's Mount Rainier, Gretchen Fraser's first chance to compete at the Winter Games (in 1940) was scuppered by the outbreak of the Second World War. The 28-year-old American's chance to shine in the Olympic sun finally came in the inaugural women's slalom event at St-Moritz 1948. She posted the fastest time in the first run and the second fastest time in the second to become the discipline's first-ever Olympic champion.

AUSTRIAN CLEAN SWEEP

If proof were ever needed of the effect a home crowd can have on a host nation team member's performance, one need look no further than the women's downhill event at the 1964 Winter Games at Innsbruck. The Austrian fans helped bring about a clean sweep of the medals by their skiers Christl Haas (gold), Edith Zimmermann (silver) and Traudl Hecher (bronze) – the first, and to date only, time the feat had been achieved in a women's alpine skiing event at the Winter Games.

PÄRSON'S RECORD HAUL OF BRONZE

Her total of 17 individual medals won at the Winter Games and World Championships make Anja Pärson the most successful female alpine skier of all time, but not every moment has been a golden one for the talented Swede. At the Olympics she has won one gold medal (in the slalom at Turin 2006), one silver medal (in the giant slalom at Salt Lake City 2002) and four bronze medals (in the slalom at Salt Lake City 2002, in the downhill and combined at Turin 2006 and in the combined at Vancouver 2010) – the bronze tally is an all-time record for a female alpine skier at the Winter Games.

Below: Four of Anja Pärson's six Olympic medals were bronze.

GOLD BY A WHISKER

Heavy snow forced a one-day postponement of the women's Super-G event at the 1998 Winter Games at Nagano, Japan, but the delay did little to dampen the excitement when the action finally got underway. The United States' Picabo Street, starting second, set the early pace with a time of 1:18.02 – and it proved enough, but only just. The 26-year-old American held out for gold by the slenderest of margins (0.01 seconds ahead of Austria's Michaela Dorfmeister) – it remains the narrowest winning margin in female alpine skiing history at the Winter Games.

LONGEST SERIES OF VICTORIES FOR DIFFERENT COUNTRIES

The last 12 editions of the women's slalom have seen winners from 10 different countries, and between 1968 and 2010 no country retained the title – which is the longest such streak in women's alpine skiing history at the Winter Games. The winners' nationalities read as follows: France-USA-East Germany-Liechtenstein-Italy-Switzerland-Austria-Switzerland-Germany-Croatia-Sweden-Croatia.

Left: Madeleine Berthod stormed to the 1956 Olympic Games downhill gold medal by a record 4.7 seconds.

BLISTERING BERTHOD SWEEPS TO HISTORIC GOLD

Considered firm favourite for the women's downhill gold medal at the 1956 Winter Games at Cortina d'Ampezzo, Italy, following the retirement of compatriot Ida Schöpfer (the 1954 world champion), Switzerland's Madeleine Berthod (a double silver medallist at the 1954 World Championships) stood in the starting gate with a time of 1:45.9 to beat. She shattered it, clocking 1:40.7 and, of the remaining competitors, only one came within five seconds of her time (Frieda Dänzer). Berthod's eventual winning margin (4.7 seconds) is the widest by a woman in Olympic alpine skiing history.

AGE NO BARRIER FOR HECHER

Such was Traudl Hecher's ability on the slopes that she earned selection for Austria's alpine skiing team for the 1960 Winter Games at Squaw Valley, California, aged just 16. And the headlines did not end there: the teenager won a bronze medal in the women's downhill event to become, aged 16 years 143 days, the youngest female medallist in alpine skiing history at the Winter Games. She won bronze again four years later at Innsbruck as part of Austria's historic medal sweep in the women's downhill. Her daughter, Elisabeth Görgl, also won a bronze medal in the same event at Vancouver 2010.

Below: Traudl Hecher won an Olympic bronze medal in the downhill almost exactly 50 years before her daughter.

FIRST FOR COBERGER

In the first 12 editions of women's alpine skiing at the Winter Games (between 1936 and 1988) every single one of the 108 medals awarded went to competitors from the northern hemisphere. That all changed at Albertville in 1992, when New Zealand's Annelise Coberger, having produced the fastest time in the second run to move her from eighth place in the standings to second, took the silver medal in the women's slalom (0.42 seconds behind Austria's Petra Kronberger) to become the southern hemisphere's first-ever medallist at the Winter Games.

Right: After retiring from skiing, 1992 Olympic silver medallist Annelise Coberger became a police officer in her native New Zealand.

VINTAGE DORFMEISTER STORMS TO GOLD

Michaela Dorfmeister was in the form of her life entering the women's Super-G event at Turin 2006, having triumphed in the downhill just five days earlier, but she knew better than anyone how dangerous the tag of favourite could be. The Austrian had been in the same position in the Super-G event at the previous year's World Championships, only to crash out of the race. But she encountered no such problems on this occasion, producing the fastest time of the day (1:32.47) to become, aged 32 years 337 days, the oldest female alpine skiing gold medallist in Winter Games history.

MOST GOLD MEDALS WON: BY EVENT

Downhill	5	Austria, Germany
Slalom	3	Germany, Switzerland, USA
Giant slalom	3	Switzerland, USA
Super-G	3	Austria
Combined	3	Austria, Germany

SINGLE CLAIM TO FAME

The following countries have only ever won one medal in women's alpine skiing at the Winter Games: Czechoslovakia (bronze, downhill); Yugoslavia (silver, slalom); Soviet Union (bronze, slalom); New Zealand (silver, slalom); Spain (bronze, slalom); Australia (bronze, slalom); Czech Republic (bronze, slalom); Russia (silver, Super-G); Finland (silver, giant slalom); and Norway (bronze, combined).

MOST MEDALS WON (BY COUNTRY): TOP TEN

Pos	Medals	Country	G	S	B
1	44	Austria	12	17	15
2	30	Germany (East/West)	13	9	8
3	25	Switzerland	10	8	7
4	24	USA	10	10	4
5	19	France	4	8	7
6	13	Italy	5	3	5
7	10	Sweden	3	2	5
8	8	Canada	4	1	3
9	6	Croatia	4	2	-
10	5	Liechtenstein	2	1	2

FIS Alpine Ski World Cup

Launched alongside the men's competition in 1967, the women's FIS Alpine Ski World Cup is an annual series of events staged around the world (in which participants compete for points) to determine both an overall champion and a winner in each of the five disciplines. Because of its week in, week out nature, many experts consider it to be the toughest alpine skiing event in the world.

MOSER-PRÖLL IS CREAM OF THE CROP

Despite her supreme talent, Annemarie Moser-Pröll enjoyed limited success in the Olympic arena, winning just one gold medal at the Games (in the women's downhill at Lake Placid 1980). Her status as the greatest female alpine skier of all time (alongside Germany's Christl Cranz) is based largely on her performances in the women's FIS Alpine Ski World Cup. The Austrian holds numerous all-time records in the competition: for the most overall titles (6) – in 1971, 1972, 1973, 1974, 1975 and 1979; the most downhill titles (7); the most career race wins (62); the most career downhill wins (36); the most podiums (113); and the most downhill wins in a single season (8) – in 1972–73.

Above: Annemarie Moser-Pröll didn't shine in Olympic competition the way she did in the FIS Alpine Ski World Cup.

MOST WORLD CUP RACE WINS: TOP TEN

Pos	Wins	Name	Country	Span	D	SG	GS	S	C
1	62	Annemarie Moser-Pröll	Austria	1969–80	36	-	16	3	7
2	55	Vreni Schneider	Switzerland	1984–95	-	-	20	34	1
3	46	Renate Götschl	Austria	1993–2009	24	17	-	1	4
4	42	Anja Pärson	Sweden	1995–	6	4	11	18	3
=	42	Lindsey Vonn	USA	2000–	21	14	1	2	4
6	36	Katja Seizinger	Germany	1989–98	16	16	4	-	-
7	33	Hanni Wenzel	Liechtenstein	1972–84	2	-	12	11	8
8	31	Erika Hess	Switzerland	1978–87	-	-	6	21	4
9	30	Janica Kostelic	Croatia	1998–2006	1	1	2	20	6
10	29	Marlies Schild	Austria	2001–	-	-	1	27	1

SERIAL CONTENDER

Austria's Renate Götschl made a sensational start to her FIS Alpine Ski World Cup career when she won her first-ever race (the slalom at Lillehammer on 14 March 1993). It was the start of a glittering 16-year association with the competition: the overall champion in 2000, she won ten discipline titles – in the downhill (1997, 1999, 2004, 2005 and 2007), Super-G (2000, 2004 and 2007) and combined (2000 and 2002), recorded 46 race wins (to stand third on the all-time list) and holds the all-time records for the most career top tens (198) and for the most Super-G race wins (17).

Left: In her 16-year career, Renate Götschl enjoyed a win in every World Cup event except the giant slalom.

GREENE TAKES INAUGURAL TITLE

Nicknamed "The Tiger" because of her aggressive approach on the slopes, Nancy Greene went on to become the most decorated Canadian alpine skier (male or female) of all time. She holds the distinction of having won the first-ever women's FIS Alpine Ski World Cup race (the slalom at Oberstaufen, Germany, on 7 January 1967) and remained the class act of the field for the rest of the season, winning seven of the 17 races to collect 176 points (four more than France's Marielle Goitschel) and become the first-ever women's overall World Cup champion. She defended her title successfully the following year.

Above: No skier is close to matching the 54 World Cup wins in slalom and giant slalom achieved by Swiss legend Vreni Schneider.

SUPER SCHNEIDER LEADS THE WAY

Vreni Schneider burst on to the World Cup scene in 1984, when she topped the podium in only her third event (in the slalom at Santa Caterina, Italy, on 17 December 1984), and soon established herself as the most proficient technical skier of her generation, winning the first of a record five giant slalom titles in 1986 and the first of three overall titles in 1989 (a season that saw her notch up a record 14 race wins and collect the first of a record six slalom titles). By the time she retired in 1995, she also held the all-time records for the most World Cup race wins in slalom (34) and giant slalom (20).

A SIGN OF GREATNESS

Eight women have achieved the notable feat of having won a World Cup event in each of the disciplines in which they could race: Nancy Greene (Canada, 1967–68), Françoise Macchi (France, 1968–72), Annemarie Moser-Pröll (Austria, 1969–80), Petra Kronberger (Austria, 1987–92), Pernilla Wiberg (Sweden, 1990–2002), Janica Kostelic (Croatia, 1998–2006), Anja Pärson (Sweden, 1998–present) and Lindsey Vonn (USA, 2000–present). Of those eight, only three – Wiberg, Kostelic and Vonn – have won a race in each of the five disciplines.

SIZZLING SEIZINGER THE QUEEN OF SUPER-G

A five-time medal winner at the FIS Junior World Championships (one of the medals a gold, in the Super-G in 1990), Katja Seizinger recorded her first FIS World Cup victory in 1990 (in the Super-G at Santa Caterina on 7 December) and went on to become a major challenger in the speed events for the next seven years, winning a total of 36 races before her retirement at the end of the 1998 season. The overall World Cup champion in 1996 and 1998, the German holds the record for the most Super-G titles – five (in 1993, 1994, 1995, 1996 and 1998).

COMBINED RACES AT THE WORLD CUP

Prior to 2005, combined events were essentially "paper races", inasmuch as the times from the separate downhill and slalom events (staged on different days) were combined on paper to give an overall combined race winner. Since 2005, however, the FIS, in an attempt to encourage skiers to compete in both disciplines, has staged "super combined" races, with both the downhill and slalom elements of this single event held on the same day. The most successful combined skier in women's Alpine Ski World Cup history is Liechtenstein's Hanni Wenzel, who recorded eight combined "paper-race" wins between 1972 and 1984.

Above: When Hanni Wenzel won her eight combined World Cup titles, the two races were held on different days.

MOST COMBINED TITLES

The FIS Alpine Ski World Cup all-time record for the most combined discipline titles is four, held by two women: Brigitte Oertli (Switzerland, in 1985, 1987, 1988 and 1989); and Janica Kostelic (Croatia, in 2001, 2003, 2005 and 2006).

MOST WORLD CUP WINS BY COUNTRY

No.	Country
15	Austria
11	Switzerland
4	USA
3	Croatia, Germany, Sweden
2	Canada, Liechtenstein
1	France, West Germany

FIS Alpine World Ski Championships

The oldest of alpine skiing's three major competitions, the FIS Alpine Ski World Championships were staged for the first time at Mürren, Switzerland, in 1931. Initially held on an annual basis (between 1931 and 1939) and then in every even-numbered year (between 1948 and 1982), they have been contested in every odd-numbered year since 1985.

MOST WORLD CHAMPIONSHIP MEDALS: TOP TEN

Pos	Medals	Name (country)	G	S	B
1	15	Christl Cranz (Germany)	12	3	-
2	11	Marielle Goitschel (France)	9	2	-
=	11	Anja Pärson (Sweden)	7	1	3
4	9	Annemarie Moser-Pröll (Austria)	5	2	2
=	9	Hanni Wenzel (Liechtenstein)	4	3	2
6	7	Erika Hess (Switzerland)	6	-	1
=	7	Renate Götschl (Austria)	2	3	2
=	7	Käthe Grasegger (Germany)	-	1	6
9	6	Pernilla Wiberg (Sweden)	4	1	1
=	6	Inge Wersin-Lantschiner (Austria)	3	3	-
=	6	Vreni Schneider (Switzerland)	3	2	1
=	6	Annie Famose (France)	1	2	1

GOITSCHEL BREAKS THE MOULD

In eight editions of the women's giant slalom at the FIS Alpine World Ski Championships, since the event was contested for the first time at Aspen, Colorado, in 1950, no champion had ever launched a successful defence of her title. That changed at the 1966 World Championships at Portillo, Chile: a day after she had claimed downhill gold, defending champion Marielle Goitschel (the Frenchwoman had won giant slalom gold at Innsbruck two years earlier) stormed to victory to make history. Three other women – Vreni Schneider (1987, 1989), Deborah Compagnoni (1996, 1997) and Anja Pärson (2003, 2005) – have equalled Goitschel's feat.

Left: It took 21 years for anyone to emulate Marielle Goitschel's feat of defending her World Championship giant slalom title.

CHRISTL CRANZ: RECORD-BREAKER

Christl Cranz was the dominant female alpine skier in the 1930s and is considered by many to be the greatest of all time. She burst on to the international scene at the 1934 World Championships in St-Moritz, winning gold in the slalom and combined and taking silver in the downhill. It was the start of a successful love affair with the event, and by the time she retired in 1941, she held numerous all-time competition records: for the most medals (15); the most gold medals (12); the most combined titles (5); the most slalom titles (4); for being the first woman to successfully defend her combined title (1934, 1935); for being the first woman to win three medals at a single World Championships (in 1937); for being the first woman to defend her slalom title (1937 and 1938); and for being the first woman to win the slalom/combined double (in 1934). She also shares the record, with Austria's Annemarie Moser-Pröll, for the most downhill titles (3).

Below: Even with more events today, Christl Cranzl's 15 World Championship medals and 12 golds are records that may never be broken.

MAGICAL MUFFIE STRIKES DOUBLE GOLD

In alpine skiing's early days, British skiers Esmé Mackinnon, known as "Muffie", and Audrey Sale-Barker were once described by *Ski* magazine as being "the first women who could be called racers", and it was the former who lived up to her lofty billing at the 1931 FIS Alpine World Ski Championships at Mürren, Switzerland. The Edinburgh-born 17-year-old stormed to gold in both the downhill and slalom events to become alpine skiing's first-ever female world champion.

BEISER STORMS TO DOUBLE GOLD

Austria's Trude Beiser first hit the headlines at the 1948 Winter Games in St-Moritz when, aged 20, she won gold in the women's combined and silver in the downhill. She confirmed her status as one of the pre-eminent skiers of her generation when she won downhill gold at the 1950 FIS Alpine Ski World Championships at Aspen, Colorado, and made history at the 1952 Winter Games in Oslo (which doubled as the World Championships) when she stormed to downhill gold (0.9 seconds ahead of Mirl Buchner) to become the first woman in the competition's history to retain her downhill title.

Left: Zali Steggall represented France at junior level, but was a world champion for Australia.

SOUTHERN HEMISPHERE SUCCESS

Born in Manly, Sydney, but raised in the French Alps, Zali Steggall learned to ski at a young age and, by the age of 14, was good enough to earn a place in France's junior skiing team. She returned to Australia shortly afterwards and, aged 18, represented the country of her birth at the 1992 Winter Games, with little success. Although progress was slow, Steggall's golden moment finally came at the 1999 FIS Alpine World Ski Championships at Vail, USA, when she won the slalom to become the southern hemisphere's first, and to date only, alpine skiing world champion.

MAIER COMES GOOD WHEN IT MATTERS

Austrian-born Ulrike Maier made her World Cup debut as a 17-year-old in December 1984 (finishing 14th in the combined at Davos, Switzerland) and secured her first podium three years later (third place in the slalom at Courmayeur, Italy), but a first victory took longer than many expected to materialize. When it finally arrived, it came on the grandest of stages: she broke her drought with a gold-medal-winning performance in the women's Super-G at the 1989 FIS Alpine World Ski Championships. Her next step to the top of the podium was a history-making one: she took Super-G gold at the 1991 World Championships to become the first woman in the competition's history to make a successful defence of her Super-G title.

COUNTRY WITH MOST MEDALS

No country has had more success at the women's FIS Alpine World Ski Championships than Austria. It leads the way in terms of gold (33), silver (36) and bronze (34) medals won.

Below: Anja Pärson shows off her 2007 medal haul.

SWEDEN'S GOLDEN GIRL

If frustration is the watchword for Anja Pärson's performances at the Winter Olympic Games (despite her undoubted talent, she has only one gold medal to show for her efforts – in the slalom at Turin 2006), then unabated joy would sum up her career to date at the FIS Alpine World Ski Championships. The Swede is the only woman in the competition's history to have won gold medals in all five disciplines: in the downhill in 2007; in the slalom in 2001; in the combined in 2007; in the giant slalom in 2003 and 2005; and in the Super-G in 2005 and 2007.

Men's Biathlon: Olympic Games

A sport that combines the disciplines of alpine skiing and rifle shooting, biathlon as we know it today appeared as a full-medal sport at the Winter Games at Squaw Valley, California, in 1960. In recent times, men contest five events: the individual (20km); the relay (4 x 7.5km); the sprint (10km); the pursuit (12.5km) and the mass start (15km).

MOST MEDALS WON: TOP FIVE

Pos	Medals	Name (country, span)	G	S	B
1	11	Ole Einar Bjørndalen (Norway, 1992–2010)	6	4	1
2	8	Sven Fischer (Germany, 1994–2006)	4	3	1
=	8	Ricco Gross (Germany, 1992–2006)	4	2	2
4	6	Halvard Hanevold (Norway, 1998–2010)	3	2	1
=	6	Sergei Tchepikov (USSR/Russia, 1994–2006)	2	3	1

BJØRNDALEN IS THE BIATHLON KING

A three-time gold medallist at the 1993 Junior World Championships and considered one of the greatest athletes of all time, Ole Einar Bjørndalen competed at the Winter Games for the first time at Lillehammer 1994 (at which he finished 36th in the individual event), won his first World Cup race two years later and arrived at the 1998 Winter Games at Nagano, Japan, as a strong contender for the medals. He did not disappoint, picking up gold in the sprint and silver in the relay. It was the start of a hugely successful association with the event and, following Vancouver 2010, the Norwegian held numerous all-time Winter Games biathlon records: for the most medals won (11); the most gold medals won (six); the most silver medals won (four); and for the most gold medals won at a single Winter Games (four, at Salt Lake City 2002).

Above: Ole Einar Bjørndalen has rewritten the Winter Olympics biathlon record books with his 11 medals.

BIATHLON IN ALL BUT NAME

Although not in its current form, the sport – at the time known as "military patrol" – did appear at the first-ever Winter Games at Chamonix, France, in 1924. The race – which consisted of teams of four members who had to ski over a 30km course, with three of the team firing 18 shots at targets set at mid-race distance – was won by Switzerland (although the medals are not considered official). Military patrol also featured as a demonstration event at the 1928, 1936 and 1948 Winter Games.

BACK-TO-BACK JOY FOR SOLBERG

Success did not come early for Magnar Solberg, but when it finally arrived it came in record-breaking fashion. The police officer was 31 years old when he travelled to the 1968 Winter Games at Grenoble, France, as part of the Norwegian men's biathlon squad, but proved that age was no barrier when he walked away with the gold medal in the individual 20km event. The success did not end there: he won individual 20km gold yet again at Sapporo four years later to become the first, and to date only, man in history to secure back-to-back Olympic titles in biathlon's toughest event.

Below: 35-year-old Magnar Solberg won his second 20km individual gold medal at Sapporo 1972.

Above: Sergei Tchepikov (second left) celebrates a relay silver at Turin in 2006, his sixth medal in five Winter Games.

MOST GOLD MEDALS WON (BY COUNTRY)

13	USSR/EUN/Russia
11	Norway
8	Germany
2	East Germany, France, Sweden, West Germany

SOVIETS SET ALL-TIME MARK

The Soviet Union's staggering victory (they finished a massive 1 minute 47.8 seconds ahead of second-placed Norway) in the first-ever men's 4 x 7.5km relay race, at Grenoble 1968, prompted a record-breaking run in the event. Untouchable, the Soviets repeated their relay success at the next five editions of the Games and, not surprisingly, their run of six successive victories is an all-time best for any biathlon event at the Winter Games. And the records don't end there: Aleksandr Tikhonov was a member of the first four gold-medal-winning teams – a Winter Games record for the most gold medals in a single event.

TCHEPIKOV LASTS THE DISTANCE

Sergei Tchepikov first appeared at the Winter Games at Calgary 1988 and won a bronze medal in the 10km sprint and a gold medal as part of the Soviet Union's 4 x 7.5km relay team. He was back at the Games four years later at Albertville, France, this time as part of the Unified Team (EUN), and won another medal, a silver, in the relay. At Lillehammer 1994 he picked up his second career gold (in the 10km sprint) and another silver (as part of Russia's relay team). Later, when he was part of Russia's silver-medal-winning relay team in his final appearance at the Games, at Turin 2006, he set a new record. The 18 years that had passed between his first and last medals is an all-time biathlon record at the Winter Games. He also holds the record for the most Winter Games biathlon competitions entered – six.

GROSS ENJOYS HIS FAIR SHARE OF OLYMPIC GLORY

World junior champion in 1989 (in the 10km sprint) and a 20-time medallist (nine of them gold) at the Biathlon World Championships, Ricco Gross is one of the most successful biathletes in Winter Games history. A sergeant in Germany's Federal Defence Force, he won gold medals at the 1992, 1994, 1998 and 2006 Winter Games as part of his country's 4 x 7.5km relay team. With another relay silver (in 2002) and three medals in individual events (silver in the 10km sprint in 1992 and 1994 and bronze in the 12.5km pursuit in 2002), he stands second on biathlon's all-time medal-winners' list at the Winter Games (with eight). He also holds the record for winning medals at the most consecutive Games (five).

Left: Sven Fischer won his fourth Olympic gold medal in the relay at Turin 2006.

FANTASTIC FISCHER PUTS EARLY CAREER FEARS BEHIND HIM

Any fears Sven Fischer might have had that a problem he'd had with his kneecaps in his youth would force him to give up his ambitions as a biathlete were soon quelled when he returned to competition in 1990 after a year spent rehabilitating and strengthening. A 20-time medallist at the Biathlon World Championships and a two-time overall Biathlon World Cup champion (in 1996–97 and 1998–99), the German enjoyed considerable success at the Winter Games, picking up eight medals (four gold, two silver and two bronze) to stand second, alongside compatriot Ricco Gross, on biathlon's all-time medal-winners' list at the Winter Games.

Other Major Championships

The Biathlon World Cup, which lasts from November to March and consists of nine to ten contest weeks, was launched in 1977. Athletes compete for points at each contest in one of four disciplines, with the leading points-scorer at the end of the season declared the overall champion. The first Biathlon World Championships were held in 1958 and are now held on an annual basis.

BIATHLON'S FIRST STAR

Frank Ullrich first came to international attention when he won a gold medal as part of East Germany's relay team at the 1975 Youth World Championships and confirmed his status as a biathlete of immense promise when he won a bronze medal at the 1976 Winter Games as part of his country's relay team. He was the Biathlon World Cup's first overall champion, in 1977–78, finished second the following season and proved his stature as the dominant biathlete of his generation when he became the first man in history to claim the overall World Cup title three seasons in a row, in 1980–81, 1981–82 and 1982–83. Only one other man, France's Raphaël Poirée, has equalled the feat.

Below: Frank Ullrich was the first biathlon World Cup winner.

CREAM OF THE CROP

The most successful competitor in biathlon history – he has won a record 11 medals at the Winter Games (six of them gold) and a staggering 36 at the Biathlon World Championships (including a seismic 16 gold medals), it comes as little surprise that Ole Einar Bjørndalen is the most successful biathlete in World Cup history. The Norwegian won his first overall title in the 1997–98 season and went on to add a further five titles to his record-breaking haul (in 2002–03, 2004–05, 2005–06, 2007–08 and 2008–09).

Below: Norway's Ole Einar Bjørndalen has 16 World Championship and six World Cup victories to go with his half-dozen Olympic gold medals.

MOST OVERALL WORLD CUP WINS: TOP FIVE

Pos	Wins	Name (country)
1	6	Ole Einar Bjørndalen (Norway)
2	4	Frank Ullrich (East Germany)
=	4	Raphael Poirée (France)
4	3	Frank-Peter Roetsch (East Germany)
5	2	Sergei Tchepikov (USSR)
=	2	Jon Age Tyldum (Norway)
=	2	Sven Fischer (Germany)

MAGICAL MEDVEDTSEV

Steeled by his rigorous training at the Soviet Union's Armed Forces Sports Society, Valery Medvedtsev burst on to the international biathlon scene in spectacular fashion at the 1986 World Championships in Oslo. He won the 10km sprint title (53.5 seconds ahead of Austria's Franz Schuler) and then stormed to gold in the gruelling 20km individual event (13.9 seconds ahead of East Germany's André Sehmisch) to become the first biathlete in history to win two individual gold medals at a single World Championships.

Left: Valery Medvedtsev was not really challenged in either the 10km or 20km individual events in 1986.

SWEDES STAR AT INAUGURAL WORLD CHAMPIONSHIPS

The first Biathlon World Championships were staged in Saalfelden, Austria, in 1958, with just two events: the 20km team events and the 20km individual. Sweden dominated the proceedings, winning the team race (11m 35s ahead of the Soviet Union), while Adolf Wiklund headed a Swedish one-two (0.69s ahead of compatriot Olle Gunneriusson) in the individual event.

SOVIETS UNION'S STREAK

Norway dominated the first two editions of the 4 x 7.5km relay race at the Biathlon World Championships, winning in 1967 and 1968, but as their superiority in the event waned, the Soviet Union began a new era of supremacy. They won for the first time in 1969, repeated their success in 1970 and, the following year, became the first team in history to record a hat-trick of titles. The run did not end there. The World Championships were not held in 1972, but the Soviet Union resumed their domination in 1973 and won their fifth successive gold the following year. It is the longest winning streak in the event's history.

SUPREME CHAMPION

A 95-time World Cup race winner and six-time overall champion who has claimed a career haul of 11 medals at the Winter Games, Ole Einar Bjørndalen is without question the greatest biathlete of all time. If further proof were needed, the Norwegian has collected a colossal 36 medals at the sport's World Championships (a sensational 16 of them gold) and also holds the all-time record for the most sprint titles (4) – in 2003, 2005, 2007 and 2009 – and for the most pursuit titles (4) – in 2005, 2007, 2008 and 2009).

MOST INDIVIDUAL WORLD CHAMPIONSHIP GOLD MEDALS (BY COUNTRY): TOP FIVE

Pos	Golds	Country
1	25	Germany (East/West)
2	23	Norway
3	21	USSR/Russia
4	9	France
5	6	Finland

PERFECTION FOR POIRÉE

A four-time overall World Cup champion (in 1999–2000, 2000–01, 2001–02 and 2003–04), France's Raphäel Poirée is considered one of the greatest biathletes in history. He confirmed that accolade at the 2004 Biathlon World Championships at Oberhof, Germany. First he claimed the 10km sprint title; four days later he won the 20km individual; and then, to round off a perfect week, he roared to victory in the 15km mass start race to become the first biathlete in history to win three gold medals at a single World Championships.

Left: Raphäel Poirée won three gold medals in one World Championships, the first man to achieve the feat.

Women's Biathlon

Women biathletes were first allowed to compete at the Winter Games in Albertville in 1992, some 32 years after the men had made their Olympic debut in the sport. The women's Biathlon World Championships were staged for the first time in 1984 (and are held on an annual basis) and the women's Biathlon World Cup was launched at the start of the 1982–83 season.

LITTLE RED RIDING HOOD STRIKES TRIPLE GOLD

A member of the Armed Forces, as is the case with the majority of German biathletes, Kati Wilhelm, nicknamed "Little Red Riding Hood" because of her characteristic red hair, started her career as a cross-country skier. After appearing in that sport at the 1998 Winter Games at Nagano, she made the switch to biathlon – and it proved a highly successful move. At Salt Lake City 2002, she picked up two gold medals (in the 7.5km sprint and in the 4 x 7.5km relay) and a silver (in the 10km pursuit). She was among the medals again at Turin 2006, winning one gold (in the 10km pursuit and two silvers (in the 12.5km mass start and 4 x 6km relay). A further bronze medal (in the relay) came at Vancouver 2010. Her haul of three gold medals at the Winter Games is an all-time record.

Left: Kati Wilhelm, in her famous red hat, shoots for gold at Turin in 2006.

MOST WINTER GAMES MEDALS WON: TOP FIVE

Pos	Wins	Name (country)	G	S	B
1	9	Uschi Disl (Germay)	2	4	3
2	7	Kati Wilhelm (Germany)	3	3	1
3	5	Albina Akhatova (Russia)	1	1	3
4	4	Katrin Apel (Germany)	2	1	1
=	4	Antje Harvey (Germany)	1	3	-

Below: Germany's Uschi Disl leads Russia's Albina Akhatova (6) on her way to bronze in the 12.5km mass start at the Turin 2006 Games.

VETERAN DISL TOPS ALL-TIME MEDAL-WINNERS' LIST

Another German biathlete who was a member of her country's Armed Forces (she served as a border-control guard), Uschi Disl enjoyed a 19-year career in international biathlon competition (winning 19 medals at the World Championships, eight of them gold) and made five appearances at the Winter Games between 1992 and 2006. A two-time gold medallist with Germany's 4 x 7.5km relay team (in 1998 and 2002), she holds the all-time record for the most medals won (nine) and for the most silver medals won (four) in Olympic competition.

WINTER GAMES MEDALS WON (BY COUNTRY)

Pos	Medals	Country	G	S	B
1	25	Germany	8	11	6
2	15	EUN/Russia	7	3	5
3	8	France	2	2	4
4	4	Norway	1	2	1
=	4	Sweden	1	1	2
6	3	Canada	2	-	1
=	3	Ukraine	-	1	2
8	2	Slovakia	1	1	-
=	2	Bulgaria	1	-	1
=	2	Belarus	-	1	1
11	1	Kazakhstan	-	1	-

THE QUEEN OF LILLEHAMMER

Born in Quebec in December 1969 and Canada's junior champion in 1987, Miriam Bédard won her first Biathlon World Cup event in 1991 and made her Winter Games debut the following year in Albertville, France, finishing third in the individual 15km event. She won her first major title the following year, with gold in the 7.5km sprint at the 1993 World Championships, and carried that form into the following year's Winter Games at Lillehammer, Norway, becoming the first woman in history to win two individual gold medals in biathlon at the Winter Games (the 15km individual and the 7.5km sprint) and the only woman to have won the individual-sprint double.

Left: Miriam Bédard won the Olympic 7.5km sprint gold medal at Lillehammer in 1994 by 1.1 seconds.

STAR OF THE SHOW

The first women's Biathlon World Championships were held in Chamonix, France, in 1984 (some 26 years after the inaugural men's competition had been staged) and the Soviet Union's Venera Chernychova was the star of the show, storming to gold in both the individual 10km and sprint 5km events. Only one other woman – Germany's Kati Wilhelm in 2009 (albeit over different distances) – has matched Chernychova's feat of claiming the individual/sprint double at the championships.

NEUNER PROVES HER POINT

The reluctance reportedly shown by Magdalena Neuner's parents when, at the age of 16, their eldest daughter opted to become a professional biathlete was utterly dispelled when her career finally got under way, for the Garmisch-Partenkirchen-born German has enjoyed nothing but unprecedented success. She claimed her first (of five) Junior World Championship titles in 2004, aged 17, won her first Biathlon World Cup event in January 2007, aged 19, and made her first appearance at the senior World Championships a month later, sensationally winning gold in the 7.5km sprint and 10km pursuit events. It was the start of a success-laden association with the championships, and by 2011 she had collected an all-time record 13 medals at the event (ten of them gold – five in individual events and five in team races).

FANTASTIC FORSBERG

A former cross-country skier (she competed in the sport from 1988 to 1996), Magdalena Forsberg's decision to switch to biathlon triggered a sequence of unparalleled success. Although the Swede suffered disappointments in Olympic competition (her total of just two bronze medals, both won at Salt Lake City 2002, belies her talent), but she was dominant at the World Championships (winning a joint record six individual gold medals) and, for a time, unbeatable in the World Cup. Her run of six straight overall titles between 1996–97 and 2001–02 is unlikely ever to be beaten and she also holds the all-time competition record for the most race wins (42).

WORLD CHAMPIONSHIPS PACE-SETTERS

Two women hold the record for winning the most gold medals in individual events at the women's Biathlon World Championships (six): Sweden's Magdalena Forsberg (in the 10km pursuit in 1997, 1998 and 2000, in the 15km individual in 1997 and 2001, and in the 12.km mass start in 2001); and Norway's Liv Grete Poirée (in the 7.5km sprint in 2000 and 2004, in the 12.km mass start in 2000 and 2004, and in the 10k pursuit in 2001 and 2004). The Norwegian also holds the record for the most individual medals won by a woman at a single championships, with three in 2004.

Left: After winning six Biathlon World Championships, Magdalene Forsberg won the 2002 Biathlon World Cup.

Men's Cross-Country Skiing: Olympic Games

Men's cross-country skiing was contested at the first-ever Winter Games, at Chamonix, France, in 1924 (with races held over 18km and 50km) and has been ever-present on the Olympic programme ever since. Today, participants compete in six events: the individual sprint, 15km and 50km races, the 4 x 10km relay, the team sprint and the combined/double pursuit.

BJØRN DAEHLIE: AN ALL-TIME BEST

Bjørn Daehlie attributes his astonishing success as a cross-country skier to the numerous activities he enjoyed as a child – including skiing, hunting, fishing, kayaking and football – and what extraordinary success he achieved. The Norwegian first came to international attention when he won two gold medals at the 1991 World Championships (in the 15km and the 4 x 10km relay) and went on to surpass those feats at the following year's Winter Games, picking up three gold medals (in the combined/double pursuit, the 50km and 4 x 10km relay) and a silver (in the 30km). Two gold medals (in the 10km and the 10km+15km combined pursuit) and two silvers (in the 30km and the 4 x 10km relay) followed at Lillehammer 1994, and he bagged three more golds (in the 10km, 50km and 4 x 10km relay) and a silver (in the 10km+15km combined pursuit) at Nagano 1998. His haul of 12 medals (eight of them gold) is an all-time record for any athlete in any sport at the Winter Games.

Above: Bjørn Daehlie shows off perfect form in the 30km race at Nagano in 1998.

MOST MEDALS WON: TOP TEN

Pos	Medals	Name (country)	G	S	B
1	12	Bjørn Daehlie (Norway)	8	4	-
2	9	Sixten Jernberg (Sweden)	4	3	2
3	7	Veikko Hakulinen (Finland)	3	3	1
=	7	Eero Mantyranta (Finland)	3	2	2
=	7	Vladimir Smirnov (USSR/EUN/Kazakhstan)	1	4	2
6	6	Thomas Alsgaard (Norway)	5	1	-
=	6	Gunde Svan (Sweden)	4	1	1
=	6	Vegard Ulvang (Norway)	3	2	1
=	6	Mika Myllylae (Finland)	1	1	4
=	6	Harri Kirvesniemi (Finland)	-	-	6

Below: Hallgeir Brenden (43) enjoyed the special glory of winning an Olympic gold medal on home soil with victory at Oslo in 1952.

BACK-TO-BACK JOY FOR BRENDEN

Born and raised in a small hamlet in Tyrsil, in the Hedmark region of southeastern Norway, Hallgeir Brenden was a farmer and a logger who developed into one of the greatest cross-country skiers in his nation's history. He first rose to international prominence when, to the delight of his home crowd, he won the 18km race at the 1952 Winter Games in Oslo. He then earned a place in the history books by retaining his title (on this occasion the race was contested over 15km) at the 1956 Winter Games at Cortina d'Ampezzo, Italy – the picture of a young Sophia Loren sitting on a smiling Brenden's lap after the victory caused a huge stir in his homeland – to become the first cross-country skier in history to succeed in defending an Olympic title.

HAUG SETS BENCHMARK

Raised on a small farm in the mountains of southern Norway, Thorlief Haug had skiing in his blood. The dominant personality in his sport in the early 1920s, he lived up to his billing at the inaugural Winter Games in Chamonix, France, in 1924, winning both of the cross-country events (the 18km and 50km) to become the sport's first-ever double Olympic champion. Remarkably, he also won gold in the Nordic combined at those Games and finished fourth in the ski jumping – and he became as famous for his exploits on the ski-jumping hills as he was for the extraordinary stamina and strength he displayed in cross-country skiing races.

ONE MAN'S DISASTER IS TWO MEN'S JOY

How quickly fortunes can change. Nine days after he had received the congratulations of King Juan Carlos for his victory in the men's combined/double pursuit race (to add to his wins in the 30km and 50km races) at Salt Lake City in 2002, Spain's Johann Mühlegg was disqualified from all three events after testing positive in a dope test. As the podiums were re-shuffled, it meant that Norway duo Thomas Allsgaard and Frode Estil – who had recorded exactly the same times in the combined/double pursuit to win a silver medal – were promoted to gold medallists. It is the only time in cross-country skiing history that two competitors have shared a gold medal at the Winter Games.

Above: Thomas Alsgaard (left) and Frode Estil left the Salt Lake City podium wearing silver medals in 2002, but returned to Norway as joint gold medallists.

MOST MEDALS WON: TOP TEN

Pos	Medals	Country	G	S	B
1	70	Norway	30	26	14
2	52	Sweden	22	13	17
3	43	Finland	11	13	19
4	38	USSR/Russia	14	11	13
5	19	Italy	4	8	7
6	8	Germany (East/West)	-	6	2
7	5	Austria	1	2	2
=	5	Switzerland	1	-	4
9	4	Estonia	2	1	1
=	4	Kazakhstan	1	2	1

ONCE ON THE PODIUM

Four countries have only ever won one medal in cross-country skiing at the Winter Games: the USA (Bill Koch, silver, in the 30km at Innsbruck 1976); Bulgaria (Ivan Lebanov, bronze, in the 30km at Lake Placid 1980); Czechoslovakia (team bronze in the 4 x 10km relay at Calgary 1988); and France (Roddy Darragon, silver, in the sprint at Turin 2006).

ADVANTAGE NORWAY

It may not come as much of a surprise, given the sport's origins, but Scandinavian countries lead the way in cross-country skiing's all-time medal-winners' table at the Winter Games. Norway leads, having won 70 of the 256 Olympic medals presented in the sport (including discontinued disciplines) – an impressive 27.34 per cent.

KAZAKHSTAN'S ONE-MAN WRECKING CREW

Born in Shuchinsk, Kazakhstan, in 1964, Vladimir Smirnov trained at the renowned Armed Forces Sports Society in Alma-Ata, made his cross-country World Cup debut in 1982 and achieved his first victory (of 29) in the event four years later. He made his Winter Games debut (representing the Soviet Union) at Calgary 1988, picking up three medals (two silver and one bronze) and appeared for the Unified Team (EUN) at Albertville 1992. Two years later, at Lillehammer 1994, he was flying the flag for his native Kazakhstan, and won not only 50km individual gold and two silvers, but also the hearts of the Norwegians for his friendly rivalry with their local hero Bjørn Daehlie. He is the only Kazakhstani to win cross-country skiing medals at the Winter Games.

Left: Vladimir Smirnov won Olympic Games medals representing the Soviet Union (1988), Unified Team (EUN, 1992) and Kazakhstan (1994 and 1998).

Other Major Championships

Men's cross-country skiing has been staged as part of the FIS Nordic World Ski Championships since 1925 and, since 2001, is held in odd-numbered years. The FIS Cross-Country World Cup, an annual competition contested over a number of races in which participants compete for points to determine an overall season winner, was held for the first time in 1973 (and has been held officially since 1981).

Below: Bjørn Daehlie averaged more than seven podium finishes in 11 World Cup seasons.

MOST WORLD CUP PODIUMS: TOP TEN

Pos	Podiums	Name (country)	G	S	B
1	81	Bjørn Daehlie (Norway)	46	23	12
2	64	Vladimir Smirnov (USSR/Kazakhstan)	31	21	13
3	46	Gunde Svan (Sweden)	31	11	5
4	36	Torgny Mogren (Sweden)	13	15	8
5	32	Vegard Ulvang (Norway)	9	15	8
6	30	Tor-Arne Hetland (Norway)	11	13	6
7	26	Thomas Alsgaard (Norway)	12	10	4
8	25	Lucas Bauer (Czech Republic)	11	10	4
=	25	Mika Myllylae (Finland)	10	7	8
=	25	Tobias Angerer (Germany)	11	5	9

THE BEST BY A COUNTRY MILE

Revered as the most successful cross-country skier in history – he won 12 medals at the Winter Games (eight of them gold) and a staggering 17 at the FIS Nordic World Ski Championships (including nine gold medals), Bjørn Daehlie's glittering performances in the FIS Cross-Country World Cup left an indelible mark on the competition. In an outstanding ten-year career between 1989 and 1999 that was strewn with success, the Norwegian superstar set all-time competition records for: the most overall titles (6); the most podium finishes (81); the most race wins (46); the most second-place finishes (23); and the most third-place finishes (12).

BRA'S BRIGHTEST MOMENT

Oddvar Bra is best known in his native Norway for the calamitous moment at the 1983 FIS Nordic World Ski Championships when he broke his ski pole in the run-up to the finishing line and squandered Norway's lead over the Soviet Union in the team relay (the two nations ultimately tied for gold) – the incident led to the popular Norwegian expression, "Where were you when Bra broke his pole?" Fortunately Bra's career was memorable for peaks as well as this trough. The overall FIS Cross-Country World Cup champion in 1974–75, he won again in 1978–79 to become the competition's first two-time winner.

SUPERB SVAN COMPLETES HAT-TRICK

An athlete renowned for his dedication and fastidious attention to detail (he famously used a lighter alloy on his ski-pole tips to make them four grams lighter), Gunde Svan made his FIS Cross-Country World Cup debut in December 1982 and recorded his first victory in only his sixth race (in the 15km at Anchorage, Alaska, on 19 March 1983). It was the start of the Swede's long and successful association with the competition: he won the overall title for the first time in 1983–84, defended it the following year and, in 1985–86, with a remarkable tally of four race victories, became the first cross-country skier in history to complete a hat-trick of titles. He was champion again in 1987–88 and 1988–89.

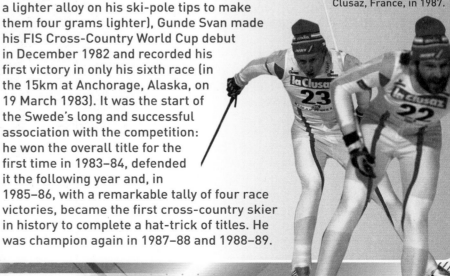

Below: Gunde Svan (23) trails his fellow Swede Thomas Wassberg in a World Cup event at La Clusaz, France, in 1987.

A STAR IN THE MAKING

Norways's Petter Northug holds the distinction of being the youngest race-winner in FIS Cross-Country World Cup history. He was just 20 years 61 days old when he won the pursuit event at Falun, Sweden, on 8 March 2006. He has gone on to record a further 11 race victories.

THE HOLMENKOLLEN HERO

A two-time gold medallist in cross-country skiing at the inaugural Winter Games at Chamonix, France, in 1924, Norway's Thorleif Haug sealed his legacy as the king of the sport at the annual Holmenkollen Ski Festival. He is the only man in history to have won the 50km race at the festival on six occasions, triumphing in 1918, 1919, 1920, 1921, 1923 and 1924.

AGE NO BARRIER FOR KIRVESNIEMI

Finland's Harri Kirvesniemi competed in the FIS Cross-Country World Cup for a staggering 19 years between 1982 and 2001 and recorded six race victories. The last of those wins was a record-breaking one: he was 41 years 305 days old when he won the 50km event in Oslo, Norway, on 11 March 2000 to become the oldest race-winner in the competition's history.

HAKULINEN AT THE GOLDEN DOUBLE

Having won 50km gold at the 1952 Winter Games in Oslo (recording the legendary time of 3:33.33), Finland's Veikko Hakulinen was already an established cross-country skiing star when he travelled to the 1954 FIS Nordic World Ski Championships in Falun, Sweden, and he confirmed that status after skiing to gold in the 15km race. He etched his name even more permanently into the sport's record books when, at the 1958 World Championships in Lahti, Finland, he won the 15km race yet again to become the first cross-country skier in history to retain a title at the event.

Above: Finnish cross-country legend Veikko Hakulinen.

MAGICAL MYLLYLAE WINS TRIPLE GOLD

Finland's Mika Myllylae showed he was a cross-country skier of considerable substance when he picked up three medals (one silver and two bronze) at the 1994 Winter Games at Lillehammer, Norway. He became world champion for the first time at Trondheim, Norway, in 1997 and went on to become the star turn at the 1999 FIS Nordic World Ski Championships at Ramsau, Austria. First he won the 30km race; three days later he stormed to victory in the 10km; and, to round out a magical nine days, he outclassed the rest of the field in the 50km event to become the first cross-country skier in history to win three individual gold medals at a single World Championships. His career would end controversially, however. In 2001, just as he was on the point of establishing himself as one of the sport's all-time greats, he was suspended for two years after failing a dope test.

Left: Mika Myllylae dominated the 1999 World Championships in Ramsau, Austria.

Women's Cross-Country Skiing: Olympic Games

Women's cross-country skiing made its first appearance at the 1952 Winter Games in Oslo (some 28 years after the inaugural men's competition) with a 10km event. At the last two Winter Games, medals have been awarded in six races, four of them in individual events (10km, 15km, 30km and sprint) and two in team races (4 x 5km relay and team sprint).

SMETANINA: THE SPORT'S FIRST STAR

The first true star of women's cross-country skiing, Raisa Smetanina secured her first success on the international stage at the 1974 FIS Nordic World Ski Championships at Falun, Sweden, when she won an individual bronze medal (in the 5km event) and a team gold (in the 4 x 5km relay). She made her debut at the Winter Games two years later, at Innsbruck, Austria, where she picked up three medals (two gold and one silver) to start what would become an astonishing and hugely successful association with the event. By the time of her final appearance in 1992, she had set all-time records for: the most medals won (ten, shared with Italy's Stefania Belmondo); the most silver medals won (five); the most years passed between winning medals (16, between 1976 and 1992); the most medals won at different Games (five, shared with Italy's Gabriella Peruzzi); and for being the oldest athlete in Winter Games history to win a gold medal (she was 39 years 354 days old when she won gold in the 4 x 5km relay with the Unified Team – EUN – in 1992).

Right: Raisa Smetanina with the Olympic gold medal she won at Albertville in 1992.

BELMONDO'S OLYMPIC STAR TURN

A two-time gold medallist at the 1989 Junior World Championships, Italy's Stefania Belmondo made a smooth transition into senior events, winning her first World Cup race later that same year, and travelled to the 1992 Winter Games as a serious contender for medals. She lived up to the hype, winning gold in the 30km event and picking up two further medals (a silver and a bronze). The success did not end there. By the time she made her final appearance at the Games, at Turin 2006 (at which she had the honour of lighting the Olympic Flame), she held the all-time competition records for the most medals won (ten – shared with Raisa Smetanina) and for the most bronze medals won (five)

Left: Stefania Belmondo of Italy drops to her knees after winning the Olympic Games 15km cross-country gold medal at Salt Lake City in 2002.

RECORD-BREAKING GOLD-MEDAL HAUL

Having enjoyed three podium finishes in her debut World Cup season (in 1989–90), Lyubov Egorova recorded her first victory in international competition at the 1991 FIS Nordic World Ski Championships at Val di Fiemme, Italy (in the 30km event), and won another gold medal with the Soviet Union's 4 x 5km relay team. She made her Winter Games debut (representing the Unified Team) at Albertville 1992 and stole the headlines, winning three gold medals (in the 10km, 15km and 4 x 5km relay) and two silvers. The success continued at Lillehammer 1994 when she won three further gold medals (in the 5km, 10km pursuit and the 4 x 5km relay) and a silver. Her haul of six gold medals is an all-time record for a female cross-country skier at the Winter Games.

Right: Lyubov Egorova made nine trips to a Winter Olympic Games podium, six times taking the top step.

PAIR'S THREE-IN-A-ROW JOY

Larissa Lazutina and Yelena Valbe's association with first the Unified Team and then Russia's 4 x 5km relay team was a record-breaking one. Not only did the pair win three successive gold medals (at Albertville 1992, Lillehammer 1994 and Nagano 1998), they also became the only women in cross-country skiing history to win three successive gold medals in the same event at the Winter Games.

OLYMPIC VETERAN

She was a world champion for the first of three times in 1978 (she was part of Finland's victorious 4 x 5km relay team), but the major highlight of Marja-Liisa Kiversniemi's career came at the 1984 Winter Games at Sarajevo when she stole the headlines by winning all three individual events (in the 5km, 10km and 20km). Although she never reached such dizzy Olympic heights again, the Finn's love of the competition is clear: she holds the record for the most Winter Games participated in by a female cross-country skier – six, between 1976 and 1994. Intriguingly, her husband, Harri, also competed at six Winter Games – they are the only married pair in history to have competed at six Olympics.

MOST MEDALS WON (INDIVIDUAL): TOP FIVE

Pos	Medals	Name (country)	G	S	B
1	10	Raisa Smetanina (USSR/EUN)	4	5	1
=	10	Stefania Belmondo (Italy)	2	3	5
3	9	Lyubov Egorova (EUN/Russia)	6	3	0
4	8	Galina Kulakova (USSR)	4	2	2
5	7	Larissa Lazutina (EUN/Russia)	5	1	1
=	7	Yelena Välbe (EUN/Russia)	3	0	4
=	7	Marja-Liisa Kirvesniemi (Finland)	3	0	4
=	7	Manuela Di Centa (Italy)	2	2	3

MOST GOLD MEDALS WON (BY COUNTRY)

Pos	Medals	Country
1	27	USSR/EUN/Russia
2	9	Finland
3	6	Norway
4	5	Italy
=	5	Sweden
6	4	Germany (East/West)
7	2	Canada
=	2	Estonia
9	1	Czech Republic
=	1	Poland

RUSSIA'S GOLDEN HAUL

The most outstanding record of national success in women's cross-country skiing competition at the Winter Games belongs to the Soviet Union/Russia. Competitors from the nation have won a total of 24 gold medals in the competition, 15 more than second-placed Finland.

RECORD-SETTING LAST HURRAH

A seven-time Norwegian champion, Hilde Gjermundshaug Pedersen ensured that her final appearance at the Winter Games, at Turin in 2006, was both a memorable and record-breaking one. When she picked up a bronze medal in the 10km event (behind Estonia's Kristina Smigun-Vähi and compatriot Marit Bjørgen), she became, aged 41 years 189 days, the oldest medallist in Winter Games history.

Right: Hilde Gjermundshaug Pedersen proved the old adage, "If at first you don't succeed, try, try again," by winning a gold medal at 41.

Other Major Championships

The women's FIS Nordic World Ski Championships were contested for the first time at Falun, Sweden, in 1954 (some 29 years after the inaugural men's event was staged) and is now held in odd-numbered years. The women's FIS Cross-Country World Cup, an annual series of races (in different disciplines) to determine an overall champion, has been staged since 1973.

MOST WORLD CUP PODIUMS: TOP TEN

Pos	Podiums	Name (country)	G	S	B
1	81	Yelena Välbe (USSR/Russia)	45	22	14
2	68	Marit Bjørgen (Norway)	45	13	10
3	66	Stefania Belmondo (Italy)	23	26	17
4	60	Larisa Lazutina (USSR/Russia)	21	19	20
5	59	Bente Skari (Norway)	41	13	5
6	49	Kristina Smigun-Vähi (Estonia)	16	18	15
7	48	Katerina Neumannova (Czech Rep)	18	16	14
8	43	Virpi Kuitunen (Finland)	20	14	9
9	40	Lyubov Egorova (USSR/Russia)	13	17	10
10	37	Justyna Kowalczyk (Poland)	15	14	8

FIRST BACK-TO-BACK CHAMPION

A three-time Olympic gold medallist (at Sarajevo 1994) and a veteran of six Winter Games, Marja-Liisa Kirvesniemi made her FIS Cross-Country World Cup debut in March 1982 and recorded her first victory in only her eighth race (in the 5km race at Lahti on 5 March 1983). A star was born: two further wins and a second-place finish were enough to ensure she ended the season as the competition's overall champion. Seven victories in the 1983–84 season (including her memorable triple success at the Olympics) saw the Finn become the first woman in history (of eight) to make a successful defence of her World Cup crown.

Right: Marja-Liisa Kirvesniemi won a World Championship 4 x 5km relay gold medal in 1978 and two Olympic Games bronze medals in 1994.

Above: Yelena Välbe represented the Soviet Union, Unified Team and Russia in an outstanding career.

VÄLBE: THE WORLD CUP QUEEN

Born in Magadan, on what is now Russia's east coast, on 20 April 1968, Yelena Välbe made her FIS Cross-Country World Cup debut as an 18-year-old in February 1987, recorded her first victory in only her fourth race (in the 15km at Campra, Switzerland, on 14 December 1988) and, thanks to six further wins, ended her first full season as the overall World Cup champion. She remained the woman to beat for the next eight years, claiming four further overall titles, in 1990–91, 1991–92, 1994–95 and 1997–98, and never finishing outside the top three in the end-of-season standings. She holds the all-time competition record for most overall titles (five) and most podium finishes (81).

SHORT BUT SWEET FOR MATIKAINEN

Marjo Matikainen's career may only have been short, but it was crowned with success. Born on 3 February 1965, the Finn made her FIS Cross-Country World Cup debut as a 19-year-old in December 1984 and recorded her first victory the following year (in the 5km at Labrador City, Canada, on 7 December 1985). It started a run of unprecedented success in the competition: she went on to claim that season's overall title, defended it successfully the following year (thanks to four race wins), and in 1987–88 she won three times en route to becoming the first woman in history to claim a hat-trick of World Cup titles (a feat since equalled by Poland's Justyna Kowalczyk). Matikainen retired from the sport in 1989 to concentrate on her studies and has since entered politics.

Above: Marjo Matikainen packed a lot of success into her very brief career.

MOST GOLD MEDALS

Yelena Välbe's star didn't only shine in Olympic and FIS Cross-Country World Cup action (she won seven medals – two gold – in the former and holds the all-time record for most overall titles and podiums in the latter); she was also the queen of the FIS Nordic World Ski Championships, winning a staggering all-time competition record 14 gold medals between 1989 and 1997. The Russian's golden moments were as follows: 1989 – 10km, 30km; 1991 – 10km, 15km, 4 x 5km relay; 1993 – 15km, 4 x 5km relay; 1995 – 30km, 4 x 5km relay; 1997 – 5km, 5km/10km combined pursuit, 15km, 30km, 4 x 5km relay.

YOUNGEST WORLD CUP WINNER

Gaby Nestler holds the distinction of being the youngest female race-winner in FIS Cross-Country World Cup history. The German was 18 years 329 days old when she won the 10km event at Les Saisies, France, on 11 January 1986. Intriguingly, it would prove to be the only victory of her career.

MAGICAL MARIT HEADS ALL-TIME WINS LIST

Initially a sprint specialist, Marit Bjørgen's hard work and dedication have turned her into one of the best all-round cross-country skiers of her generation. The Norwegian's first FIS Cross-Country World Cup win came in the 2km sprint race at Düsseldorf, Germany, on 26 October 2002. She claimed her first overall World Cup title in 2004–05, retained it the following year and, although since then she has failed to add to her overall honours haul, she has been overall runner-up on three occasions and race wins have continued to come her way. Her tally of 49 World Cup race wins is an all-time record for a cross-country skier of either sex.

FIRST THREE-TIME WINNER

Remembered chiefly for being the first cross-country skier in history to be awarded the prestigious Holmenkollen medal at the traditional annual Nordic skiing festival in Oslo, the Soviet Union's Alvetina Kolchina first came to international attention when she won 10km and 3 x 5km relay gold at the 1958 FIS Nordic World Ski Championships in Lahti, Finland. She retained her 10km title four years later (as well as winning the 5km race and another gold medal in the 3 x 5km relay), and in 1970 she became the first three-time winner of an event at the championships when she struck gold in the 10km once again.

OLDEST WORLD CUP WINNER

Norway's Hilde Gjermunudshaug Pedersen only recorded one individual victory in her career, but when that winning moment finally arrived it was a record-breaking one. Aged 41 years 60 days when she won the 10km event at Otepaeae, Estonia, on 7 January 2006, she had become the oldest race-winner in FIS Cross-Country World Cup history.

Below: Hilde Gjermundshaug Pedersen enjoyed an *annus mirabilis* in 2006.

Men's Freestyle Skiing: Olympic Games

Freestyle skiing has its roots in Scandinavia (in the 1930s, Norwegian cross-country skiers practised ski acrobatics as part of their cross-country training), was popularized in North America in the 1960s and '70s, and made its debut as a full-medal sport at the Winter Games at Albertville 1992. Three events were staged at Vancouver 2010 – moguls, aerials and ski cross.

THE MOGUL MASTER

Janne Lahtela's first medal at the Winter Games came at Nagano 1998 when, despite the fact that he had never won a World Cup race, he finished a surprise second in the moguls behind the USA's Jonny Moseley. His success four years later came as no surprise, however. By the time he arrived at Salt Lake City in 2002 he had become a world champion (in 1999), had won 14 World Cup races and was the class act of the field, qualifying for the finals in second place and edging the USA's Travis Mayer to the gold medal by 0.38 points. One of only two men in the sport's history to win gold and silver medals at the Winter Games, the five-time overall World Cup champion went on to become one of the dominant personalities in mogul skiing.

Right: A shock silver medalist at Nagano in 1998, Janne Lahtela was a hot favourite at Salt Lake City in 2002 and won again.

SUCCESSFUL SWITCH

Vancouver-born Dale Begg-Smith moved to Australia at the age of 16 because the country's ski programme offered him sufficient flexibility to combine skiing with his burgeoning business interests. It was a move that paid dividends for both parties, as not only did Begg-Smith become a wealthy man, he also represented his adopted country with huge success. After qualifying for Australian citizenship in 2003–04, he made a sensational Winter Games debut at Turin 2006, winning both the qualifying and final rounds to take moguls gold ahead of Finland's Mikko Ronkainen. Four years later in Vancouver he put up a strong defence of his title, only to lose out in the battle for gold by 0.17 points to Canada's Alexandre Bilodeau. It is the closest any man has come to date to successfully defending his moguls title at the Winter Games.

MEDALS WON (BY COUNTRY)

Pos	Medals	Country	G	S	B
1	8	United States	2	3	3
2	5	France	1	2	2
3	4	Canada	2	1	1
=	4	Belarus	1	1	2
=	4	Finland	1	2	1
6	2	Switzerland	2	–	–
=	2	Australia	1	1	–
=	2	China	1	–	1
=	2	Russia	–	1	1
10	1	Czech Republic	1	–	–
=	1	Austria	–	1	–
=	1	Norway	–	–	1

Above: It was almost a happy homecoming for Dale Begg-Smith, but the Australian just missed out at Vancouver in 2010.

MEDAL-TABLE LEADERS

No country has enjoyed more success in men's freestyle competition at the Winter Games than the United States. The country has claimed eight medals (two gold, three silver and three bronze). France lies in second place in the medals table with a haul of five (one gold, two silver and two bronze), ahead of three countries – Canada, Belarus and Finland – sharing third place with four medals.

SCHONBACHLER'S SWANSONG

Twenty-four competitors contested the first-ever men's aerials event at the Winter Games, at Lillehammer in 1994, with a host of American and Canadian skiers widely tipped to battle it out for the gold medal. Instead, Switzerland's Sonny Schönbächler (who had only just come out of retirement, specifically to savour the Olympic atmosphere, and who had placed a lowly tenth in the qualifying rounds) won both rounds in the finals to become the Winter Games' first-ever aerials champion.

PERSISTENCE PAYS OFF FOR VALENTA

At Nagano 1998, Ales Valenta's penchant for choosing moves with a high degree of difficulty failed to pay dividends when he finished outside the medals in fourth place. But he reaped the rewards in Salt Lake City four years later: with only five points separating the top seven aerialists as the competition moved into the final round, the 29-year-old Czech successfully executed the first triple back flip with five twists ever seen and stormed to the gold medal with a 4.62-point winning margin. He is the Czech Republic's only ever medallist in men's freestyle skiing at the Winter Games.

Above: Ales Valenta's high-risk moves earned him aerials gold at Salt Lake City in 2002.

Left: Han Xiaopeng flies the flag for China after winning his country's first Winter Games gold medal.

HAN SECURES CHINA'S FIRST GOLD

A former acrobat who had never won a World Cup event and so was considered a rank outsider for the medals in the men's aerials competition at the 2006 Winter Games in Turin, Han Xiaopeng of China caused something of a stir when he led the standings after the qualifying round. And the 22-year-old proved that his performance had been far from a one-off when he finished third in the first of the two final rounds and second in the second to win the gold medal by 1.09 points. In the process, he had become China's first-ever gold medallist at the Winter Games.

SCHMID STORMS TO INAUGURAL SKI-CROSS GOLD

Michael Schmid was the outstanding performer in the enormously successful inaugural men's ski-cross competition at the 2010 Winter Games in Vancouver. In front of packed stands, the 25-year-old Swiss star set the pace in the qualifying round and then won every one of his subsequent four races (including the final, ahead of Austria's Andreas Matt) to become the first-ever men's ski-cross Olympic champion.

SKI BALLET

Ski ballet was included as a demonstration sport at both the 1988 and 1992 Winter Games, in Calgary and Albertville respectively. However, despite the fact that authorized competitions had been held from the late 1960s until 2000, the International Ski Federation then ceased all formal competitions in ski ballet, following a decline in its popularity, and the sport never achieved full Olympic medal status.

Other Major Championships

The FIS Freestyle World Ski Championships were held for the first time at Tignes, France, in 1986 and are now staged in odd-numbered years. Events currently contested at the championships are moguls, dual moguls, aerials, ski cross, slopestyle and half-pipe. The FIS Freestyle Skiing World Cup – for moguls, aerials and ski cross – has been running on an official basis every year since 1988.

GOLDEN START FOR LANGLOIS
Given that, thanks to six victories, he had won the overall title at the unofficial World Cup in 1984–85 (the FIS did not sanction the event until 1988), Lloyd Langlois was a strong favourite for the aerials gold medal at the inaugural FIS Freestyle World Ski Championships at Tignes, France, in 1986. And the 23-year-old American did not disappoint, beating Canada's Yves Laroche into second place to become the sport's first world champion. He defended his title three years later in Oberjoch, Germany.

ACROSKI'S DOUBLE WORLD CHAMPION
Formerly known as ski ballet, acroski was staged at each of the first seven FIS Freestyle World Ski Championships until the FIS discontinued the sport in 2000 due to a marked slide in its popularity. During that time (between 1986 and 1999), only one man managed to claim the World Championship crown on more than one occasion: France's Fabrice Becker, who triumphed in 1993 and 1997.

Right: The No. 1 bib was appropriate for Fabrice Becker.

DOUBLE COMBINED WORLD CHAMPION
Sergei Shuplestov would have travelled to the 1991 FIS Freestyle World Ski Championships in Lake Placid, USA, full of confidence – just a month earlier, at La Plagne, France, he had won the first World Cup competition of his career, in the combined event (consisting of moguls, aerials and acroski). And that confidence would have been justified: the Russian walked away with the combined World Championship crown. He defended his title successfully two years later in Altenmarkt-Zauchensee, Austria, and remains the only skier in history to achieve the feat. The event has not been staged at the World Championships since 1997.

WORTHINGTON'S ONE-MAN SHOW
The grandson of US athlete Harry Worthington, who competed in track and field at the 1912 Olympic Games in Stockholm, Trace Worthington won the Junior World Championships aerials title in 1986 and achieved the first of his career haul of 37 World Cup victories at La Clusaz, France, in 1990. He returned to La Clusaz five years later for the FIS Freestyle World Ski Championships and stole the show, winning both the aerials and combined titles. It remains the only time in history that a skier has won two gold medals at a single World Championships.

Left: Trace Worthington had a special fondness for the snow of La Clusaz, France.

BILODEAU BREAKS DUAL MOGULS HOODOO

Introduced at the FIS Freestyle World Ski Championships for the first time at Meiringen-Hasliberg, Switzerland, in 1999, the dual moguls is an event in which two skiers compete against each other rather than against the clock. The first six editions of the race at the championships saw six different winners, until 2011, when Canada's Alexandre Bilodeau, the 2009 champion, came to defend his title. Bilodeau, who at Vancouver 2010 had become the first Canadian in history to win a Winter Games gold medal on Canadian soil, now became the first skier at the World Championships to defend his dual moguls title.

Left: Dual moguls ace Alexandre Bilodeau.

SUCCESSFUL SWITCH FOR KRAUS

A former alpine skier whose best finish was 28th place in the slalom at both the 1997 and 2003 FIS World Ski Championships, Tomas Kraus switched to ski cross in 2002 and achieved instant success. The Czech won on his World Cup debut, at Tignes, France, on 30 November 2002, and also took the inaugural ski cross event at the FIS Freestyle World Ski Championships in Ruka, Finland, in 2005. Two years later, at Madonna di Campiglio, Italy, he became the first, and to date only, man in ski cross history to retain his World Championship crown.

Above: Tomas Kraus (left) enjoyed little success on the alpine skiing circuit, but he was an instant star at ski cross.

STAR OF THE WORLD CUP SLOPES

An eight-time Norwegian acroski champion and a world champion in the event in 1995, Rune Kristiansen has achieved unrivalled success in the FIS Freestyle World Cup. He made his debut in the competition as a 20-year-old in 1985, secured his first event victory on 12 December 1987, at Tignes, France, and went on to enjoy a glittering career. By the time he retired in 1996, he had amassed 67 podium finishes and an all-time World Cup record 38 victories.

YOUNGEST AND OLDEST

The youngest winner of an event in FIS Freestyle World Cup history is the USA's Torin Yater-Wallace, who was a mere 15 years 108 days old when he won the half-pipe event at La Plagne, France, on 20 March 2011. The competition's oldest event winner is the USA's Ian Edmondson, who was 42 years 319 days old when he won the acroski event at Ovindoli, Italy, on 4 March 2000.

MOST WORLD CHAMPIONSHIP MEDALS WON (BY COUNTRY): TOP TEN

Pos	Medals	Country	G	S	B
1	44	Canada	17	15	12
2	30	United States	11	8	11
3	27	France	11	6	10
4	12	Finland	4	4	4
5	7	Belarus	1	3	3
6	6	Austria	1	3	2
=	6	Switzerland	-	3	3
8	5	USSR/Russia	3	-	2
9	4	Australia	1	1	2
10	3	Germany	2	-	1
=	3	Czech Republic	2	1	-
=	3	Norway	1	1	1
=	3	Japan	-	2	1
=	3	Sweden	-	2	1

Women's Freestyle Skiing: Olympic Games

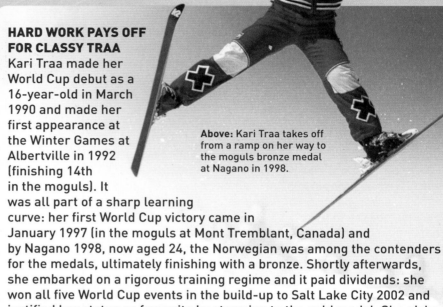

Women's freestyle skiing made its debut as a full-medal sport at the Winter Games at Albertville 1992 with a moguls event. An aerials competition was added to the programme at Lillehammer 1994 (having been a demonstration sport in both 1988 and 1992) and ski cross made a hugely successful debut at the 2010 Games in Vancouver.

HARD WORK PAYS OFF FOR CLASSY TRAA

Kari Traa made her World Cup debut as a 16-year-old in March 1990 and made her first appearance at the Winter Games at Albertville in 1992 (finishing 14th in the moguls). It was all part of a sharp learning curve: her first World Cup victory came in January 1997 (in the moguls at Mont Tremblant, Canada) and by Nagano 1998, now aged 24, the Norwegian was among the contenders for the medals, ultimately finishing with a bronze. Shortly afterwards, she embarked on a rigorous training regime and it paid dividends: she won all five World Cup events in the build-up to Salt Lake City 2002 and justified her status as favourite by storming to the gold medal. She picked up a silver at Turin 2006 too, to become the only freestyle skier (male or female) to have won three medals at the Winter Games.

Above: Kari Traa takes off from a ramp on her way to the moguls bronze medal at Nagano in 1998.

MEDALS WON (BY COUNTRY)

Pos	Medals	Country	G	S	B
1	7	Norway	2	2	3
2	6	United States	3	2	1
3	5	Canada	2	2	1
4	4	China	-	3	1
5	3	Australia	2	-	1
6	2	Japan	1	-	1
=	2	Switzerland	1	-	1
=	2	France	-	-	2
9	1	Uzbekistan	1	-	-
=	1	Unified Team	-	1	-
=	1	Sweden	-	1	-
=	1	Germany	-	1	-
=	1	Russia	-	-	1

Below: Tae Satoya gave Japan its only Olympic freestyle skiing gold medal and did it on home snow.

SHOCK WIN FOR SATOYA

When pre-tournament favourite Candice Gilg (the 1997 world champion and that season's overall World Cup leader) crashed out of the moguls event in the qualifying round at Nagano 1998, everyone knew the competition had been blown wide open, but few at that stage would have backed Japan's Tae Satoya to win the gold medal. Although extremely popular in her homeland – her every turn on the moguls was greeted with chants of "Tae, Tae" – the 21-year-old had never recorded a podium finish in a World Cup race and was considered a journeyman on the international circuit. But Satoya surpassed herself, recording the highest points total in her final run (and the third fastest time) to win an unlikely gold medal. She is Asia's only gold medallist in women's freestyle skiing at the Games.

SKI BALLET AT THE WINTER GAMES

For the women as with the men, ski ballet (or acroski as it came to be known) has only been included as a demonstration sport at the Winter Games and was never granted full Olympic medal status. France's Christine Rossi won the event at Calgary 1988, and Switzerland's Conny Kissling at Albertville 1992.

WEINBRECHT WINS FIRST GOLD

When freestyle skiing made its full-medal debut at Albertville 1992 with a moguls competition, the USA's Donna Weinbrecht, the 1991 world champion, who had led the FIS Freestyle World Cup moguls standings between 1990 and 1992, started as the firm favourite. And the 26-year-old American lived up to her billing, running a conservative race (she was only fourth fastest) but, pointedly, without any errors. It was enough: as other competitors floundered around her, she held on to beat the Unified Team's Jelisaweta Koschewnikowa by 0.19 points to become the sport's first-ever female Olympic champion.

CLOSE, BUT NOT CLOSE ENOUGH

In six editions of the moguls event at the Winter Games between Albertville 1992 and Vancouver 2010, no woman has ever made a successful defence of her title – although two have come mighty close. At Turin 2006, defending champion Kari Traa won a silver medal, losing out to Canada's Jennifer Heil. It was a similar story for the 26-year-old Canadian at Vancouver 2010. With only one runner left to race, she was in line for the gold medal, but America's Hannah Kearney produced a flawless, last-gasp run to pip her to the Olympic title.

CHERYAZOVA HITS THE HEIGHTS

Although Lina Cheryazova won every aerials event on the World Cup circuit in the build-up to the 1994 Winter Games at Lillehammer, doubts were raised about her pre-competition billing as favourite when she only qualified for the final in 12th place. But the mark of a true champion is to produce the goods when it really matters, and the 25-year-old Uzbekistan aerialist not only did that but showed star quality. She produced a stunning jump in the first of the final rounds to take an 11-point lead over her nearest rival (Sweden's Marie Lindgren) and held on in the second round to win her country's first-ever Olympic gold medal.

AUSTRALIAN SURPRISE

Australia's hopes of winning aerials gold at Salt Lake City 2002 appeared to lie in tatters just a week before the start of the Games when pre-event favourite Jacqui Cooper (the overall World Cup winner in 1999, 2000 and 2001) suffered a torn knee ligament and was forced to withdraw from the competition. But her compatriot Alisa Camplin, a former gymnast, picked up the mantle in spectacular fashion, placing third in both of the final two rounds to become the southern hemisphere's first female freestyle skiing gold medallist. And Australia has enjoyed further success in the event, Melbourne-born Lydia Lassila taking aerials gold at Vancouver 2010.

Left: Alisa Camplin went from the gymnasium to the ski slopes and won aerials gold at Salt Lake City in 2002.

FIRST SKI CROSS CHAMPION

At Vancouver 2010, it seemed for a while that to have been placed among the pre-event favourites group for gold in the Winter Games' first-ever ski cross competition was nothing but a curse. Of the group of four, first France's Ophélie David crashed out in the quarter-finals and then Kelsey Serwa (Canada) and Anna Holmlund (Sweden) failed to progress past the semi-finals. That left Vancouver-born Ashleigh McIvor as the last favourite standing, and the 26-year-old did not disappoint, leading the final from start to finish to become the event's first female Olympic champion.

Left: Ashleigh McIvor was the first ski cross Olympic gold medallist and she won in front of home fans at Vancouver.

Other Major Championships

The first women's FIS Freestyle World Ski Championships were staged at Tignes, France, in 1986, with moguls and aerials events. The dual moguls event was added to the programme in 1999, ski cross and half pipe joined the party in 2005, and slope style was contested for the first time in 2011. The FIS Freestyle World Cup has been staged annually since 1980.

DOUBLE WORLD CHAMPIONSHIPS JOY FOR GILG

Although she may have endured nothing but misery at the Winter Games (finishing 24th at Albertville 1992, fifth at Lillehammer 1994 and, despite her favourite's status, crashing out in the qualifying rounds at Nagano 1998), Candice Gilg showed her true class on the moguls fields at the FIS Freestyle World Ski Championships. The diminutive 5ft 3in Frenchwoman became world champion for the first time at La Clusaz, France, in 1995 and retained her title in Lizuna Kogen, Japan, two years later. She is the only woman in World Championships history to have made a successful defence of her moguls title.

Right: Candice Gilg is one of the greatest moguls skiers of all time.

TRAA: A SERIAL RECORD BREAKER

The most successful freestyle skier in Olympic history (she has won three medals at the Winter Games – one gold, one silver and one bronze), Kari Traa has also enjoyed her fair share of success at the FIS Freestyle World Ski Championships. She won both the moguls and double moguls events at the 2001 championships in Whistler, Canada (to become the first woman to win more than one gold medal at a single championships), defended her dual moguls title in 2003 (becoming the first person to achieve the feat) and, by the time she bowed out of international competition in 2007, held the all-time record for the most medals won by a female skier at the championships (seven).

HEIL STRIKES TRIPLE GOLD

Jennifer Heil made her FIS Freestyle World Cup debut as a 16-year-old in 1999, appeared at the FIS Freestyle World Ski Championships for the first time in 2001 (finishing a creditable seventh in the moguls) and won her first event the following year (at Inawashiro, Japan). She recorded her first-ever career victory in the dual moguls at the 2005 World Championships in Ruka, Finland, defended her title two years later in Madonna di Campiglio, Italy, and claimed the crown for a third time at Deer Valley, USA, in 2011. She is the only woman in World Championship history to have won the dual moguls on three occasions.

CHINA'S SNOW PRINCESS

Nicknamed "The Snow Princess", former gymnast Nina Li made her first international appearance as an 18-year-old at the 2001 FIS Freestyle World Championships at Whistler, Canada, and finished 15th in the aerials. The Chinese aerialist showed her immense promise with a second-place finish in her first-ever FIS Freestyle World Cup event (at Mount Buller, Australia, on 8 September 2001), finished 11th in the World Championships two years later and became world champion for the first time at Ruka, Finland, in 2005. By then the dominant aerialist on the circuit, she surprisingly had to settle for a silver medal at the 2006 Winter Games. However, she defended her title successfully at the 2007 World Championships in Madonna di Campiglio, Italy (becoming the first woman in history to do so), and then etched her name into the history books when she won the title for a third successive time at Inawashiro, Japan, in 2009.

Below: Nina Li does a spectacular flip on the way to becoming a three-time aerials world champion.

UEMURA THRILLS THE LOCALS

Although success at the Winter Games eluded her (she finished seventh, sixth and fifth in 1998, 2002 and 2006 respectively), Aiko Uemura has enjoyed success in both the FIS Freestyle World Cup (notching up 11 event victories) and at the sport's World Championships, particularly the 2009 event held in her native Japan (at Inawashiro). To the delight of the home crowd, the Nagano-born skier became only the second woman in the competition's history (following in the footsteps of Norway's Kari Traa – in 2001 and 2003) to win gold in both the moguls and dual moguls competitions, and the first Japanese woman to win a gold medal at the championships.

Left: Aiko Uemura of Japan matched Kari Traa's moguls and dual moguls successes.

MOST MEDALS WON (BY COUNTRY): TOP TEN

Pos	Medals	Country	G	S	B
1	26	Canada	10	7	9
2	23	United States	6	8	9
3	10	Norway	5	4	1
4	9	France	5	2	2
=	9	Germany	1	3	5
6	8	Australia	4	1	3
7	7	China	4	2	1
8	6	Switzerland	1	4	1
=	6	Sweden	-	4	2
10	5	Japan	2	1	2

AMERICAN MEDAL SWEEP

The inaugural FIS Freestyle World Ski Championships, held at Tignes, France, in 1986, saw a curiosity in the event's history. The USA's Mary Jo Tiampo saw off the challenge of her compatriot Hayley Wolff to become the first-ever moguls world champion, and another American, Maria Quintana, struck gold in the aerials competition. It is the only time in the championships' history that all the medals on offer have been won by competitors from one nation.

IN A LEAGUE OF HER OWN

Because her specialist sport, acroski (also known as ski ballet), never attained full-medal status at the Winter Games – it only ever featured as a demonstration sport, at Calgary 1988 (when she took bronze) and at Albertville 1992 (when she won gold) – Conny Kissling's supreme talent never achieved the international recognition it deserved. And it was some talent: the Swiss star dominated her sport for a decade, winning the overall FIS Freestyle World Cup title ten years in a row between 1983 and 1992. It is a record that seems certain to stand the test of time.

Right: Champion Anais Caradeux is flanked by second-placed Mirjam Jaeger, left, and Marta Ahrenstedt after the World Cup half-pipe in 2006.

YOUNGEST AND OLDEST

The FIS Freestyle World Cup's youngest event winner is Anais Caradeux (France), who was 15 years 199 days old when she won the half-pipe event at Les Contamines, France, on 15 January 2006. The competition's oldest event winner is Austria's Katharina Gutensohn, who was 42 years 357 days old when she won the ski cross event at Meiringen-Hasilberg, Switzerland, on 14 March 2009.

Men's Nordic Combined: Olympic Games

Nordic combined – an event that combines the disciplines of ski jumping and cross-country skiing (and which is also known as the Gundersen method) – was contested at the inaugural Winter Games in Chamonix, France, in 1924, with a single event. Today, three events are contested: the 10km individual normal hill; the 10km individual large hill; and the team normal hill (4 x 5km).

Above: Austria's Felix Gottwald sails through the night sky after jumping off the large hill at Vancouver in 2010.

MOST MEDALS WON

Pos	Medals	Name (country)	G	S	B
1	7	Felix Gottwald (Austria)	3	1	3
2	6	Johan Grøttumsbraten (Norway)	3	1	2
3	5	Samppa Lajunen (Finland)	3	2	-
4	4	Fred Børre Lundberg (Norway)	2	2	-
=	4	Bjarte Engen Vik (Norway)	2	1	1
=	4	Georg Hettich (Germany)	1	2	1
=	4	Klaus Sulzenbacher (Austria)	-	1	3

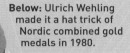

Below: Ulrich Wehling made it a hat trick of Nordic combined gold medals in 1980.

UNBEATABLE WEHLING

A fourth-place finish in the ski-jumping section of the Nordic combined event at the 1972 Winter Games in Sapporo, Japan, left 19-year-old Ulrich Wehling needing to beat his closest rival, Finland's Rauno Miettinen, by approximately one minute in the cross-country skiing race if he was to win the gold medal. As it turned out, the young East German beat the Finn by almost two minutes to start what turned out to be extraordinary Olympic career. Having added the World Championship title to his collection in 1974, Wehling was the dominant contestant at Innsbruck 1976 and cruised to victory in his defence of his Olympic title; and, four years later, although the result was far from a formality at Lake Placid (he was pushed all the way by Finland's Jouko Karjalainen), Wehling hung on to complete a hat-trick of Olympic titles. He is the only man in Nordic combined history to achieve this feat.

ALL-ROUNDER HAUG TAKES INAUGURAL GOLD

The first-ever Nordic combined event at the Winter Games, at Chamonix, France, in 1924, started with an 18km cross-country skiing race (integrated into the normal 18km race) that saw four Norwegians – led by Thorlief Haug – open a clear lead over the rest of the field. The ski-jumping section of the event was held on the same day as the main ski-jumping competition and Haug astonished the crowd with his superb style to hold on to his lead (following a fourth-place finish) and become Nordic combined's first-ever Olympic champion.

GOTTWALD HEADS THE MEDALS LIST

Felix Gottwald is the most decorated athlete in Olympic Nordic combined history. The Austrian won three gold medals (in the individual large hill and 4 x 5km team event at Turin 2006 and in the team event at Vancouver 2010), one silver medal (in the normal hill at Turin 2006) and three bronze medals (in the normal hill, large hill and 4 x 5km team events at Salt Lake City 2002) to stand alone at the top of the sport's all-time Winter Games medal table with seven.

ASIAN SURPRISE

Takanori Kono was part of Japan's 3 x 10km team that eased to a surprise gold medal at the 1992 Winter Games in Albertville and that retained its title two years later at Lillehammer – where he also enjoyed Olympic success in an individual capacity. His compatriot Kenji Ogiwara (the 1993 world champion and overall World Cup winner) was the strong pre-event favourite, but it was Kono who prospered, finishing fourth in the ski jumping and 11th in the cross-country to pick up the silver medal and become Japan's first, and to date only, Nordic combined individual medallist at the Winter Games.

LAJUNEN'S GAMES TO REMEMBER

Twenty-two-year-old Samppa Lajunen was the undoubted star of the Nordic combined competition at the 2002 Winter Games at Salt Lake City. The 1996–97 and 1999–2000 World Cup winner beat another Finn, Jaako Tallus, by 24.7 seconds to win gold in the normal hill event, then formed part of his country's four-man team that narrowly won gold ahead of Germany in the team event and rounded out an astonishing Olympic campaign by triumphing in the inaugural edition of the large hill event. He is the only athlete in Nordic combined history to win three gold medals at a single Winter Games.

Above: Samppa Lajunen won gold medals in all three Nordic combined Olympic events in 2002.

Below: Japan's superior jumping talent helped them to repeat as Nordic combined gold medallists at Lillehammer in 1994.

DOMINANT JAPAN EASES TO BACK-TO-BACK GOLD

Japan's Nordic combined relay team had first shown its potential when it won a surprise bronze medal at the 1991 FIS Nordic World Ski Championships in Val di Fiemme, Italy, but it still came as something of a surprise when, at the 1992 Winter Games in Albertville, it stole a commanding lead after the ski-jumping section of the event. Its 29.5-point lead equated to a start margin of 2:27 in the cross-country relay, which proved more than enough, and the Japanese cruised to gold with a 1:26.4 winning margin over Norway. Its performance at Lillehammer 1994 was even more commanding: a phenomenal exhibition of ski jumping left the Japanese with a start margin of 5:07 over Norway and the race for gold was effectively over. Japan completed the formalities to become the first country in Winter Games history to retain its Nordic combined team title.

MOST MEDALS WON (BY COUNTRY): TOP FIVE

Pos	Medals	Country	G	S	B
1	26	Norway	11	8	7
2	18	Germany (East/West)	7	4	7
3	13	Finland	4	7	2
4	12	Austria	3	2	7
5	4	France	2	1	1
=	4	United States	1	3	-
=	4	Switzerland	1	2	1
=	4	USSR/Russia	-	1	3

NORWEGIAN DOMINATION

Norway's absolute domination of Nordic combined's all-time medal table at the Winter Games – the country has won 26 Olympic medals in the sport (11 of them gold) – is largely to do with its early supremacy in the event. Norwegians won all of the first 12 available medals in the competition, and it wasn't until the 1948 Winter Games in St-Moritz that a non-Norwegian (Finland's Heikki Hasu, who won gold) found himself among the medals.

Other Major Championships

Nordic combined has been contested at the FIS Nordic World Ski Championships since 1925, when there was just a 10km individual normal hill event. A large hill team event was staged for the first time in 1982, the 10km individual large hill debuted in 1999, the 10km mass start was added to the programme in 2009 and the normal hill team event in 2011. The annual FIS Nordic Combined World Cup has been running since 1983–84.

Below: Hans Vinjarengen was the first superstar of Nordic combined.

GERMANY'S GOLDEN BOY

Born on 16 May 1977, Ronny Ackermann learned to ski at the age of five, took up ski jumping two years later, collected a silver medal with the German relay squad at the 1997 Junior World Championships and notched up his first FIS Nordic Combined World Cup victory two years after that (in the 15km individual normal hill event at Vuokatti, Finland). He picked up a bronze medal in the individual large hill event at the 2001 FIS Nordic World Ski Championships and won two silver medals at the 2002 Winter Games. If not winning gold was a disappointment, he put it behind him by becoming world champion (in the 15km individual normal hill) for the first time in 2003. He defended his title successfully at Obertsdorf, Germany, in 2005 and again at Sapporo, Japan, in 2007 to become the event's first three-time winner. Olympic success, however, has continued to elude him.

Left: Few Nordic combined skiers have started younger than Ronny Ackermann – and none have been more successful.

MOST WORLD CHAMPIONSHIP MEDALS WON (BY COUNTRY): TOP FIVE

Pos	Medals	Country	G	S	B
1	62	Norway	23	22	17
2	38	Germany (East/West)	14	15	9
3	22	Finland	5	9	8
4	16	Austria	4	4	8
5	7	Japan	5	-	2
=	7	Czechoslovakia	3	3	1

LORRY DRIVER TRIUMPHS

A lorry driver by day, with an enormous passion for the outdoors and a huge talent at cross-country skiing, Hans Vinjarengen first came to international prominence when, aged 23, he won a silver medal in the Nordic combined at the 1928 Winter Games in St-Moritz, Switzerland. He added to his growing reputation by taking gold at the following year's FIS Nordic World Ski Championships in Zakopane, Poland, and, to the delight of his home crowd, led Norway's clean sweep of the medals at the 1930 championships in Oslo to become the sport's first back-to-back world champion.

WEST GERMANS BREAK THE RELAY MOULD

Introduced in 1982, the team event at the FIS Nordic World Ski Championships (a three-man event until 1995 and a four-man one thereafter) sees each team member taking two jumps from the large hill for points, with the points difference between teams used to determine the starting times for the cross-country skiing relay race. The first three editions of the event saw three different winners – East Germany (at Oslo 1982), Norway (at Rovaniemi 1984) and West Germany (at Seefeld 1985). At Oberstdorf 1987, however, the West German trio broke the mould by becoming the first team in the history of the championships to retain its title.

THE STAR OF THE SHOW

Nordic Combined's overall World Cup winner in 1997–98 and 1998–99, Bjarte Engen Vik won a gold medal at the FIS Nordic World Ski Championships for the first time at Trondheim in 1997 as part of Norway's victorious relay team. At the 1999 World Championships in Ramsau am Dachstein, Austria, however, he was the individual star of the show. First, he cruised to gold in the individual normal hill event (with a comfortable 34.5-second winning margin over Finland's Samppa Lajunen) and then, a week later, secured an equally dominant victory in the championships' first-ever individual large hill event (by 30.2 seconds ahead of Austria's Mario Stecher) to become the first man in history to win two individual gold medals at a single World Championships.

Above: Bjarte Engen Vik (4) won two World Championship golds in 1999.

MOST WORLD CUP EVENT WINS: TOP FIVE

Pos	Wins	Name (country, span)
1	52	Hannu Manninen (Finland, 1994–)
2	28	Ronny Ackermann (Germany, 1997–2010)
3	26	Bjarte Engen Vik (Norway, 1991–2001)
4	24	Felix Gottwald (Austria, 1993–2011)
5	22	Samppa Lajunen (Finland, 1996–2004)

YOUNGEST AND OLDEST

Austria's Mario Stecher is the youngest person to win an FIS Nordic Combined World Cup event: he was 16 years 182 days old when he won the 15km individual normal hill event at Oslo, Norway, on 15 January 1994. Felix Gottwald is the oldest competitor to win a World Cup event. The Austrian was 34 years 360 days old when he won the 10km individual normal hill event at Schonach, Germany, on 8 January 2011.

FABULOUS FINN

Although Hannu Manninen was edged out in FIS Nordic World Ski Championships competition by his great rival Ronny Ackermann (who won ten medals to his six), no one has surpassed Manninen's record in the FIS Nordic Combined World Cup. A three-time gold medallist at the Junior World Championships (in 1995 and 1997), the Finn recorded his first World Cup victory at Falun, Sweden, on 8 March 1996, a month before his 18th birthday, became a senior world champion for the first time in 1999 (as part of Finland's victorious relay team) and became an Olympic champion (in the relay) in 2002. His great breakthrough came when he won the overall World Cup title in 2003–04, the victory triggering a sensational run of success. He held on to his crown the following year, made it a hat-trick in 2005–06 and then, in 2006–07, became the first man in history to win the overall title four years in a row. By 2011, he also held the all-time record for the most World Cup victories, with 52.

Right: Hannu Manninen has claimed almost twice as many World Cup Nordic combined victories as anyone else.

TRIPLE WORLD CUP JOY FOR OGIWARA

Kenji Ogiwara shot to international prominence when he formed part of Japan's Nordic combined relay team, surprise winners of the gold medal at the 1992 Winter Games in Albertville, but it was in an individual capacity that he would write his name into the history books. In 1993 he became individual normal hill world champion and ended the season as the overall FIS Nordic Combined World Cup winner. He won five times in the 1993–94 season to retain his title and six times in 1994–95 to become the first man in Nordic Combined history to win the overall World Cup title on three occasions.

Men's Ski Jumping: Olympic Games

Ski jumping is one of only six sports – cross-country skiing, figure skating, ice hockey, Nordic combined and speed skating are the others – to have been contested at every Winter Games since Chamonix 1924. Today's programme involves three events: the individual large hill (the K120, from a 90m jump), the individual normal hill (the K90, from a 70m jump) and the team large hill.

KING OF THE OLYMPIC HILL

The first-ever ski-jumping event at the Winter Games was held on a hill known as "Du Mont", which had a K-point of 71m and was situated at Les Bossons, near Chamonix, the 1924 Games' host town in France. Norwegian-born jumpers dominated the event, with Jacob Tullin producing two jumps of 49m (both with excellent style points) to become the sport's first-ever Olympic champion. The longest jump of the competition was 50m, made by the USA's Norwegian-born Anders Haugen (who ended up with the bronze medal).

Below: Finnish ski-jumpers have followed Antti Hyvärinen's lead.

THE GAMES' FIRST DOUBLE CHAMPION

Going into the 1932 Winter Games in Lake Placid, New York, 19-year-old Norwegian Birger Ruud, winner of the World Championship title earlier in the year, was considered the strongest challenger to his 24-year-old brother Sigmund, who had won the silver medal at St-Moritz 1928. And it was the younger of the two brothers who triumphed: Birger Ruud produced jumps of 66.5m in the first round and 69m in the second (both with high style marks) to take gold. He was again the star of the show at the 1936 Games in Garmisch-Partenkirchen, Germany. In front of a colossal crowd (reported to be 106,000), the Norwegian, now aged 24, lay in second place after the first round (with a leap of 75m) and then in the second, when it mattered, produced a stylish leap of 74.5m to become the first man in history to retain his Olympic ski-jumping title.

Above: Norway's Birger Ruud won gold medals in 1932 and 1936 and a silver, aged 36, in 1948.

HYVÄRINEN ENDS NORWAY'S RUN OF SUCCESS

Norwegian jumpers had dominated the first six editions of ski jumping at the Winter Games, producing the sport's first six Olympic champions and winning 14 of the possible 18 medals on offer, but that all changed at the 1956 Games at Cortina d'Ampezzo, Italy. To Norway's great shock, not one of the nation's team members finished in the top eight; instead, Finland's 23-year-old Antti Hyvärinen, who had finished seventh at the 1952 Games in Oslo, produced jumps of 81m in the first round and 84m in the second (the longest in the competition) to become the sport's first-ever non-Norwegian Olympic champion.

KANKKONEN DIGS DEEP TO TAKE INAUGURAL GOLD

The Winter Games' first normal hill event (known as the K70 and contested on a jump 70m in length over three rounds) was staged at Innsbruck 1964, with Norway's Toralf Engan (the 1962 normal hill world champion) and Finland's Veikko Kankkonen (winner of that year's Four Hills tournament) expected to vie for the gold medal. After the first round, Czechoslovakia's Josef Matous held a surprise lead, with Engan in second and Kankkonen a distant 29th, and seemingly out of contention. But cometh the hour ... In the second round the Finn produced the longest jump of the day (80m) and, with the excellent style points, propelled himself up the leaderboard. He hadn't finished there: a final-round jump of 79m saw him pip Engan for gold to become the Winter Games' first-ever normal hill champion.

FUNAKI THRILLS EXPECTANT HOME CROWD

A huge crowd of 30,000 gathered at the foot of the Hakuba Ski Jump prior to the individual large hill competition at the 1998 Winter Games at Nagano, full of expectation that Japan could end its 26-year wait for further ski-jumping success (following Yukio Kasaya's individual normal hill gold-medal success at Sapporo 1972). And there was every reason for hope: the nation's team contained reigning world champion Masahiko Harada and Kazuyoshi Funaki, who had already claimed a silver medal in the normal hill event. Austria's Andreas Widhölzl held the lead at the halfway stage, but Funaki leapt a staggering 132.5m in the second round to send the crowd into raptures and become the Winter Games' first, and to date only, non-European large hill champion.

Right: Japan have only won ski-jumping gold medals when they are Winter Olympic Games' hosts.

MOST MEDALS WON (BY COUNTRY): TOP TEN

Pos	Medals	Country	G	S	B
1	29	Norway	9	9	11
2	23	Austria	6	7	10
3	22	Finland	10	8	4
4	16	Germany (East/West)	6	6	4
5	9	Japan	3	4	2
6	7	Czechoslovakia	1	2	4
7	5	Switzerland	4	1	-
=	5	Poland	1	3	1
9	2	Sweden	-	1	1
=	2	Yugoslavia	-	1	1

AWESOME AMMANN SETS THE BENCHMARK

In December 1997, an unknown 16-year-old Swiss ski jumper named Simon Ammann made his World Cup debut at Oberstdorf, Germany, and finished a creditable 15th. He qualified for the following year's Winter Games at Nagano, finishing 35th in the normal hill and 39th in the large hill, but his best was yet to come. Although he had yet to record a World Cup victory, he arrived at the 2002 Winter Games off the back of five successive podium finishes and in the form of his life, but it still came as a shock when he walked away with the gold medals in both the normal and large hill events. At Turin 2006 he lost both of his titles (finishing a disappointing 36th in the normal hill and 15th in the large hill), but by Vancouver 2010 he had recaptured his form and there he again completed the normal hill/large hill double. In terms of individual gold medals won, he is the most successful ski jumper in Olympic history.

NYKANEN LEAPS INTO GLORY

Matti Nykänen had already enjoyed plenty of ski-jumping success by the time he arrived at the 1988 Winter Games – he had taken the large hill World Championships title at Oslo in 1982 and Olympic normal hill gold at the 1984 Games at Sarajevo – but his performances in Calgary would catapult him to legendary status. First he crushed the rest of the field to win gold in the individual normal hill event; then he leapt 120.5m in the first round of the large hill competition to storm into a lead he would never relinquish; and, finally, he rounded out a perfect competition by forming a part of Finland's victorious quartet in the team event. He was the first man in history to win both individual ski-jumping events at the Winter Games.

Left: Simon Ammann shows off his record third and fourth Winter Olympic Games gold medals, won at Vancouver in 2010.

Other Major Championships

Ski jumping was contested at the FIS Nordic World Ski Championships for the first time in 1925, with a large hill competition; the normal hill was added to the programme in 1962, the team large hill in 1982 and the team normal hill in 2001. The FIS Ski-Flying World Championships, now staged in even-numbered years, were held for the first time in 1972. The FIS Ski Jumping World Cup has been held annually since 1979–80.

SKI JUMPING DISTANCE WORLD RECORD PROGRESSION: LAST TEN

Length (m)	Year	Name (country)	Location (country)	Hill
246.5	2011	Johan Remen Evensen (Norway)	Vikersund (Norway)	Vikersundbakken
243.0	2011	Johan Remen Evensen (Norway)	Vikersund (Norway)	Vikersundbakken
239.0	2005	Bjorn Einar Romoren (Norway)	Planica (Slovenia)	Letalnica Brator Gorisek
235.5	2005	Matti Hautamaki (Finland)	Planica (Slovenia)	Letalnica Brator Gorisek
234.5	2005	Bjorn Einar Romoren (Norway)	Planica (Slovenia)	Letalnica Brator Gorisek
231.0	2005	Tommy Ingebrigtsen (Norway)	Planica (Slovenia)	Letalnica Brator Gorisek
231.0	2003	Matti Hautamaki (Finland)	Planica (Slovenia)	Letalnica Brator Gorisek
228.5	2003	Matti Hautamaki (Finland)	Planica (Slovenia)	Letalnica Brator Gorisek
227.5	2003	Matti Hautamaki (Finland)	Planica (Slovenia)	Letalnica Brator Gorisek
225.0	2003	Adam Malysz (Poland)	Planica (Slovenia)	Letalnica Brator Gorisek
225.0	2000	Andreas Goldberger (Austria)	Planica (Slovenia)	Letalnica Brator Gorisek

A DAY TO REMEMBER FOR EVENSEN

Although not considered to be among the best ski jumpers in the world – he had only ever achieved four podium finishes on the FIS Ski Jumping World Cup circuit and had won a bronze medal with Norway in the team event at the 2010 Winter Games in Vancouver – Johan Remen Evensen had a couple of days to remember at Vikersund, Norway, in February 2011. On 11 February, in the training round of a World Cup event, he leapt a distance of 243m to break compatriot Bjorn Einar Romoren's world record (239m, set at Planica, Slovenia) that had stood since 2005. In the qualification round staged later that day, the 25-year-old did even better, launching himself a staggering distance of 246.5m to set a new mark. The following day, he recorded his first, and to date only, World Cup victory.

Left: Johan Remen Evensen rewrote the record books.

PLANICA STAGES FIRST 200M JUMP IN HISTORY

The Letalnica hill at Planica, Slovenia, sometimes referred to as "the mother of all jumping hills", was first constructed in 1968 and earned its reputation as a hill for big jumps in the very first event it held – the first five jumps were all world records. Re-modified in time for the 1994 FIS Ski-Flying World Championships, the hill hit the headlines again when Finland's Toni Nieminen launched himself down the slope and recorded an incredible distance of 203.0m – the first 200m-plus leap in history. The Letalnica hill lost its status as the world's biggest ski-jumping hill in 2011 following the redevelopment of Vikersundbakken in Norway.

Right: Speeding down the slope at Vikersund.

GRINI BOUNCES BACK

Two days in February 1967 saw a succession of record-breaking jumps at the Heini Klopfer ski-flying hill in Oberstdorf, Germany. On 10 February, Norway's Lars Grini broke compatriot Bjørn Wirkola's world record of 146m, set in 1966, with a jump of 147m. His moment in the spotlight was short-lived – later that day, Sweden's Kjell Sjöberg bettered his mark with a jump of 148m. Grini, however, bounced straight back: the following day, 11 February, he became the first man in history to produce a jump of 150m. This time his record would last for a year.

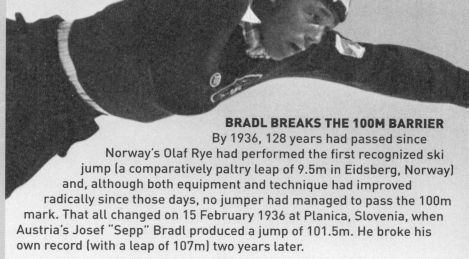

BRADL BREAKS THE 100M BARRIER

By 1936, 128 years had passed since Norway's Olaf Rye had performed the first recognized ski jump (a comparatively paltry leap of 9.5m in Eidsberg, Norway) and, although both equipment and technique had improved radically since those days, no jumper had managed to pass the 100m mark. That all changed on 15 February 1936 at Planica, Slovenia, when Austria's Josef "Sepp" Bradl produced a jump of 101.5m. He broke his own record (with a leap of 107m) two years later.

Above: Josef Bradl's place in the history of ski jumping is safe as the first man to clear 100m.

DOUBLE JOY FOR WIRKOLA

Although he would later become famous for becoming the only person ever to win the legendary Four Hills Tournament (Oberstdorf and Garmisch-Partenkirchen in Germany and Innsbruck and Bischofshofen in Austria) three years in a row (in 1967, 1968 and 1969), Norway's Bjørn Wirkola first made a name for himself at the 1966 FIS Nordic World Ski Championships in Oslo. The 23-year-old won the individual large hill competition (7.7 points ahead of Japan's Takashi Fujisawa) and then took the honours in the normal hill competition (4.0 points ahead of East Germany's Dieter Neuendorf) to become the first jumper in World Championship history to complete the normal hill/large hill double.

ENGAN TAKES INAUGURAL NORMAL HILL TITLE

The individual normal hill competition at the 1962 FIS Nordic World Ski Championships took place at Zakopane, Poland, and 25-year-old Toralf Engan denied the home crowd its moment of glory. The Norwegian pipped Poland's Antoni Laciak for the gold medal to become the event's first-ever world champion. He would go on to win gold in the individual large hill event at the 1964 Winter Games in Innsbruck, Austria.

THE BEST OF HIS GENERATION

Winner of the FIS Ski Jumping World Championships title in 1931 at Oberstdorf, Germany, Birger Ruud confirmed his status as one of the outstanding ski jumpers of his generation when he took Olympic individual large hill gold at the 1932 Winter Games at Lake Placid, USA. But more was to come: the Norwegian regained his World Championship title at Vysoké Tatry, Czechoslovakia, in 1935 (to become the event's first two-time winner) and won it again at Chamonix, France, two years later – the first jumper in history to make a successful defence of the title.

THE FLEA LEAPS INTO THE RECORD BOOKS

The most successful German ski jumper of all time, Jens Weissflog, known as "The Flea" because of his small stature, leapt into public consciousness when, in 1983–84, at the age of 19, he won the Four Hills Tournament. The following year he won individual normal hill gold at the Winter Games in Sarajevo and in 1985 confirmed his status as the best in the business by becoming normal hill world champion for the first time. He had to spend the next few seasons in the shadow of his great rival, Finland's Matti Nykänen, but he was back in the headlines once more at the 1989 World Championships in Lahti, Finland, where he reclaimed the individual normal hill title to become the event's first two-time winner.

Left: Jens Weissflog enjoyed most of his success as part of East Germany's team, but he competed and won World Championship medals with the unified Germany team in both 1991 and 1993.

HARADA'S DAYS TO REMEMBER

Masahiko Harada is best remembered for his spectacular and very public meltdown in the final round of the team large hill competition at the 1994 Winter Games at Lillehammer. With his Japan team holding a virtually unassailable lead and with him needing only to record a distance of 105m to win gold, he produced a disappointing leap of 97m to hand victory to Germany. But the Japanese star did enjoy plenty of success in his career: he won the individual normal hill competition at the 1993 FIS Nordic World Ski Championships at Falun, Sweden, and individual large hill gold at the 1997 Championships at Trondheim, Norway, to become the first non-European winner of either event.

Right: Masahiko Harada had a terrible day at Lillehammer in 1994, but his career had many golden moments.

MOST WORLD CUP EVENT WINS: TOP TEN

Pos	Wins	Name (country)
1	46	Matti Nykänen (Finland)
2	39	Adam Malysz (Poland)
=	39	Gregor Schlierenzauer (Austria)
4	36	Janne Ahonen (Finland)
5	33	Jens Weissflog (East Germany)
6	28	Martin Schmitt (Germany)
7	25	Andreas Felder (Austria)
8	21	Thomas Morgenstern (Austria)
9	20	Andreas Goldberger (Austria)
=	20	Simon Ammann (Switzerland)

TEAM RECORDS

No country has enjoyed greater success in the team large hill competition at the FIS Nordic World Ski Championships than Finland. They won the title for the first time at Engelberg, Switzerland, in 1984, became the first team to retain the title a year later, in Seefeld, Austria, completed a hat-trick of titles at Oberstdorf, Germany, in 1987 and made it four in a row at the 1989 Championships at Lahti, Finland. They have since added three further titles (in 1995, 1997 and 2003). Austria are the kings of the team normal hill competition, having won all three editions of the event (in 2001, 2005 and 2011).

KING OF THE WORLD CUP HILL

A four-time gold medallist at the Winter Games, Matti Nykänen's success wasn't solely confined to Olympic ski-jumping hills. He also won nine medals at the FIS Nordic World Ski Championships (five of them gold) and was one of the early stars of the FIS Ski Jumping World Cup, claiming the overall title in 1982–83, 1984–85, 1985–86 and 1987–88 to become the competition's first three- and four-time winner. By the time he bowed out of the competition following the 1990–91 season, the Finn held the all-time World Cup record for the most event wins (46).

CONSISTENCY THE KEY FOR AHONEN

A five-time gold medallist at the FIS Nordic World Ski Championships who was renowned for his icy, expressionless demeanour during competition, Finland's Janne Ahonen has spent more time in the thick of the action in FIS Ski Jumping World Cup competition than any other competitor. The two-time overall champion (in 2003–04 and 2004–05), who lies third in the all-time event winners' list, the Finn holds the all-time competition records for the most podium finishes (108) and for the most top tens (245).

Below: Matti Nykänen is the most decorated of all Finland's World Cup ski jumpers with 46 event victories.

Right: Showing off perfect form, Adam Malysz won his third World Championship in 2007.

MAGICAL MALYSZ

After six years of moderate success on the international circuit, which yielded only three FIS Ski Jumping World Cup victories, Adam Malysz kick-started his career by winning individual normal gold at the 2001 FIS Nordic World Ski Championships at Lahti, Finland. The Pole defended his title successfully at Val di Fiemme, Italy, two years later (becoming the first man in history to achieve the feat) and made it a competition to remember by winning the large hill event. Four years later, at the 2007 World Championships at Sapporo, Japan, he won the normal title yet again to confirm his status as one of the best jumpers of his generation and become the event's only three-time winner.

ROOKIE NIEMINEN'S EXPLOSIVE DEBUT

Toni Nieminen's mastery of the new V-style technique – as opposed to the traditional Daescher technique (in which jumpers set their skis in a parallel position and place their arms behind the hips), which had dominated the sport since the 1950s – was the principal reason behind the most explosive debut season in FIS Ski Jumping World Cup history. In 1991–92, the Finn recorded eight victories on the circuit to become, aged 16 years 303 days, the youngest overall World Cup champion in history.

STEINER STRIKES DOUBLE SKI FLYING GOLD

Held on the sport's biggest hills, with a K-spot (the point at which jumpers leave the hill) usually positioned in excess of 185m, the FIS Ski Flying World Championships were held for the first time at Planica, Slovenia, in 1972, with 20-year-old Walter Steiner taking the gold medal. The Swiss star finished second the following year (behind East Germany's Hans-Georg Aschenbach), and although he did not take part in the event in 1975, he was the class of the field once again at the 1977 World Championships at Vikersund, Norway, beating second-placed Anton Innauer (Austria) by 17.5 points to become the competition's first two-time champion. Only two other jumpers – Germany's Sven Hannawald (in 2000 and 2002) and Norway's Roar Ljøkelsøy (in 2004 and 2006) – have since equalled his feat.

A SEASON TO REMEMBER FOR SCHLIERENZAUER

A former world junior champion who made his FIS Ski Jumping World Cup debut as a 16-year-old at the Holmenkollen Ski Festival on 12 March 2006 (at which he finished a creditable 24th), Gregor Schlierenzauer won his first World Cup event in the 2006–07 season, became a senior world champion later that year (as an Austrian team member in the team large hill) and finished runner-up in the overall World Cup standings in 2007–08. The following season was one to remember for the young Austrian: he won 13 events, secured 20 podium finishes and won his first overall World Cup title with a haul of 2,083 points – all three of which are all-time World Cup records.

Right: Gregor Schlierenzauer celebrates winning the World Cup in January 2009.

Women's Ski Jumping

Although women's ski jumping has never appeared at the Winter Games (it will make its first appearance at Sochi, Russia, in 2014), the sport has been contested internationally for a number of years. The FIS Ladies Grand Prix has been held annually since 1999 and the FIS Ski Jumping Continental Cup since 2004–05; a women's event was staged at the FIS Nordic World Ski Championships in 2009; and the inaugural season of the women's FIS Ski Jumping World Cup took place in 2011–12.

Above: Anette Sagen has won four World Cups, five Continental Cups and four Grands Prix.

IRASCHKO SHOWS HER CLASS

Famous both for her three victories at the Holmenkollen Ski Festival (in 2000, 2001 and 2003) and for being the first woman ever to record a jump of more than 200m (during practice at Bad Mitterndorf, Austria, on 29 January 2003), Daniela Iraschko first showed her potential when she won the overall FIS Ladies Grand Prix title in 2000 – the first of a record five titles in the competition (the others were in 2001, 2002, 2005 and 2010). Runner-up to Anette Sagen in the FIS Ski Jumping Continental Cup in 2007–08 and 2008–09, the Austrian finally burst out of her rival's shadow in 2009–10, claiming the overall title for the first time and defending it successfully the following season. Still going strong after a decade in the sport she took gold in the women's normal hill competition at the 2011 FIS Nordic WorldSki Championships at Midtstubakken, Norway.

Left: Daniela Iraschko is used to showing off her gold medals.

SAGEN STARTS THE DEBATE

Considered one of the greatest female ski jumpers of all time, Norway's Anette Sagen hit the headlines in 2004 when, despite her undoubted talent, she was denied the opportunity to jump from the K185 hill in Vikersund. The news did much to trigger an extended debate over sexual equality in the sport and could be considered the real catalyst that led to the sport's inclusion at the 2014 Winter Games. On the hill, however, Sagen has enjoyed a glittering career, winning the overall FIS Ski Jumping Continental Cup a record five years in a row (between 2004–05 and 2008–09) and the FIS Ladies Grand Prix on four occasions (in 2003, 2004, 2006 and 2008). At the 2009 FIS Nordic World Ski Championships at Liberec, Czech Republic, when a women's ski jumping event was held at the championships for the first time, Sagen picked up a bronze medal.

CONTINENTAL CUP: OVERALL TOP THREE PLACINGS

Year	First	Second	Third
2004–05	Anette Sagen (NOR)	Lindsey Van (USA)	Daniela Iraschko (AUT)
2005–06	Anette Sagen (NOR)	Lindsey Van (USA)	Jessica Jerome (USA)
2006–07	Anette Sagen (NOR)	Ulrike Gässler (GER)	Lindsey Van (USA)
2007–08	Anette Sagen (NOR)	Daniela Iraschko (AUT)	Jacqueline Seifriedsberger (AUT)
2008–09	Anette Sagen (NOR)	Daniela Iraschko (AUT)	Ulrike Gässler (GER)
2009–10	Daniela Iraschko (AUT)	Ulrike Gässler (GER)	Anette Sagen (NOR)
2010–11	Daniela Iraschko (AUT)	Coline Mattel (FRA)	Eva Logar (SLO)
2011–12	Daniela Iraschko (AUT)	Sarah Hendrickson (USA)	Maja Vtic (SLO)

Left: Lindsey Van was the first American ski jumper to win a top international competition.

VAN BOUNCES BACK TO TAKE INAUGURAL TITLE

After years of being upstaged by Anette Sagen and Daniela Iraschko, Lindsey Van's first moment in the spotlight came when she won the overall FIS Ladies Grand Prix title for the first time in 2007 (having finished as runner-up the previous three seasons). Just when it appeared she had made the breakthrough, however, she suffered a career-threatening knee injury, which was followed by a painfully slow return to fitness – but it was worth it. On 20 February 2009, at the FIS Nordic World Ski Championships at Liberec, Czech Republic, she beat off the challenge of Ulrike Gässler (Germany) and Anette Sagen (Norway) to become women's ski jumping's first-ever world champion.

YOUNG GUN MATTEL MAKES HER MARK

One of the brightest prospects on the women's international ski-jumping circuit, France's Coline Mattel first took up the sport at the age of seven, was taking part in adult competitions by the age of ten and made her debut in the FIS Ski Jumping Continental Cup on 17 February 2007 at the age of 11 (finishing 37th). She was still only 15 when she recorded her first victory in the competition, on 18 December 2010; a month later, she became junior world champion; in February 2011, she picked up a bronze medal at the FIS Nordic World Ski Championships; and she ended the year as the overall FIS Ladies Grand Prix champion. Greater honours surely await this supremely talented Frenchwoman.

Above: The sky's the limit for French teenage sensation Coline Mattel.

MOST FIS CONTINENTAL CUP WINS: TOP FIVE

Pos	Wins	Name (country)
1	45	Daniela Iraschko (AUT)
2	42	Anette Sagen (NOR)
3	15	Ulrike Gässler (GER)
4	9	Coline Mattel (FRA)
5	8	Lindsey Van (USA)

KAISER: THE FIRST CHAMPION

The first season-long international women's ski-jumping tournament in history, the FIS Ladies Grand Prix competition began in 1999, with five events (four in Germany and one in Austria). Austria's Sandra Kaiser was the star of the show, winning three of the events and finishing second in another to become the competition's first-ever champion.

WOMEN'S WORLD CUP: UP AND RUNNING

The women's FIS Ski Jumping World Cup was held for the first time in 2011–12 (some 32 years after the launch of the men's event) with 14 events staged around Europe. The USA's Sarah Hendrickson took the honour of winning the first-ever event (at Lillehammer, Norway, on 3 December 2011).

FIS LADIES GRAND PRIX: OVERALL TOP THREE PLACINGS

Year	First	Second	Third
1999	Sandra Kaiser (AUT)	Karla Keek (USA)	Daniela Iraschko (AUT)
2000	Daniela Iraschko (AUT)	Eva Ganster (AUT)	Heidi Roth (GER)
2001	Daniela Iraschko (AUT)	Henriette Smeby (NOR)	Eva Ganster (AUT)
2002	Daniela Iraschko (AUT)	Anette Sagen (NOR)	Helena Olsson (SWE)
2003	Anette Sagen (NOR)	Eva Ganster (AUT)	Lindsey Van (USA)
2004	Anette Sagen (NOR)	Lindsey Van (USA)	Eva Ganster (AUT)
2005	Daniela Iraschko (AUT)	Lindsey Van (USA)	Ulrike Gässler (GER)
2006	Anette Sagen (NOR)	Lindsey Van (USA)	Juliane Seyfarth (GER)
2007	Lindsey Van (USA)	Ulrike Gässler (GER)	Katie Willis (CAN)
2008	Anette Sagen (NOR)	Maja Vtic (SLO)	Atsuko Tanaka (JAP)
2009	Not contested		
2010	Daniela Iraschko (AUT)	Anette Sagen (NOR)	Ulrike Gässler (GER)
2011	Coline Mattel (FRA)	Daniela Iraschko (AUT)	Jessica Jerome (USA)

Men's Speed Skiing

Speed skiing, one of alpine skiing's oldest disciplines, has its roots in North America's Rocky Mountains when, more than a century ago, woodcutters and gold miners organized competitions on the mountains' slopes. The first official races were held in 1930; the World Championships (now staged every two years) took place for the first time in 1981; the sport made its only appearance at the Winter Games (as a demonstration sport) at Albertville 1992; and a World Cup circuit was launched in 2002.

FASTEST SPEEDS RECORDED: TOP TEN

Pos	Speed (km/h)	Name (country)	Year	Location
1	251.400	Simone Origone (Italy)	2006	Les Arcs, France
2	250.700	Philippe Goitschel (France)	2002	Les Arcs, France
3	250.700	Ivan Origone (Italy)	2006	Les Arcs, France
4	250.170	Jonathan Moret (Switzerland)	2006	Les Arcs, France
5	250.000	Philippe May (Switzerland)	2006	Les Arcs, France
6	249.650	Laurent Sistach (France)	2002	Les Arcs, France
7	248.790	Jukka Viitasaari (Finland)	2006	Les Arcs, France
8	248.450	Jukka Viitasaari (Finland)	2005	Les Arcs, France
9	248.280	Philippe May (Switzerland)	2005	Les Arcs, France
10	248.105	Harry Egger (Austria)	1999	Les Arcs, France

Right: Philippe May is one of five men to reach 250km/h on skis.

THE ANGEL OF THE SNOW

In 1932, Leo Gasperl had the courage to go where others had feared to tread. On a fenced track on the slopes of St-Moritz, Switzerland, and using specially constructed skis 2.4m in length, the Austrian-born son of a woodcutter set the first-ever official speed-skiing world record – known as the "flying kilometre". To the amazement of the huge crowd gathered at the foot of the slope, he reached a speed of 136.600km/h. News of his achievement spread quickly around the world and Gasperl – who had become known as "The Angel of the Snow" – had secured his status as speed skiing's greatest pioneer.

Right: Michael Prüfer won the gold medal at Albertville in 1992 when the Winter Olympic Games included speed skiing as a demonstration event.

McKINNEY BREAKS THE MYTHICAL 200KM/H BARRIER

A former downhill specialist with the US ski team, Steve McKinney learned the art of speed skiing from his friend Dick Dowarth and took up the sport seriously following a trip to watch speed-skiing races held at Cervina, Italy, in 1973. He returned the following year and set the first of his world records (189.473km/h), which lasted a year. In 1977, at Portillo, Chile, he set another world's best speed (198.020km/h) and, at the same venue a year later, went even faster, becoming the first man in history to break the 200km/h barrier (200.222km/h). This record would stand for four years.

ONLY APPEARANCE AT THE WINTER GAMES

Speed skiing has made only one appearance at the Winter Games, as a demonstration sport at Albertville 1992 at the Les Arcs speed-skiing course. France's Michael Prüfer, a 31-year-old medical doctor from Savoie who had broken the world record in 1988 (with a speed of 223.741km/h), broke his own record (registering 229.229km/h) to win the event. However, the competition was marred by the death of Swiss speed skier Nicolas Bochatay – he collided with a snow-grooming vehicle on a public slope outside the racing area on the morning of the speed skiing finals – and, mainly because of safety concerns, the sport has not featured at the Games again.

GOITSCHEL SURPASSES 250KM/H

A four-time world champion (in 1995, 1999, 2000 and 2002), a silver-medal winner at the sport's one and only appearance at the Winter Games, in 1992, and a former world record holder (when he reached 233.615km/h in 1993), France's Philippe Goitschel etched his name into the record books at Les Arcs, France, on 23 April 2002 when he became the first man in the sport's history to break the 250km/h barrier (with 250.700km/h). The 40-year-old celebrated his record-breaking achievement by announcing his immediate retirement from the sport.

WEBER BECOMES SPEED SKIING'S FIRST WORLD CHAMPION

The first-ever FIS Speed Skiing World Championships were staged at Storm Peak, USA, in 1981, with Austria's Franz Weber clocking the fastest time of the day (175.695km/h) to become the sport's first-ever world champion. He made a successful defence of his title three years later at Les Arcs, France, with a speed of 208.937km/h.

BRIT WILKIE BECOMES THE FASTEST MAN ON SKIS

Describing himself as a frustrated downhill skier, Briton Graham Wilkie abandoned his alpine skiing ambitions in 1984 and turned his attention to speed skiing. And with spectacular results: in April 1987, at the FIS Speed Skiing World Championships at Les Arcs, France, the 28-year-old smashed the world record (the first to do so at the championships), clocking a speed of 212.514km/h. In doing so, he became Britain's first, and to date only, speed-skiing world champion.

OTHER SPEED SKIING WORLD RECORDS

Monoski:	Xavier Cousseau (FRA), 212.260km/h Les Arcs, 2002.
VTT speed racing (with parachute):	Eric Barone (FRA), 222.223km/h Les Arcs, 2002.
Speed downhill:	Mathieu Sage (FRA), 210.770km/h Les Arcs, 2006.

UNSTOPPABLE ORIGONE

Born and raised in Italy's north-western alpine region of Aosta, Simone Origone first tried his hand at speed skiing at Les Arcs, France, in 2004 and had an immediate affinity with the discipline, proving himself good enough to earn selection for Italy's national squad shortly afterwards. Success came immediately: he won his first World Cup race at only his second attempt, claimed the overall World Cup title in his first season (2004) and, remarkably, ended the season as the sport's world champion (a title he has yet to relinquish, winning it again in 2005, 2006, 2007, 2009 and 2011). He proved his status as the best in the business when, on 20 April 2006, again at Les Arcs, he set a new speed record of 251.400km/h (that stands to this day). The Italian has further confirmed his as-yet-unchallenged superiority in the sport by winning further overall World Cup titles in 2005, 2006, 2007, 2009, 2010 and 2011. His record in that event makes stunning reading: he has notched up 45 podium finishes (with 24 wins) in the 51 events he has entered.

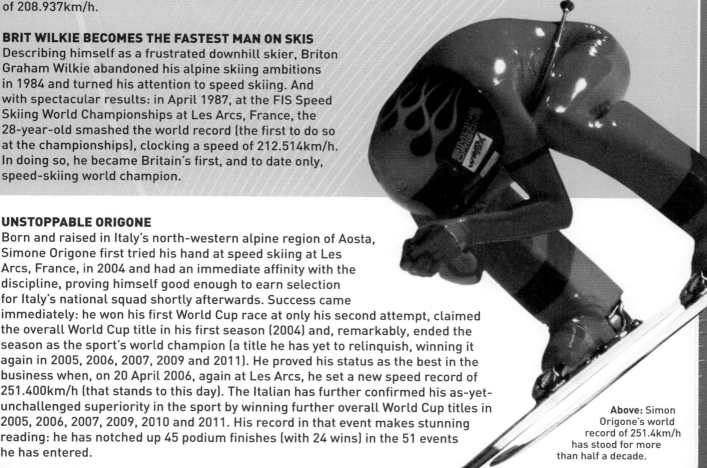

Women's Speed Skiing

Unusually, women's international speed-skiing competitions have run in parallel to the men's, so the first women's FIS Speed Skiing World Championships were held at Storm Park, USA, in 1981; a women's competition was held once at the Winter Games (as a demonstration sport), at Albertville 1992; and women have contested the FIS Speed Skiing World Cup on an annual basis since 2002.

Above: Elena Banfo has recorded the two fastest speeds by any Italian woman speed skier.

FASTEST SPEEDS RECORDED: TOP TEN

Pos	Speed (km/h)	Name (country)	Year	Location
1	242.590	Sanna Tidstrand (Sweden)	2006	Les Arcs, France
2	242.260	Karine Dubouchet Revol (France)	2002	Les Arcs, France
3	239.200	Sanna Tidstrand (Sweden)	2005	Les Arcs, France
4	238.570	Tracie Sachs (USA)	2006	Les Arcs, France
5	238.410	Elena Banfo (Italy)	2006	Les Arcs, France
6	237.780	Kati Metsapelto (Finland)	2006	Les Arcs, France
7	234.528	Karine Dubouchet Revol (France)	1999	Les Arcs, France
8	234.070	Elena Banfo (Italy)	2005	Les Arcs, France
9	232.110	Karine Dubouchet Revol (France)	2002	Les Arcs, France
10	231.214	Carolyn Skyer-Curl (USA)	1997	Les Arcs, France

FIRST OFFICIAL WOMEN'S RECORD

The first official speed skiing record was set by Emanuel Spreafico on the slopes of Cervinia, under the admiring gaze of the Matterhorn, in 1963. In front of an ecstatic home crowd, the Italian recorded a speed of 127.138km/h. The mark would stand as a record for two years until Austria's Kristl Staffner reached 143.230km/h at the same venue in 1965.

Right: Sanna Tidstrand is a multiple World Cup champion.

SENSATIONAL SWEDE SETS NEW MARK

A winner in the skicross event at the 2005 X Games at Aspen, Colorado, Sanna Tidstrand made her mark on speed skiing in spectacular style in the Pro Mondial event at Les Arcs, France, in April 2006. The Swedish star hit the headlines by recording a speed of 242.590km/h to beat Karine Dubouchet Revol's world record of 242.260km/h (set in 2002). Tidstrand confirmed her status as one of the sport's biggest stars by winning gold at the 2007 FIS Speed Skiing World Championships and by claiming the overall FIS Speed Skiing World Cup title in 2008, 2009 and 2011.

DIMINO-SIMONS BREAKS 200KM/H BARRIER

An air stewardess by profession with a passion for speed skiing in her spare time, the United States' Melissa Dimino-Simons, a native of Olympic Valley, California, made history on 19 April 1984 at Les Arcs, France. She became the first woman in history to clock a speed in excess of 200km/h (200.780km/h) – her record stood until 1987, when France's Jacqueline Blanc clocked a speed of 201.005km/h on the same Les Arcs course.

CULVER BECOMES FIRST DOUBLE WORLD CHAMPION

One of the early stars of the women's speed-skiing circuit, Salt Lake City's Kirsten Culver broke the record on 23 April 1983 when she recorded a speed of 194.384km/h at Silverton, Colorado, USA. Two years later, at Les Arcs, France, she became world champion for the first time (with a speed of 166.358km/h), and in 1986, at La Clusaz, France, clocked a speed of 191.950km/h to become the first woman in history to mount a successful defence of her title at the World Championships.

OTHER SPEED SKIING RECORDS

Speed downhill: Charlotte Bar (France) – 200.110km/h at Les Arcs, France, in 2006.
Monoski: Patty Moll (Switzerland) – 145.450km/h at Les Arcs, France, on 2–3 April 2004.

WOMEN'S SPEED SKIING'S BIGGEST STAR

There had been no bigger star in women's speed skiing than France's Karine Dubouchet Revol. She burst on to the international scene in 1996 when she took gold at the FIS Speed Skiing World Championships at Vars, France. It was the start of a hugely successful association with the event that saw her claim further victories in 1998, 1999, 2000, 2001, 2009 and 2011. A former world record holder (she clocked 242.260km/h at Les Arcs, France, in 2002), the talented Frenchwoman also won the overall FIS Speed Skiing World Cup title in its inaugural season in 2002.

Above: Karine Dubouchet Revol was the first woman to achieve 240km/h.

SPEED SKIING AT THE WINTER GAMES

Women's speed skiing was introduced, as a demonstration sport, at the Winter Games in Albertville in 1992. Finland's Tarta Mulari won the event (with a speed of 219.245km/h – a new world record) ahead of Norway's Liss Pettersen and Switzerland's Renata Kolarova. That remains the sport's only Olympic appearance.

THE WORLD CUP QUEEN

Tracie Sachs, from Long Island, New York, took up speed skiing seriously in 1999 and ended her first full year in the sport ranked third in the world. A glistening career had begun: she won the first of a record five straight overall FIS Speed Skiing World Cup titles in 2003 (her haul of 180 points in 2005 is an all-time competition record) and became world champion for the only time in her career at Breuil/Cervinia, Italy, in 2005. The only honour missing from her star-studded resumé is the world speed record, but she came mighty close: at Les Arcs, France, in April 2006, she reached a speed of 238.570km/h – only two women in history (Sweden's Sanna Tidstrand and France's Karine Dubouchet Revol) have gone faster.

Right: Tracie Sachs quickly surpassed Carolyn Skyer-Curl as the USA's greatest ever speed skier.

Chapter 2 ICE SKATING

Skating on ice is an ancient practice, whose origins date back some 4,000 years to southern Finland. Today the term ice skating covers sports in which competitors move on ice using ice skates on specially prepared indoor and outdoor tracks. Modern-day competitive disciplines include figure skating (singles, pairs and ice dancing – in which competitors perform prepared routines to music) and speed skating (short-track and long-track racing), both of which are governed by the International Skating Union, which sanctions numerous other events at World Championships.

Above: Germany's Aliona Savchenko and Robin Szolkowy are almost perfectly synchronized as they perform in the pairs free skating event of the 2011 ISU World Figure Skating Championships in Moscow. The German couple rebounded from their silver medal at Vancouver 2010 – when it doubled as the Winter Olympic Games competition – to win a third gold medal in Russia (and a fourth would come at the 2012 World Championships in Nice).

Men's Figure Skating – Singles: Olympic Games

Men's figure skating first appeared at the Summer Olympic Games in London in 1908, returned at the 1920 Games in Antwerp and has been part of the programme of events at every Winter Games since Chamonix 1924. The United States has been the event's most successful nation, winning 15 medals, seven of them gold.

Below: Ronnie Robertson (left, silver), Hayes Alan Jenkins (centre, gold) and David Jenkins (right, bronze); a US clean sweep in 1956.

FIRST OLYMPIC CHAMPION

Men's figure skating's first true star, Ulrich Salchow claimed a record ten World Championships titles between 1901 and 1911, as well as nine European Championships gold medals and an Olympic gold medal, and landed the first jump in competition (taking off on the back inside edge of his skate on one foot and landing on the back outside edge of the skate on his other foot – the move was later dubbed the "salchow"). When men's figure skating made its first appearance at the Summer Olympic Games at London in 1908, the 30-year-old Swede was the firm favourite to capture gold. He built a huge lead with his opening routine and, although he placed second in the free skating programme (behind compatriot Richard Johansson), he had done enough to become the sport's first-ever Olympic champion. He would make one further appearance at the Olympic Games, at Antwerp in 1920, at which he finished fourth.

ONLY MEDAL SWEEP AT THE WINTER GAMES

There has only ever been one medal sweep in men's figure skating at the Winter Games, at Cortina d'Ampezzo, Italy, in 1956, when competitors from the United States won all three medals. The sweep also saw the only occasion in Olympic figure skating history in which two brothers – Hayes Alan Jenkins (gold) and David Jenkins (bronze) – finished on the podium. When younger brother David went on to win gold at the 1960 Games at Squaw Valley, California, the pair became the only brothers to have won Olympic figure skating gold medals.

YOUNG GUN BUTTON STRIKES OLYMPIC GOLD

The United States' Dick Button made a sensational Olympic debut at the 1948 Winter Games in St-Moritz. The young Harvard freshman had won his first senior US Championships title in 1946 and had finished runner-up – behind Switzerland's Hans Gerschwiler – at the 1947 World Championships. At the Games, Button took a slender lead over Gerschwiler in the compulsory programme and then, in his free programme routine, wowed the judges by landing a double axel (the first skater in competition history to do so) to become, aged 18 years 205 days, the youngest male figure skating gold medallist in history. He would go on to retain his title at the 1952 Winter Games in Oslo, Norway.

Above: Dick Button became men's figure skating's youngest-ever Olympic gold medallist at the 1948 Winter Games.

THREE IN A ROW FOR GOLDEN BOY GRAFSTRÖM

The first major international figure skating competition since the end of the First World War took place at the 1920 Olympic Games in Antwerp, Belgium (the last time the event would be staged at the Summer Games), with Gillis Grafström overcoming both a leg injury and a pair of broken skates to claim gold. The Swede, by then 30, retained his title at the inaugural Winter Games at Chamonix, France, in 1924 and, four years later at St-Moritz, Switzerland, beat off the challenge of his closest rival, Austria's Will Böckl, to claim his third Olympic gold medal. He is the only male figure skater in history to achieve the feat.

CLOSE BUT NOT CLOSE ENOUGH

Despite being strongly tipped for the gold medal at the 2002 Winter Games at Salt Lake City, Utah, Yevgeny Plyushchenko's shot at glory effectively disappeared when he fell during his first routine. However, in finishing second in the free skating programme he did enough to claim the silver medal behind fellow Russian Aleksey Yagudin. He achieved his goal at the 2006 Games in Turin, winning both the short and free programmes to take gold. He took a sabbatical from the sport shortly afterwards and only returned to competitive skating a few months before Vancouver 2010; the lack of competitive edge showed, and the Russian fell short of Evan Lysacek's overall total (by a slender 1.31 points) to become the only man in figure skating history to win two Olympic silver medals.

Right: The Czech Republic's Petr Barna spins during his bronze-medal-winning routine at the 1992 Winter Games in Albertville, France.

THE ONLY THING THAT GLISTENS IS GOLD FOR GREAT BRITAIN

Great Britain may only have ever won two medals in men's singles figure skating at the Winter Games, but both of them have been golden moments. At Innsbrück in 1976, John Curry beat off the challenge of Vladimir Kovalev (Soviet Union) to win gold with a supremely elegant and balletic performance. Four years later, at Lake Placid, Robin Cousins was likewise the star of the show, beating East Germany's Jan Hoffmann (silver) and the United States' Charles Tickner (bronze).

Right: Britain's John Curry celebrates his gold-medal-winning moment at the 1976 Winter Games in Innsbruck, Austria.

MOST MEDALS WON (BY COUNTRY): TOP TEN

Pos	Medals	Country	G	S	B
1	15	United States	7	3	5
2	10	USSR/EUN/Russia	5	4	1
3	8	Austria	3	3	2
=	8	Canada	-	4	4
5	7	Sweden	4	2	1
6	5	France	-	1	4
7	4	Czechoslovakia	1	1	2
8	3	Germany (East/West)	1	2	-
=	3	Switzerland	-	2	1
10	2	Great Britain	2	-	-

FIRST QUADRUPLE JUMP

Although he didn't win the gold medal (that honour went to the Unified Team's Viktor Petrenko), Petr Barna wowed the audience with his free skating programme at the 1992 Winter Games at Albertville. During his routine, the 25-year-old Czech became the first skater in history to land a quadruple jump in competition. His effort was enough to earn him a bronze medal.

ISU World Figure Championships

Considered the most prestigious of the International Skating Union's (ISU) competitions, the World Figure Skating Championships were held for the first time at St Petersburg, Russia, in 1896 and are staged on an annual basis. As is the case with the Olympic Games, the United States has been the event's most successful nation, winning 63 medals (23 of them gold).

Left: Britain's Madge Syers shocked the world when she won silver at the 1902 Championships in London.

SYERS BREAKS THE GENDER BARRIER

It may not have appeared in the competition's small print but, nonetheless, in the competition's formative years it was widely assumed that only men would enter the ISU World Figure Skating Championships. Someone forgot to tell Britain's Madge Syers: the London-born skater entered the event held in her home town in 1902 and, to the delight of everyone (including winner Ulrich Salchow, who afterwards presented her with his gold medal), finished in second place. Syers remains the event's sole female medallist – her participation led to the creation of the separate Ladies' World Championships (which were held for the first time in 1906).

Left: Ulrich Salchow is the World Championships' most successful skater with ten gold medals.

SALCHOW IN A LEAGUE OF HIS OWN

If proof were needed of Ulrich Salchow's absolute domination of men's international figure skating in the early years of the twentieth century, his performances in the ISU World Figure Skating Championships alone provide it. Runner-up in 1897, 1899 and 1900 (finishing behind Gustav Hügel on each occasion), the legendary Swede took the crown for the first time at Stockholm in 1901 and retained his title in 1902, 1903, 1904 and 1905. Having refused to enter the 1906 Championships (fearing that, because it was staged in Munich, the judges would be biased in favour of his great rival Gilbert Fuchs), he won again in 1907 and held on to his crown until 1911. His ten victories in the event are an all-time competition record.

FUCHS BECOMES FIRST CHAMPION

A self-taught figure skater who, in his youth, practised gymnastics and weightlifting, Austrian-born Gilbert Fuchs was famed for his legendary, bitter rivalry with Ulrich Salchow in the early years of the twentieth century (the pair would refuse to take part in competitions held in each other's countries because they feared the judges would be biased). But arguably Fuchs's greatest moment on the ice came as early as 1896 at the inaugural World Figure Skating Championships in St Petersburg, Russia. Fuchs, representing the German Empire, saw off the challenge of Austria's Gustav Hügel and hometown favourite Georg Sanders to become the sport's first-ever world champion. He went on to collect a second title in Munich, Germany, in 1906 – a competition in which Salchow had refused to take part.

BRILLIANT BUTTON BECOMES THE MAN TO BEAT

Dick Button made a career out of defying the words of the coach who told him, at the age of 12, that he would never be a good skater. He became the United States national champion within four years, picked up a silver medal at the 1947 World Championships and, the following year in St-Moritz (still only 18), became the youngest-ever Olympic champion in men's figure skating. Having confirmed his pre-eminence by winning the 1948 World Championships, Button then proceeded to win every competition he entered until he turned professional in 1952, including six consecutive victories at the World Championships. He remains the most successful figure skater since the Second World War.

A FIRST FOR TAKAHASHI

As far as gold medals were concerned, the first 113 years of the ISU World Figure Skating Championships were a wholly European and North American affair, with every one of the champions hailing from one of those two continents. That all changed at Turin in 2010, when Japan's Daisuke Takahashi (runner-up three years earlier) beat off the challenge of Canada's Patrick Chan (silver) and France's Brian Joubert (bronze) to become the event's first, and to date only, Asian champion.

Right: Japan's Daisuke Takahashi made history at the 2010 ISU World Championships in Turin, Italy.

MEDAL SWEEPS

There have been six medal sweeps at the ISU World Figure Skating Championships, shared by two countries. The first came in Vienna in 1925, when Austrian competitors thrilled the home crowd by occupying all three places on the podium: Willy Böckl (gold), Franz Kachler (silver) and Otto Preissecker (bronze). Other medal sweeps came in 1927 (Austria), 1928 (Austria), 1952 (United States), 1955 (United States) and 1956 (United States).

KING KARL

Just as Ulrich Salchow dominated men's figure skating in the early years of the twentieth century, Karl Schäfer reigned supreme in the 1930s. The Austrian burst on to the international scene at the age of 19, winning a bronze medal at the 1927 World Championships, became world champion for the first time in 1930 and held on to the crown for a record-breaking seven consecutive years until he retired from international competition following his 1936 success to become a coach in the United States.

Left: Austria's Karl Schäfer (right) won a record-breaking seven consecutive titles in the 1930s.

MOST MEDALS WON (BY COUNTRY): TOP TEN

Pos	Medals	Country	G	S	B
1	63	United States	23	22	18
2	53	Austria	22	16	15
3	30	Canada	12	12	6
4	24	Germany	3	11	10
5	22	Sweden	15	4	3
6	19	France	3	7	9
7	18	USSR	4	7	7
8	15	Russia	7	3	5
=	15	Great Britain	2	8	5
10	8	Czechoslovakia	3	4	1
=	8	East Germany	2	2	4
=	8	Hungary	-	2	6

Women's Figure Skating – Singles: Olympic Games

Right: The USA's Tara Lipinski thrills the crowd en route to her record-breaking gold medal at Nagano 1998.

Women's singles figure skating formed part of the programme at the 1908 and 1920 Summer Olympic Games (held at London and Antwerp respectively) and has been part of every Winter Games since the inaugural event at Chamonix in 1924. The competition has featured 398 competitors from 48 countries, with skaters from the United States enjoying the most success, winning 23 medals (seven of them gold).

LIPINSKI THE PRODIGY CLAIMS RECORD-BREAKING GOLD

A champion roller-skater in her youth, Tara Lipinski first tried her hand at figure skating at the age of six and came to national prominence in 1994 when she won the US Olympic Festival competition at the age of 12 – becoming the youngest in any event to achieve the feat. She finished 15th at the 1996 ISU World Figure Skating Championships, became US national champion for the first time in 1997 and, the following year, still only 15 years old, went on to become the sport's youngest-ever world champion. She faced stiff competition from her compatriot Michelle Kwan at the 1998 Winter Games in Nagano, but skated superbly in the free skating programme (having trailed Kwan after the short programme) to claim gold and become, aged 15 years 255 days, the youngest female Olympic champion (in any event) in history.

A CUT ABOVE THE REST

Although she had claimed her first (of ten) World Championship titles the year before (at the tender age of 14), Sonja Henie wasn't everybody's automatic pick for gold at the 1928 Winter Games in St-Moritz, Switzerland, with many expecting her to face stiff competition from the American and Canadian contingents as well as from Austria's 17-year-old sensation Fritzi Burger. But the Norwegian (making her second appearance at the Games following her eighth-place finish, as an 11-year-old, at Chamonix 1924) was the undoubted star of the show, winning both the compulsory and free-skating programmes to win gold. Her dominance continued at Lake Placid four years later, as she became the first woman in history to retain her Olympic title. The success did not end there: having won every World and European title in the inter-Olympic years preceding Garmisch-Partenkirchen 1936, she eased to a hat-trick of gold medals to become the first skater in Olympic history to win three successive gold medals.

Left: Norway's Sonja Henie was the dominant force in women's figure skating in the 1920s and '30s.

COLLEDGE'S RECORD-BREAKING MOMENT

The best years of Cecilia Colledge's career would ultimately be stymied by the outbreak of the Second World War and she only ever appeared at one edition of the Winter Games (at Garmisch-Partenkirchen in 1936), but her performance there was a record-breaking one. The British star finished second behind Norwegian sensation Sonja Henie (unluckily according to some) to become, aged 15 years 79 days, the youngest female medallist in any event in Olympic history.

MOST SUCCESSFUL POST-WAR SKATER

A product of East Germany's Kinder- und Jugendsportschule (a school for athletically talented children and young people), Katarina Witt travelled to the 1984 Winter Games in Sarajevo, Bosnia, as a two-time European champion, but was still considered an outsider for the gold medal, which was expected to go to one of the two previous world champions: Elaine Zayak (1982) and Rosalyn Sumners (1983), both of the United States. However, Witt won both the short and free skating programmes to take gold. She was favourite to win again at Calgary in 1988 and, despite finishing only third in the short programme and second in the free skating section of the competition, did enough to collect a second successive title. She is the only female post-war skater to have made a successful defence of her Olympic singles title.

MOST MEDALS WON (BY COUNTRY): TOP TEN

Pos	Medals	Country	G	S	B
1	23	United States	7	8	8
2	7	Austria	2	4	1
3	6	Great Britain	2	1	3
4	5	East Germany	3	1	1
=	5	Canada	1	2	2
6	3	Norway	3	-	-
=	3	Japan	1	2	-
=	3	Netherlands	1	2	-
=	3	Sweden	1	1	1
10	2	Germany	-	1	1
=	2	Russia	-	1	1
=	2	China	-	-	2

Right: Two-time Olympic gold medallist Katarina Witt was women's figure skating's pin-up girl in the 1980s.

Right: Japan's Shizuka Arakawa became Asia's first women's figure skating gold medallist at Turin 2006.

ARAKAWA DEFIES THE FORMBOOK

By 2006, the 21 previous women's singles figure skating Olympic champions had all hailed from either Europe or from North America and few expected that to change in Turin, with the USA's Sasha Cohen and Russia's Irina Slutskaya (world champion in 2002 and 2005) widely tipped for gold. Instead, Japan's Shizuka Arakawa (the 2004 world champion) took advantage of falls from both Cohen (in the short programme) and Slutskaya (in the free skating programme) to take gold and become the event's first, and to date only, Asian champion.

FRITZI'S CONSECUTIVE SILVER MEDALS

Austria's Fritzi Burger, a supremely talented skater in her own right, had the misfortune to spend the prime of her career competing against the phenomenal Sonja Henie when she too was at the peak of her powers. The Austrian never defeated her Norwegian nemesis in competition, including her two appearances at the Winter Games (in 1932 and 1936). There may have been some consolation, however small, in this distinction: Burger is the only woman in Olympic figure skating history to have won two successive silver medals. Talking about her rivalry with Henie in 1994, Burger mused: "I had two husbands. She [Henie] even beat me at that. She had three."

AN EVENT TO REMEMBER FOR THE USA

No country has enjoyed more success in women's singles figure skating at the Olympic Games than the United States. The country has collected 23 medals in the event (16 more than second-placed Austria), consisting of seven gold, eight silver and eight bronze.

ISU World Figure Skating Championships

The ISU Championships for Ladies were staged for the first time at Davos, Switzerland, in 1906 (some ten years after the equivalent inaugural event for men), although it wasn't until 1924 that the event's winners were accorded world champion status. The United States has enjoyed the most success in the competition, winning 71 medals (a massive 26 of them gold).

MOST SUCCESSFUL POST-WW2 SKATERS

Two skaters hold the record for the most World Championships titles won in the post-Second World War era: the USA's Carol Heiss, who won five consecutive titles between 1956 and 1960 (after which she retired to pursue a career in film, notably playing the lead role in *Snow White and the Three Stooges*); and her compatriot Michelle Kwan, who struck gold at the 1996, 1998, 2000, 2001 and 2003 World Championships.

MOST MEDALS WON (BY COUNTRY): TOP TEN

Pos	Medals	Country	G	S	B
1	71	United States	26	21	24
2	36	Austria	7	17	12
3	22	Great Britain	6	9	7
4	19	East Germany	9	8	2
5	14	Japan	7	3	4
6	13	Norway	10	1	2
=	13	Canada	4	5	4
=	13	Germany	1	8	4
9	11	Hungary	7	1	3
=	11	Russia	3	4	4

Left: The USA's Michelle Kwan was the dominant skater of the late 1990s and early 2000s, winning five titles.

THE FIRST GREAT POST-WW1 CHAMPION

Born in Vienna, the daughter of Christa von Szabo, herself twice a medallist in the pairs at the World Championships, Herma Szabo was the first star of women's figure skating in the years following the First World War. The first female figure skater in history to wear a skirt cut above the knee (which permitted greater movement), she won five consecutive world titles between 1922 and 1926 (a record subsequently bettered by Sonja Henie) and retired in 1927 following a second-place finish (behind Henie) at that year's World Championships.

Right: Austria's Herma Szabo (far left) was the first woman in the competition's history to win five consecutive titles.

MARVELLOUS MADGE TAKES INAUGURAL CROWN

Given that her silver-medal-winning performance at the 1902 ISU World Figure Skating Championships did much to precipitate the creation of a separate ladies' event, it seems highly appropriate that Madge Syers should hold the honour of winning the first two editions of the ISU Championships for Ladies (which would achieve World Championships status in 1924). The British star won at Davos, Switzerland, in 1906 and in Vienna, Austria, the following year, ahead of Jenny Herz (silver) and Hungary's Lily Kronberger (bronze) on both occasions.

ASIAN INVASION

There has been a notable shift in talent at the ISU Ladies World Figure Skating Championships in recent years. After an 83-year wait, Asia finally celebrated its first world champion in 1989 (when Japan's Midori Ito struck gold); the continent enjoyed further success in 1994 (Japan's Yuka Sato) and 1995 (China's Chen Lu). In recent years there has been an explosion of talent, with competitors from southeast Asia winning the last five championships: Miki Ando (Japan, in 2007 and 2011); Mao Asada (Japan, in 2008 and 2010); and Kim Yuna (Korea, in 2009).

THE ONLY CHINESE CHAMPION

China's Chen Lu was famed in the early part of her career for her ability to produce breathtaking jumps – notably triple jumps, which had started to dominate women's figure skating. While it brought her numerous plaudits, it failed to win her any prizes, but then came the breakthrough: she picked up bronze medals at the 1992 and 1993 ISU Ladies World Figure Skating Championships, added a further bronze medal to her growing collection at the 1994 Winter Games in Lillehammer (becoming the first Chinese figure skater to medal at the Olympics), and reached the zenith of her career when she struck gold at the 1995 World Championships in Birmingham, England. She remains the event's only Chinese winner.

Right: China's Chen Lu celebrates her gold-medal-winning performance at the 1995 World Championships in Birmingham.

Left: Tonya Harding (left), Kristi Yamaguchi (centre) and Nancy Kerrigan (right) were on top form for the United States in Munich, Germany, in 1991.

KRONBERGER RAISES THE BAR

Bronze medallist at the first two editions of the ISU Championships for Ladies in 1906 and 1907, Lily Kronberger struck gold for the first time at Troppau (now Opava in the Czech Republic) in 1908 and retained her title in Bucharest, Romania, the following year (albeit that she was the competition's only entrant). She won again in Davos, Switzerland, the following year and once again in 1911 (in Vienna, Austria) to become the event's first four-time winner. Interestingly, during her final success, she became the first figure skater in history to perform her routine to music.

ONLY MEDAL SWEEP

There has only ever been one medal sweep at the ISU Ladies World Figure Skating Championships – at Munich, Germany, in 1991, when figure skaters from the United States occupied all three places on the podium: Kristi Yamaguchi won the gold medal, Tonya Harding the silver, and Nancy Kerrigan the bronze.

Figure Skating – Pairs: Olympic Games

As is the case with the men's and women's singles events, pairs skating – an event for which International Skating Union (ISU) rules specify teams consisting of "one lady and one man" – made two appearances at the Summer Games (at London 1908 and Antwerp 1920) and has been part of every Winter Games programme since Chamonix 1924. The Soviet Union has been the event's most successful nation, winning 20 medals (12 of them gold).

EVERY CLOUD HAS A GOLDEN LINING FOR RODNINA

The 1972 Winter Games marked a golden, if turbulent denouement for Soviet pair Irina Rodnina and Alexei Ulanov. The pair had claimed the four previous European titles and had been world champions in 1970 and 1971, but the story that dominated the build-up to the event at Sapporo was that Ulanov (even though he knew that Rodnina had strong feelings for him) had become romantically linked with Rodnina's great rival Lyudmila Smirnova (the pairs silver medallist, with Andrei Suraikin, at the 1972 Winter Games). So even though they won gold by a clear margin, Rodnina left the ice in tears following their final free skating programme. Ulanov and Smirnova teamed up shortly afterwards (and would later marry), while Rodnina, too, found a new partner, Alexandr Zaitsev, and went on to enjoy record-breaking success, winning pairs gold at Innsbrück 1976 and Lake Placid 1980 to become the only woman in history to win three consecutive gold medals at the Winter Games.

Left: Irina Rodnina found a new partner in Alexandr Zaitsev and the pair went on to enjoy record-breaking success, claiming back-to-back gold medals in 1976 and 1980.

Above: Ludowika Jakobsson (née Eilers) and husband Walter struck gold at the 1920 Games in Antwerp.

FIRST MARRIED PAIR TO TAKE OLYMPIC GOLD

The first truly great pair in figure skating history, Germany's Ludowika Jakobsson and Finland's Walter Jakobsson first came to international prominence when they won a silver medal at the 1910 ISU World Figure Skating Championships. They married in 1911 and, representing Finland, became world champions for the first time later the same year (a title they won again in 1914 and 1923). The class of the field at the 1920 Olympic Games in Antwerp, they topped every one of the judges' scorecards to become the first married pair to win Olympic gold for figure skating.

UP AND RUNNING

Having won the inaugural pairs title at the ISU World Figure Skating Championships earlier in the year at St Petersburg, Russia, Germany's Anna Hübler and Heinrich Burger were widely expected to win the pairs gold medal at the 1908 Olympic Games in London (one of only two times the event made an appearance at the Summer Games). And they duly lived up to their billing, fending off the challenge of British pairs Phyllis and James Johnson and Madge and Edgar Syers to become the first Olympic pairs champions. As a footnote, in winning a bronze medal, Madge Syers (who took gold in the singles competition) became the first skater of either sex to medal in both the individual and pairs events (Germany's Ernst Baier equalled her feat in 1936).

DRAMA AT SALT LAKE CITY

Controversy reigned in the pairs competition at the 2002 Winter Games in Salt Lake City. Following the short programme, Russian pair Elena Berezhnaya and Anton Sikharulidze held the advantage over Canada's Jamie Salé and David Pelletier (who had fallen during their routine), but low technical scores for the Russians in the free skating programme handed Salé and Pelletier a chance for gold. They skated flawlessly and for the crowd, at least, there was no doubt they were the champions. But then came the marks – and Berezhnaya and Sikharulidze were declared the winners. The story did not end there: a few days later news emerged that the French judge had been pressured into voting for the Russians, and eventually the IOC decided to award gold medals to both pairs. It is the only time in pairs figure skating history that the Olympic gold medal has been shared.

Above: Russia's Anton Sikharulidze and Elena Berezhnaya and Canada's Jamie Salé and David Pelletier shared pairs gold in 2002.

MOST MEDALS WON (BY COUNTRY): TOP TEN

Pos	Medals	Country	G	S	B
1	20	USSR/EUN/Russia	12	7	1
2	12	Germany (East/West)	3	3	6
3	7	Canada	2	1	4
4	5	Austria	2	2	1
=	5	China	1	2	2
=	5	USA	-	3	2
=	5	Hungary	-	2	3
8	3	France	2	-	1
=	3	Great Britain	-	1	2
10	2	Finland	1	1	-

YOUNGEST CHAMPIONS

Not only did Ekaterina Gordeeva and Sergei Grinkov continue the Soviet Union's absolute domination of pairs figure skating at the Winter Games when they won gold at Calgary 1988 (it marked the nation's seventh consecutive triumph in the event), they also made history. As Gordeeva was 16 years 264 days old at the time and Grinkov was 21 years 12 days old, their average age of 18 years 324 days made them the event's youngest-ever champions.

OLDEST CHAMPIONS

Soviet pair Ludmila Belousova and Oleg Protopotov ensured their final appearance at the Winter Games, at Grenoble in 1968, was both a gold-medal-winning and record-breaking one. With Belousova 32 years 84 days old at the time and Protopotov 35 years 243 days old, their average age of 33 years 354 days made them the event's oldest-ever champions.

A GOLDEN FIRST FOR ASIA

China's Shen Xue and Zhao Hongbo first teamed up in 1992 and, by the end of the decade, started to challenge for major international honours, winning back-to-back silver medals at the 1999 and 2000 ISU World Figure Skating Championships (becoming the first Chinese skaters to medal at the event) and bronze in 2001 before hitting golden heights with victories in 2002 and 2003. But they found ultimate success at the Winter Games harder to come by: they finished fifth at Nagano 1998 and in bronze medal position at both Salt Lake City 2002 and Turin 2006 before finally laying their hands on that elusive gold medal at Vancouver 2010. In doing so, they had become the first Asian gold medallists in the event's history.

Above: China's Shen Xue (left) and Zhao Hongbo put in gold-medal-winning performances at the 2010 Winter Games in Vancouver.

World Championships

The first ISU Championships for Pairs Figure Skating were staged at St Petersburg, Russia, in 1908 (the event would become known as the World Championships from 1924) – despite the fact that, in some countries, pairs skating was regarded as indecent, or even illegal. Competitors from the former Soviet Union enjoyed most success in the competition, winning 52 medals (25 of them gold).

EARLY STARS

Germany's Anna Hübler and Heinrich Burger (a lawyer outside the rink) were the class of the field at the first-ever ISU Championships for Pairs Figure Skating at St Petersburg, Russia, in 1908 and claimed a comfortable victory – ahead of Great Britain's Phyllis and James Johnson – to become the event's first champions. After becoming Olympic champions later the same year, they skipped the 1909 Championships in Stockholm, Sweden, but made a triumphant return in 1910 in Berlin, Germany, to become the competition's first two-time winners.

BROTHER AND SISTER ACT

The first 28 editions of the pairs competition at the ISU World Figure Skating Championships had seen three married couples strike gold, but the 1950 Championships in London saw partnerships of another kind hit the headlines. For the only time in the event's history, all three places on the podium were occupied by brother-and-sister partnerships, with the United States' Karol and Peter Kennedy taking gold, Great Britain's Jennifer and John Nicks claiming silver, and Hungary's Marianna and Laszlo Nagy winning bronze.

Left: In 1950, the USA's Karol and Peter Kennedy became the first brother-and-sister partnership to become world pairs champions.

WORLD CHAMPIONSHIPS JOY FOR THE JOLYS

The event's biggest stars in the late 1920s and early 1930s, France's two-time Olympic champions Andrée Joly-Brunet and Pierre Brunet (known collectively as the "Jolys" after they were married), took gold in the pairs World Figure Skating Championships for the first time in 1926, won again in 1928, completed their third triumph in 1930 and became the first pair in championship history to win on four occasions when they took the gold medal in Montreal, Canada, in 1932.

Right: Four-time champions Andrée Joly-Brunet and Pierre Brunet were the leading pairs partners in the late 1920s and early 1930s.

FIRST THREE-TIME WINNERS

Having finished as runners-up (behind Anne Hübler and Heinrich Burger) in Berlin, Germany, the previous year, Finland's Ludowika and Walter Jakobsson became world pairs champions for the first time in 1911 in Vienna, Austria, in highly unusual circumstances – they were the competition's only entrants. There was nothing unusual about their triumph in 1914 in St-Moritz, Swizerland, however, when they outperformed Austrian pairs Helene Engelmann and Karl Mejstrik and Christa von Szabo and Leo Horwitz to take a comfortable gold. Still going strong after the resumption of the championships following the First World War, they finished as runners-up in 1922 and, the following year in Oslo, Norway, became the first pair in history to win the event for a third time.

MOST MEDALS WON (BY COUNTRY): TOP TEN

Pos	Medals	Country	G	S	B
1	52	USSR	25	19	8
2	32	Germany	15	8	9
3	27	Austria	7	13	7
4	26	Canada	10	7	9
5	25	USA	2	6	17
6	22	Russia	7	7	8
7	16	China	5	7	4
8	14	East Germany	1	6	7
9	13	Hungary	5	3	5
10	11	Great Britain	3	3	5

ASIAN SUCCESS

China's Shen Xue and Zhao Hongbo had been knocking on the door of ISU World Figure Skating Championships success for some time, winning back-to-back silver medals in 1999 and 2000 and a bronze medal in 2001, but they finally made their history-making breakthrough at the 2002 Championships in Nagano, Japan, winning gold ahead of Russia's Tatiana Totmianina and Maxim Marinin to become the event's first-ever Asian champions. The Chinese pair defended their title in Nice, France, the following year.

MEDAL SWEEPS

There have been three medal sweeps in the pairs competition at the ISU World Figure Skating Championships. The first came in 1939, when German pairs occupied all three positions on the podium, with Maxi Herber and Ernst Baier taking gold, Ilse and Erich Pausin claiming silver (the pair had previously represented Austria, but by 1939 the country had been annexed by Nazi Germany), and Ilse Koch and Gunther Noach winning bronze. Other medal sweeps occurred in 1969 and 1988 (both by the Soviet Union).

Left: Elena Valova and Oleg Vasiliev led a Soviet Union clean sweep of the medals at the 1998 Championships in Budapest.

Below: No skater enjoyed as much success at the World Championships as Irina Rodnina (pictured here with partner Alexander Zaitsev).

IRINA RODNINA: IN A LEAGUE OF HER OWN

The most successful pairs skater in history, the Soviet Union's Irina Rodnina began her career with Alexei Ulanov and together they won three European titles (in 1970, 1971 and 1972), Olympic gold (at Sapporo in 1972) and four world titles (in 1969, 1970, 1971 and 1972). A change of partner (to Alexander Zaitsev) following the 1972 World Championships did little to change her fortunes: the pair claimed seven European titles between 1973 and 1980, enjoyed golden Olympic success in 1976 and 1980 and won six consecutive World Championships between 1973 and 1978. Rodnina's haul of ten consecutive World Championship successes is a pairs record that will surely never be broken.

FOUR IN A ROW FOR HERBER AND BAIER

Famed for being the first pair in history to perform side-by-side jumps in competition, Germany's Maxi Herber and Ernst Baier (both highly accomplished skaters in singles) became national pairs champions for the first time in 1934 and picked up a bronze medal at that year's World Championships. Their breakthrough year came in 1936, when they became world and Olympic champions for the first time. From that point on until international competitions were suspended following the outbreak of the Second World War they were the pair to beat, and nobody did: they added further world titles in 1937, 1938 and 1939 to become the first pair in the event's history to win four titles in a row.

Ice Dancing: Olympic Games

Ice dancing differs from pairs skating in several ways. It requires different lifts; competitors must perform spins as a team in a dance hold; throws and jumps are not allowed; and partners are not permitted to perform more than two arms' lengths apart. The event made its first full-medal appearance at the 1976 Winter Games in Innsbruck (having appeared as a demonstration sport in 1948 and 1968) and has been part of the programme ever since.

FIRST BACK-TO-BACK CHAMPIONS

The ice dancing competition at the 1994 Winter Games in Lillehammer was full of intriguing subplots. First, the change of rules allowing professionals to compete for the first time saw the return of 1984 champions Torvill and Dean. Second came the riveting rivalry between Russian pairs Maya Usova and Alexandr Zhulin (who were married) and Pasha Grishuk and Evgeny Platov, in which an alleged affair between Zhulin and Grishuk resulted in a punch-up in a Los Angeles restaurant. On the ice, Torvill and Dean took the bronze medal, while Grishuk and Platov edged their Russian rivals to gold. The couple were the star performers at Nagano 1998, where they became the first ice dancing pair in history to make a successful defence of their Olympic title.

Above: Natalia Bestemianova and Andrei Bukin's moment in the limelight came at the 1988 Winter Games in Calgary.

FIRM FAVOURITES DELIVER THE GOODS

Having won every ice dancing title they contested between 1970 and 1976 (i.e. all except the 1975 ISU World Figure Skating Championships, which they did not attend), Soviet pair Lyudmila Pakhomova and Aleksandr Gorschov were the overwhelming favourites to take ice dancing gold at the 1976 Winter Games in Innsbruck. And they duly delivered, winning all three phases of the competition – compulsory, original set pattern and free dance – to become the event's first-ever Olympic champions.

Left: Soviet pair Aleksandr Gorschov and Lyudmila Pakhomova made history at Innsbruck 1976, becoming the first pair to win Olympic ice dancing gold medals.

SECOND TIME LUCKY

Natalia Bestemianova and Andrei Bukin's silver-medal-winning performance at the 1984 Winter Games in Sarajevo almost passed unacknowledged amid the torrent of fanfares directed towards the gold-medal-winning excellence of Jayne Torvill and Christopher Dean, but the Soviet pair would go on to enjoy their time in the limelight – particularly after the British pair left the amateur ranks to skate professionally. The Soviets won three successive gold medals at the ISU World Figure Skating Championships between 1985 and 1987, and then won all three phases of the competition at the 1988 Winter Games in Calgary to become the first ice dancing pair in history to win silver and gold medals at successive Games.

TOP TWO STEPS OF THE PODIUM HAS A NEW LOOK

The ice dancing competition at the 2010 Winter Games provided an anomaly in the event's history: it was the only time a Russian or Soviet pair had not finished in the top two. Canada's Tessa Virtue and Scott Moir took gold (to become not only the youngest gold medallists in the event's history – with an average age of 20 years 170 days – but also the first ice dance pair to win Olympic gold on home ice and on their Winter Games debut) and the United States' Meryl Davis and Charlie White took silver.

Left: Great Britain's Jayne Torvill and Christopher Dean came close to ice dancing perfection at the 1984 Winter Games in Sarajevo.

BRITAIN'S GOLDEN COUPLE

No pair has taken Olympic ice dancing gold in more emphatic fashion than Jayne Torvill and Christopher Dean at the 1984 Winter Games in Sarajevo. The British pair, the overwhelming favourites for gold following their stunning performance at the European Championships earlier in the year (at which they received 18 perfect scores of 6.0), held a comfortable lead after the compulsory and set-dance routines and wowed both the crowd and the judges in the free dance: skating to Ravel's Bolero, they finished their routine to a standing ovation that lasted close to five minutes and were awarded 12 out of 18 perfect scores.

CLOSEST FINISH

The ice dancing competition at the 1980 Winter Games in Lake Placid, New York, ended with the closest finish in the event's history. By the time the three dances were over, four judges had ranked Soviet pair Natasha Linichuck and Gennady Karponosov in first place and four judges had plumped for Hungarian couple Krisztina Regorczy and Andras Sallay, while the British judge had them tied. This meant that, for the first time in the event's history, the gold medal was decided by a tiebreaker – the count-up of total ordinals (as well as awarding points, each judge ranked the competitors in 1st, 2nd, 3rd etc, and these numbers were added together) – which the Soviets won 13–14.

Above: Soviet pair Marina Klimova and Sergei Ponomarenko completed a full set of medals with gold at Albertville 1992.

MEDALS WON (BY COUNTRY)

Pos	Medals	Country	G	S	B
1	17	USSR/EUN/Russia	7	6	4
2	3	France	1	1	1
=	3	USA	-	2	1
4	2	Canada	1	-	1
=	2	Great Britain	1	-	1
6	1	Hungary	-	1	-
=	1	Italy	-	-	1
=	1	Ukraine	-	-	1

FIRST TO WIN BRONZE, THEN SILVER, THEN GOLD

Practice made perfect for Soviet pair Marina Klimova and Sergei Ponomarenko at the Olympic Games. They won a bronze medal at Sarajevo 1984 (to become the youngest medallists by average age in the event's history: Klimova was 17 years 201 days old at the time and Ponomarenko 23 years 131 days old – average 20 years 170 days; they then took silver at Calgary 1988 and finally won the gold medal at Albertville 1992. They are the only pair in the competition's history to have won bronze, silver and gold medals in ice dancing at successive Winter Games.

ISU World Figure Skating Championships

Ice dancing made its debut at the ISU World Figure Skating Championships in 1952 in Paris (some 24 years before the discipline made its debut at the Winter Games) and has been contested every year since (with the exception of 1961, when the event was cancelled following the Sabena Flight 548 disaster). Competitors from the Soviet Union and Russia have enjoyed the most success, winning 59 medals (29 of them gold).

BUCKING THE BRITISH TREND

The British run of success in ice-dancing competition at the ISU World Figure Skating Championships (British pairs had triumphed in the first nine editions of the event), finally came to an end in Prague, Czechoslovakia, in 1962 when home skaters Eva Romanova and Pavel Roman took gold to become ice dancing's first non-British world champions. The Czech pair would add further victories in 1963, 1964 and 1965.

Above: Czech pair Eva Romanova and Pavel Roman ended Britain's run of ice-dancing success with gold at Prague in 1962.

MEDAL SWEEPS

There have been five medals sweeps in ice dancing at the ISU World Figure Skating Championships: three by Great Britain (in 1955, 1956 and 1968); one by the Commonwealth of Independent States, a team made up of skaters from former Soviet states (in 1992); and one by Russia (in 1993).

ICE DANCING'S FIRST SHINING STARS

Jean Westwood and Lawrence Demmy formed the outstanding pair in the early years of the ice dancing competition at the ISU World Figure Skating Championships. The British partnership took gold at the inaugural event in Paris in 1952, retained their title in Davos, Switzerland, the following year, completed a hat-trick of titles in Oslo, Norway, in 1954 and made it four in a row when they triumphed in Vienna, Austria, in 1955. Their run of four consecutive victories stood as a record until 1974, when Soviet pair Lyudmila Pakhamova and Alexandr Gorshkov recorded their fifth consecutive victory in the event.

FIRST TO WIN GOLD, SILVER AND BRONZE

Natalia Linichuk and Gennadi Karponosov's climb to the top of the ice-dancing tree was a progressive one. The Soviet pair took bronze at the 1974 and 1977 ISU World Figure Skating Championships before claiming back-to-back victories in 1978 and 1979. When they finished second behind Hungary's Krisztina Regoczy and Andras Sallay at the 1980 Championships in Dortmund, Germany, they became the first ice-dancing pair in the competition's history to have won a complete set of gold, silver and bronze medals. After claiming gold at the 1980 Winter Games in Lake Placid, the pair retired the following year.

Right: Soviet pair Natalia Linichuk and Gennadi Karponosov became the first pair in history to win World Championship gold, silver and bronze medals.

Above: From left, Tessa Virtue/Scott Moir, Meryl Davis/Charlie White and Maia/Alex Shibutani in 2004.

POWER SHIFT

The 2003 success of Canada's Shae-Lynn Bourne and Victor Kraatz marked the beginning of a shift in power in ice dancing at the ISU Figure Skating World Championships. The following year, in Moscow, the United States' Meryl Davis and Charlie White took gold, Canada's Tessa Virtue and Scott Moir won silver and Maia Shibutani and Alex Shibutani (also from the United States) finished third. It was the first time in the competition's history that non-European pairs occupied all three places on the podium.

SOVIET PAIR SETS A NEW STANDARD

Lyudmila Pakhamova and Alexandr Gorshkov made their first appearance at the ISU World Figure Skating Championships in Vienna, Austria, in 1967 and finished in a lowly 13th position, but better times lay ahead for the Soviet pair. They finished sixth in 1968, took the silver medal (behind Britain's Diane Towler and Bernard Ford) in 1969 and became world champions for the first time in 1970. Their victory prompted a run of unprecedented success in the event: they retained their title for the next four years (their run of five consecutive victories is an all-time competition record), took the silver medal in 1975, and won for a record-breaking sixth and final time in Gothenburg, Sweden, in 1976.

MOST MEDALS WON (BY COUNTRY): TOP TEN

Pos	Medals	Country	G	S	B
1	59	USSR/CIS*/Russia	29	19	12
2	34	Great Britain	17	10	7
3	26	USA	1	9	16
4	22	Canada	2	9	11
5	12	France	3	6	3
6	5	Germany	–	3	2
7	4	Czechoslovakia	4	–	–
=	4	Bulgaria	2	1	1
9	3	Hungary	1	1	1
=	3	Italy	1	1	1

* Former Soviet Union states competed as the Commonwealth of Independent States team in 1992.

FIRST NON-EUROPEAN CHAMPIONS

The road to the top of the ISU World Figure Skating Championships hill was a slow one for Shae-Lynn Bourne and Victor Kraatz. The Canadian pair picked up a record four consecutive bronze medals in the competition in 1996, 1997, 1998 and 1999 and won the silver medal in 2002 before finally striking gold at the 2003 championships in Washington DC. Their victory was a first in the competition for a non-European pair.

Right: Canada's Shae-Lynn Bourne and Victor Kraatz in action at the 2003 World Championships in Washington DC.

Men's Speed Skating: Olympic Games

Speed skating, a form of ice skating in which competitors race against each other around a track over a specified distance, is one of six sports to have appeared at every Winter Games. The current men's programme consists of six events: over 500m, 1000m, 1500m, 5000m, 10,000m and the team pursuit. Norway has been the event's most dominant nation, winning 76 medals (24 of them gold).

OSLO JOY FOR ANDERSEN

Hjalmar Andersen's first experience of the Winter Games, at St-Moritz in 1948, was a miserable one: he won the qualifying round for the 1500m but was not selected for Norway's team; instead he was chosen for the 10,000m event – which was cancelled because of adverse weather conditions. However, he had a Winter Games to remember at Oslo in 1952, winning the 1500m, 5000m and 10,000m events to become the first speed skater in history to win three race events at a single Winter Games.

Right: Hjalmar Andersen enjoyed triple gold-medal-winning success at the 1952 Winter Games in Oslo.

Left: Norway's Ivar Ballangrud picked up a record-equalling seven medals at three editions of the Winter Games.

TERRIFIC THUNBERG SETS THE BENCHMARK

A relatively late starter to speed skating, Helsinki-born Clas Thunberg did not start to skate competitively until he was 18. Although he took some time to become established as a speed skater of international class (he was 27 when he became Finland's national champion for the first time), he then wasted little time in putting together one of the most successful careers in the sport's history. He became European all-round champion for the first time in 1922, world all-round champion the following year and was the star of the show at the 1924 Winter Games in Chamonix, taking bronze in the 500m, silver in the 10,000m, gold in the 1500m and 5000m and winning a further gold medal after being awarded the all-round title (the only time in the event's history the accolade was handed out). The success did not end there: when he won two further gold medals at the 1928 Winter Games in St-Moritz (in the 500m and 1500m) he became the first speed skater in Winter Games history to win five gold medals (a feat later equalled by the USA's Eric Heiden at the 1980 Winter Games at Lake Placid).

MOST MEDALS WON

Two speed skaters share the record for the most medals won at the Winter Games (seven): Finland's Clas Thunberg (who achieved the feat at the 1924 and 1928 Games); and Norway's Ivar Ballangrud (who equalled Thunberg's feat at three editions of the Winter Games between 1928 and 1936).

HEROIC HEIDEN ACHIEVES THE IMPOSSIBLE

There has never been more interest in the speed skating event at the Winter Games than that which preceded the competition at Lake Placid, New York, in 1980. And the reason for the fervour was the form of home favourite Eric Heiden. After competing at the 1976 Games as a 17-year-old (at which he finished seventh in the 1500m and 19th in the 5000m), Heiden established himself as the best speed skater in the world, claiming the all-round world title at the 1977, 1978 and 1979 World Championships. And he simply blew the opposition away at Lake Placid, winning every event he entered – the 500m, 1000m, 1500, 5000m and 10,000m – to become the only athlete in history to win five gold medals at a single Winter Games. It is a feat that will surely never be equalled.

Above: The USA's Eric Heiden was unstoppable at Lake Placid in 1980, winning up gold medals in every one of the five events he entered.

SHARED GOLD MEDALS

There have been two instances of skaters sharing the gold medal at the Winter Games, on both occasions in the 1500m. The first instance occurred at Cortina d'Ampezzo 1956, when Soviet star Yevgeny Grishin (who had already won 500m gold) posted a new world record time of 2:08.6, only to see compatriot Yury Mikhaylov match it. The next instance occurred at Squaw Valley four years later: this time Norway's Roald Aas (skating in the ninth pair) set the pace with 2:10.4; his lead lasted until Grishin (who had already launched a successful defence of his 500m crown) skated in the 13th pair, and although the Soviet star led the splits until the last lap, he could only match the Norwegian's time. Amazingly, the 1500m gold medal honours were shared for the second successive Winter Games.

MOST MEDALS WON (BY COUNTRY): TOP TEN

Pos	Medals	Country	G	S	B
1	76	Norway	24	27	25
2	56	Netherlands	15	21	20
3	40	USA	21	13	6
4	36	USSR/Russia	12	13	11
5	17	Finland	5	6	6
6	16	Sweden	7	4	5
7	14	Canada	3	4	7
8	11	Japan	1	4	6
9	10	Germany (East/West)	6	1	3
10	6	Korea	2	3	1

LANDMARK MOMENT FOR GRISHIN

The first seven editions of the 500m speed skating event at the Winter Games saw seven different winners, but that all changed at Squaw Valley, California, in 1960. Reigning champion Yevgeny Grishin of the Soviet Union (who had not lost a race over the distance in the four years since his gold-medal-winning triumph at Cortina d'Ampezzo) overcame a stumble on the home stretch (which cost him at least a second in time) to become the first speed skater in Olympic history to retain the 500m title.

SUPER SHANI BREAKS THE MOULD

United States speed skater Shani Davis made history at Turin 2006: the Chicago-born star took gold in the men's 1000m to become the first black athlete to win any event at the Winter Games. And the records did not stop there: the 27-year-old made a successful defence of his Olympic crown at Vancouver four years later to become the first speed skater in history to win back-to-back 1000m gold medals at the Winter Games.

Right: The USA's Shani Davis won back-to-back 1000m gold medals at Turin 2006 and Vancouver 2010 to earn his place in the record books.

Other Major Championships

Speed skaters contest three major events beyond the Olympic arena: the ISU World All-Round Speed Skating Championships (held on an annual basis since 1893); the ISU World Single Distance Championships (currently staged in non-Olympic years and held for the first time in 1996); and the ISU Speed Skating World Cup (a season-long series of events held on an annual basis since 1985–86).

ISU WORLD ALL-ROUND CHAMPIONSHIPS: MOST MEDALS – TOP FIVE

Pos	Medals	Name (country, span)	G	S	B
1	42	Ivar Ballangrud (Norway, 1924–38)	19	14	9
2	29	Oscar Mathisen (Norway, 1907–14)	21	4	4
=	29	Clas Thunberg (Finland, 1922–33)	19	6	4
=	29	Michael Staksrud (Norway, 1927–37)	8	11	10
5	27	Ard Schenk (Netherlands, 1965–72)	12	4	11

FANTASTIC FIVE FOR THUNBERG

One of only two men in history to have won five gold medals in speed skating at the Winter Games (the other being the United States' Eric Heiden), Finland's Clas Thunberg also enjoyed considerable success in the World All-Round Speed Skating Championships. A star of the sport in the years following the First World War, he won the overall title for the first time in Stockholm, Sweden, in 1923, and went on to enjoy further successes in 1925, 1928, 1929 and 1931 to equal Oscar Mathisen's record of five overall titles.

Left: Five-time overall champion Clas Thunberg was speed skating's biggest star in the 1920s.

Below: Gianni Romme is the only man ever to win three 10,000m ISU World Single Distance Championship gold medals.

A YEAR TO REMEMBER FOR ROMME

1998 was the best year of Gianni Romme's hugely successful career. He took double speed skating gold at the Winter Games in Nagano (in the 5000m and 10,000m) and then became the first person in history to win the 5000m–10,000m double at the ISU World Single Distance Championships. His victory in the 10,000m also saw him become the first, and to date only, person to win the event on three occasions (following his previous success in 1996 and 1997).

FIRST CHAMPION

Jaap Eden competed at the unofficial World All-Round Speed Skating Championships in 1891 (finishing third in the half-mile event and fourth in the mile). Having become the Dutch all-round champion for the first time only days before, he entered the 1893 World All-Round Championships (the first to be sanctioned by the ISU) as overwhelming favourite and duly delivered, winning the 500m, 1500m and 5000m to become the event's first overall champion, a feat he repeated in 1895 and 1896. Remarkably, he was also a two-time world champion in cycling (in 1894 and 1895).

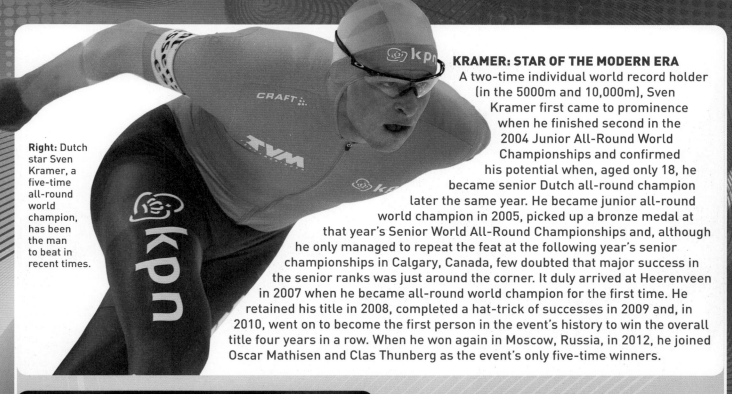

KRAMER: STAR OF THE MODERN ERA

Right: Dutch star Sven Kramer, a five-time all-round world champion, has been the man to beat in recent times.

A two-time individual world record holder (in the 5000m and 10,000m), Sven Kramer first came to prominence when he finished second in the 2004 Junior All-Round World Championships and confirmed his potential when, aged only 18, he became senior Dutch all-round champion later the same year. He became junior all-round world champion in 2005, picked up a bronze medal at that year's Senior World All-Round Championships and, although he only managed to repeat the feat at the following year's senior championships in Calgary, Canada, few doubted that major success in the senior ranks was just around the corner. It duly arrived at Heerenveen in 2007 when he became all-round world champion for the first time. He retained his title in 2008, completed a hat-trick of successes in 2009 and, in 2010, went on to become the first person in the event's history to win the overall title four years in a row. When he won again in Moscow, Russia, in 2012, he joined Oscar Mathisen and Clas Thunberg as the event's only five-time winners.

RECORD-BREAKING MEDAL HAUL FOR BALLANGRUD

A member of the famous "Hadeland Trio" of speed skaters (alongside Michael Staksrud and Hans Engnestangen), Norway's Ivar Ballangrud was one of the best speed skaters in the world in the mid-1920s and 1930s. A four-time gold medallist at the Winter Games, he also made his mark at the World All-Round Speed Skating Championships, claiming the overall title on four occasions (in 1926, 1932, 1936 and 1938) and winning a record-breaking 42 individual medals, 21 of them gold.

ISU WORLD SINGLE DISTANCE CHAMPIONSHIPS: GOLD MEDALS (BY COUNTRY)

Pos	Golds	Country
1	36	Netherlands
2	10	USA
3	7	Japan
=	7	Norway
5	6	Canada
6	3	Korea
7	1	Russia

DOUBLE GOLD FOR RITSMA

A four-time world all-round champion (in 1995, 1996, 1999 and 2001), Netherlands speed skating star Rinje Ritsma also made a record-breaking mark in the ISU World Single Distance Championships. At the 1997 event held in Warsaw, Poland, he took gold in both the 1500m and 5000m to become the first speed skater in the event's history to win two gold medals at the same edition of the championships.

Left: The Netherlands' Rinje Ritsma breaks down after winning double gold at the 1997 ISU World Single Distance Championships.

SHIMIZU: THE 500M KING

No one has enjoyed more success in the 500m competition at the ISU World Single Distance Championships than Hiroyasu Shimizu. The Japanese speed skater, who became a hero in his homeland following his 500m gold-medal-winning triumph at the 1998 Winter Games in Nagano, took the title for the first time in 1996 and went on to enjoy further victories in 1998, 1999, 2000 and 2001. He is the event's only five-time winner.

Above: Japan's Hiroyasu Shimizu won five titles in 500m event at the ISU World Single Distance Championships in the late 1990s and early 2000s.

THE UNTOUCHABLES

The Dutch were unbeatable in the team pursuit race at the ISU World Single Distance Championships following the race's introduction to the event in 2005. They won the inaugural race and went on to defend their title successfully in 2007, 2008 and 2009. The run finally came to an end when the United States took the title for the first time at Inzell, Germany, in 2011.

Above: (left to right) Dutch skaters Erben Wennemars, Mark Tuitert and Carl Verheijen won team pursuit gold in 2005.

THE MAN TO BEAT

The best long-track speed skater of the modern era, five-time all-round world champion Sven Kramer was the man to beat in the 5000m/10,000m discipline at the ISU World Single Distance Championships. He is the only man in history to have won the discipline's overall season title (scores for both events were combined) on three occasions, triumphing in 2007, 2008 and 2009.

STAR OF THE LONG TRACK

Two-time Olympic champion Gianni Romme (he won the 5000m-10,000m double at the 1998 Winter Games in Nagano) enjoyed enormous success in the 5000m-10,000m discipline at the ISU Speed Skating World Cup. The Dutch star is the only man in the event's history to have won the overall long-track title on four occasions: in 1997–98, 1999–2000, 2000–01 and 2001–02.

HAPPIER TIMES FOR JENSEN IN THE WORLD CUP

United States speed skater Dan Jansen will ultimately be remembered mainly for the series of heart-breaking near misses he endured (he left the 1988 and 1992 Winter Games medal-less despite being overwhelming favourite for 500m and 1000m gold on both occasions) before he finally secured that elusive Olympic gold medal in his last-ever race (in the 1000m at Lillehammer 1994). In the ISU Speed Skating World Cup, however, Jansen enjoyed happier times. In 1985–86, the event's inaugural season, he took the overall titles in both the 500m and 1000m (a feat since repeated on eight occasions – and by Jensen for a second time in 1993–94).

Above: Although remembered for his near-misses at the Winter Games, the USA's Dan Jansen enjoyed success in the ISU Speed Skating World Cup.

ONLY THREE-TIME 100M CHAMPION

The 100m was only contested for six seasons at the ISU Speed Skating World Cup. China's Yu Fengong took the first two overall titles, but Japan's Yuya Oikawa later surpassed his exploits, clocking up three overall titles in the discipline: in 2005–06, 2006–07 and 2008–09.

ISU SPEED SKATING WORLD CUP – MOST RACE VICTORIES: TOP TEN

Pos	Wins	Name (country, span)
1	67	Jeremy Wotherspoon (Canada, 1998–2008)
2	48	Uwe-Jens Mey (East Germany/Germany, 1986–92)
3	47	Shani Davis (USA, 2006–)
4	46	Dan Jansen (USA, 1986–94)
5	35	Hiroyasu Shimizu (Japan, 1993–2005)
6	30	Igor Zhelezovsky (USSR/Belarus, 1986–93)
=	30	Adne Sondral (Norway, 1991–2002)
8	29	Rintje Ritsma (Netherlands, 1992–2001)
9	25	Erben Wennemars (Netherlands, 2001–08)
10	23	Johann Olav Koss (Norway, 1990–4)

THE WORLD CUP'S BIGGEST STAR

Even though success on the biggest stage of all eluded him (despite his obvious talent he only won one medal at the Winter Games – a silver in the 500m at Nagano in 1998), Jeremy Wotherspoon is generally acknowledged to be the best sprint skater of the modern era. Before his retirement in 2009, the Canadian, who set ten world records during the course of his career, was the dominant force in the ISU Speed Skating World Cup, taking a record 13 overall titles (eight in the 500m and five in the 1000m) and recording an all-time record 67 race wins (19 more than second-placed Uwe-Jens Mey).

Above: Canada's Jeremy Wotherspoon has won more World Cup races than any other speed skater in history.

Women's Speed Skating: Olympic Games

Women's speed skating was a demonstration sport at the 1932 Winter Games in Lake Placid, New York, and has been a full-medal event since the 1960 Games in Squaw Valley, California. Women currently contest six events: the 500m, 1000m, 1500m, 3000m, 5000m and Team Pursuit. German speed skaters (from East and West) have enjoyed the most success in the competition, winning 62 medals (19 of them gold).

Left: Germany's Claudia Pechstein shows off the two gold medals she won at the 2002 Winter Games in Salt Lake City.

PERSISTENCE PAYS FOR PECHSTEIN

She spent the early part of her career in the considerable shadow of her compatriot Gunda Niemann-Stirnemann, but perseverance paid for Germany's Claudia Pechstein and she went on to put together the most impressive record by a female speed skater in Winter Games history. Uniquely she has won nine medals, five of them gold – in the 5000m in 1994, 1998 and 2002 (she is the only person to have won more than one gold medal in the event); in the 3000m in 2002; and in the Team Pursuit in 2006. She is also the only woman in history to have won speed skating medals at five editions of the Winter Games.

ONLY COUNTRY TO WIN TEAM PURSUIT TITLE

The women's Team Pursuit event was contested for the first time at the 2006 Winter Games in Turin, with the German team (comprising Daniela Anschütz-Thoms, Anni Friesinger, Lucille Opitz, Claudia Pechstein and Sabine Völker) taking gold. The Germans successfully defended their title in Vancouver four years later – with a team made up of Anschütz-Thoms, Stephanie Beckert, Friesinger and Katrin Mattscherodt – and remain the event's only winners.

Right: Lidiya Skoblikova won all four of the events she entered at the 1964 Winter Games.

STUNNING SKOBLIKOVA'S GOLDEN CLEAN SWEEP

The only question asked before the women's speed skating competition at the 1964 Winter Games in Innsbrück, Austria, was whether the USSR's Lidiya Skoblikova (who had taken two gold medals – in the 1500m and 3000m – at Squaw Valley 1960) could repeat her performance at the 1963 World Championships where she had won all four individual gold medals (in the 500m, 1000m, 1500m and 3000m). The biggest question mark hung over the 500m – where the shorter distance made the outcome more unpredictable – and the 24-year-old Soviet star had to be at her very best, posting an Olympic record time of 45.0 seconds to snatch the gold medal from compatriot Irina Yegorova (whose time of 45.4 seconds had earlier broken the previous Olympic best). The following day, Skoblikova stormed to gold in the 1500m (with a 2.9-second winning margin); a day later, she cruised to victory in the 1000m; and she duly completed her history-making clean sweep when she destroyed the rest of the field in the 3000m (by 3.6 seconds). It is the only time in women's speed skating history that an athlete has won all of the individual medals available to her.

BRILLIANT BLAIR ROARS INTO THE RECORD BOOKS

Considered one of the greatest speed skaters of all time, Bonnie Blair made her first appearance at the Winter Games in 1984 in Sarajevo and, aged 19, finished eighth in the 500m. But better times lay ahead for the star from Champaign, Illinois. She travelled to Calgary 1988 ranked among the favourites for 500m gold – alongside East Germans Karin Kania and Christa Rothenburger – and bested Kania's new world record time (39.10) by two-hundredths of a second to take gold. Four years later she won a far more comfortable victory (and became the first woman in history to retain her 500m title) at Albertville, France, where she also struck gold in the 1000m. She completed the double again at Lillehammer 1994, to become not only the first, and to date only, woman to have secured the 500m/1000m double twice, but also the only woman to have claimed 500m gold at three consecutive Winter Games.

Above: The United States' Bonnie Blair completed the 500m-1000m double at the 1994 Winter Games in Lillehammer.

DUTCH DELIGHT FOR VAN GENNIP

Yvonne van Gennip may have been in the form of her life at the 1988 Winter Games in Calgary, but still few expected her to challenge for gold-medal honours; in fact, she produced one of the greatest performances in speed skating history. The 23-year-old Dutchwoman beat off the challenge of pre-event favourites Gabi Zange, Karin Kania and Andrea Ehrig-Mitscherlich to take a surprise gold in the 3000m, overcame the odds to win the 1500m, and then completed a stunning Games by cruising to gold (with a 3.1-second winning margin) in the 5000m (the first time the event had been staged at the Winter Games). She remains the only woman in history to have completed the 1500m/3000m/5000m treble at the Winter Games.

SUMMER AND WINTER OLYMPIAN

Japan's Seiko Hashimoto is unique in that she represented her country at seven separate Olympics, making four appearances in speed skating at the Winter Games (between 1984 and 1994 – her best result was a bronze medal in the 1500m at Albertville 1992) and three in cycling at the Summer Games (in 1988, 1992 and 1996 – her best result was a ninth-place finish in the women's points race at Atlanta 1996). She became head of the Japanese Skating Federation in 1996 and is also a member of Japan's House of Councillors.

FIRST ASIAN CHAMPION

Asian speed skaters had come mighty close to winning the 500m gold medal at the Winter Games – China's Ye Qiabo (in 1992) and Wang Manli (in 2006) had both secured the silver medal – but it wasn't until Vancouver 2010 that a competitor from the continent enjoyed the thrill of becoming Olympic champion in the event. Korea's Lee Sang-Hwa beat pre-event favourite Jenny Wolf (Germany) to become the first-ever Asian Olympic female speed-skating champion.

Below: Korea's Lee Sang-Hwa celebrates on the podium after winning the gold medal in the 500m at the 2010 Winter Games in Vancouver.

MOST MEDALS WON (BY COUNTRY): TOP TEN

Pos	Medals	Country	G	S	B
1	62	Germany (East/West)	19	27	16
2	33	USSR/Russia	14	8	11
3	27	USA	10	8	9
4	26	Netherlands	12	8	6
5	16	Canada	4	6	6
6	6	China	-	3	3
7	5	Finland	1	2	2
8	4	Japan	-	1	3
9	3	Czech Republic	2	-	1
=	3	Austria	1	1	1
=	3	Poland	-	1	2

Other Major Championships

Women speed skaters compete in three major competitions beyond the Winter Games: the ISU World All-Round Speed Skating Championships (held annually since 1936); the ISU World Single Distance Championships (now contested in non-Olympic years and staged for the first time in 1996); and the ISU Speed Skating World Cup (a season-long series of events to determine overall discipline winners which has been contested on an annual basis since 1985–86).

CINDERELLA OF VIYATKA

A naturally fast skater in her youth, Maria Isakova, who was nicknamed "The Cinderella of Viyatka" (after the city of her birth), competed at the Soviet All-Round Championships for the first time in 1936, at the age of 15, and finished fifth. It was a sign of what was to come. Robbed of her prime competitive years by the Second World War (she was 21 when it started), she competed at the ISU World All-Round Championships for the first time in 1948 (aged 30) and won. She retained her title the following year and in 1950, in Moscow, in what would be her final appearance at the competition, became the first woman in history to win the event three years in a row.

Right: The Soviet Union's Maria Isakova was one of the early stars of women's speed skating.

Below: With 32 gold medals to her name, Gunde Niemann-Stirnemann's record at the ISU World All-Round Speed Skating Championships will probably never be surpassed.

KIT KLEIN: THE FIRST CHAMPION

Winner of the 500m and 1500m events when speed skating was staged as a demonstration sport at the 1932 Winter Games at Lake Placid, New York, US star Kit Klein took an overall bronze medal at the unofficial (non-ISU-sanctioned) World All-Round Championships in Oslo, Norway, in 1935. Klein returned to Europe the following year for the first official ISU World All-Round Championships, held in Stockholm, Sweden, and won the overall gold medal to become the championships' first official winner.

NIEMANN-STIRNEMANN SETS NEW STANDARDS

Although she never achieved the dominance in the Olympic arena that was expected of her (despite her glittering success in other speed skating competitions, she only won three gold medals – in the 3000m and 5000m at Albertville 1992 and in the 3000m at Nagano 1998), Gunde Niemann-Stirnemann (who first competed under her maiden name, Kleemann) more than made up for it with her performances at the ISU World All-Round Speed Skating Championships, for in this competition the German was almost unbeatable. Between 1991 and 1998, she won the overall title on an incredible eight occasions and in the process picked up 42 individual medals (an astonishing 32 of them gold) – an achievement unlikely to be equalled.

ISU WORLD ALL-ROUND CHAMPIONSHIPS – MOST MEDALS: TOP FIVE

Pos	Medals	Name (country, span)	G	S	B
1	42	Gunde Niemann-Stirnemann (East Germany/Germany, 1989–2000)	32	8	2
2	39	Claudia Pechstein (Germany, 1996–2003)	6	27	6
3	30	Karin Kania (East Germany, 1981–88)	20	9	1
=	30	Stien Baas-Kaiser (Netherlands, 1965–72)	10	15	5
5	29	Inga Artamonova-Voronina (USSR, 1957–65)	16	8	5

Below: Canada's Catriona Le May Doan is a three-time 500m ISU World Single Distance champion.

LE MAY DOAN MAKES HER MARK

A two-time Olympic champion over 500m (at Nagano 1998 and Salt Lake City 2002), for which she earned the moniker "the fastest woman on ice", Canada's Catriona Le May Doan, a five-time world champion, also showed her class at the ISU World Single Distance Championships. She took the 500m title for the first time in 1998, retained it the following year (becoming the first woman to achieve the feat), finished third in 2000 and won the title for the third time at Salt Lake City, Utah, in 2001.

RUSSIAN DOMINATION

Speed skaters from the Soviet Union dominated the ISU World All-Round Speed Skating Championships between 1952 and 1966, setting a competition record by winning 15 consecutive titles: Lidia Selikhova (1952 and 1954); Kalida Shchegoleteva (1953); Rimma Zhukova (1955); Sofya Kondakova (1956); Inga Artamonova (1957, 1958, 1962 and 1965); Tamara Rylova (1959); Valentina Stenina (1960, 1961 and 1966); and Lidiya Skoblikova (1963 and 1964). The record-breaking sequence finally came to an end when Dutch star Stien Kaiser took the title at the 1967 championships in Deventer, Netherlands.

A NEW STAR IS BORN

Germany's Jenny Wolf made a dramatic entrance to the ISU World Single Distance Championships at Salt Lake City, Utah, in 2007 when, in only her second-ever race in the event, she broke the 500m world record. It marked the arrival of a new speed skating star: Wolf went on to win gold, retained her title the following year and, in Vancouver in 2009, became the first woman in championship history to complete a hat-trick of 500m successes. She put aside the disappointment of only winning 500m silver at the 2010 Winter Games by claiming her fourth consecutive World Single Distance Championships 500m title at Inzell, Germany, in 2011.

Above: Germany's Jenny Wolf has been the standout performer in the 500m in recent times, winning four consecutive titles at the ISU World Single Distance Championships.

FIRST TO RETAIN TITLE

A four-time national champion and considered one of the pioneers of speed skating for women both domestically and internationally, Norway's Laila Schou-Nilsen won the last of the unofficial World All-Round Championships in her home capital, Oslo, in 1935. She took official all-round gold at the 1937 Championships in Davos, Switzerland, in stunning fashion, winning all four events (the 500m, 1000m, 3000m and 5000m) and breaking the world record for each – her record in the 5000m would last until 1950. When she took the title for a second time in Oslo the following year, she became the first woman in the history of the championships to make a successful defence of her title.

MOST GOLD MEDALS FOR FRIESINGER

A three-time gold medallist at the Winter Games (in the 1500m at Salt Lake City 2002 and in the Team Pursuit at both Turin 2006 and Vancouver 2010), Anni Friesinger has won more gold medals than any other competitor at the ISU World Single Distance Championships. The German's successes are as follows: 1000m gold in 2003, 2004 and 2008; 1500m gold in 1998, 2001, 2003, 2004, 2008 and 2009 (the latter saw her overhaul compatriot Gunde Niemann-Stirnemann's record of 11 gold medals); as well as gold in the 3000m in 2003, in the 5000m in 2005, and in the Team Pursuit in 2005.

PECHSTEIN TOPS MEDAL COUNT

The most prolific medal winner in women's speed skating history at the Winter Games (she has won nine, five of them gold), Claudia Pechstein has also enjoyed remarkable success at the ISU World Single Distance Championships. Between 1996 and 2011, the German has picked up an all-time competition record 23 medals, five of them gold – in the 1500m in 2000; in the 3000m in 2000 and 2004; and in the 5000m in 1996 and 2003.

Left: Germany's Anni Friesinger has won more gold medals at the ISU World Single Distance Championships than any other female speed skater in history.

Below: The United States' Bonnie Blair first showed her class in the ISU Speed Skating World Cup in 1986.

THE SHORT DISTANCE QUEEN

Bonnie Blair first showed her incredible talent in speed skating's shorter distances – a talent that would eventually lead her to winning five gold medals at the Winter Games – during the 1986–87 ISU Speed Skating World Cup season. The United States star became the first female skater in the event's history to win the 500m/1000m overall season title double. She repeated the feat in 1991–92, 1993–94 and 1994–95 before her retirement in March 1995.

THE BEST IN HISTORY

Without a doubt the most dominant female speed skater in history, Gunde Niemann-Stirnemann, who represented both East Germany and Germany in her career, has been the most successful competitor in the ISU Speed Skating World Cup. She made her debut in the competition in 1989, claimed her first overall season victory (in the 1500m) in 1990–91 and, from that moment on, could not stop winning, notching up an all-time record 19 overall season titles (nine in the 1500m and ten in the 3000m/5000m) and recording an incredible 98 race wins (some 29 more than second-placed Bonnie Blair).

TEAM PURSUIT AT THE WORLD CUP

The Team Pursuit event was introduced to the ISU Speed Skating World Cup programme for the first time in 2005–06, with Germany the first to take the overall season title. Canada, who took the title for the first time in 2007–08, became the event's first two-time winners when they won again in 2009–10. The Netherlands (champions in 2006–07 and 2010–11) have since equalled Canada's feat.

Right: Canada's Team Pursuit trio on its way to gold during the 2009–10 ISU Speed Skating World Cup season.

MOST WORLD CUP RACE WINS: TOP TEN

Pos	Wins	Name (country, span)
1	98	Gunde Niemann-Stirnemann (East Germany/Germany, 1989–2001)
2	69	Bonnie Blair (USA, 1986–95)
3	59	Jenny Wolf (Germany, 2004–)
4	56	Anni Friesinger (Germany, 2000–09)
5	36	Monique Garbrecht-Enfeldt (Germany, 1991–2004)
6	34	Catriona Le May Doan (Canada, 1998–2003)
7	26	Christine Nesbitt (Canada, 2008–)
8	23	Claudia Pechstein (Germany, 1996–2009)
=	23	Martina Sablikova (Czech Republic, 2007–)
10	21	Karin Kania (East Germany, 1986–8)

WOMEN'S SPEED SKATING WORLD RECORDS

Event	Time	Name (country)	Date	Venue
500m	36.94	Yu Ying (China)	29/01/2012	Calgary
500m (x2)	1:14.17	Jenny Wolf (Germany)	16–17/11/2007	Calgary
1000m	1:12.68	Christine Nesbitt (Canada)	28/01/2012	Calgary
1500m	1:51.79	Cindy Klassen (Canada)	20/11/2005	Salt Lake City
3000m	3:53.34	Cindy Klassen (Canada)	18/03/2006	Calgary
5000m	6:42.66	Martina Sablikova (Czech Rep)	18/02/2011	Salt Lake City
10,000m	13:48.33	Martina Sablikova (Czech Rep)	15/03/2007	Calgary
Team Pursuit	2:22.79	Canada	06/12/2009	Calgary

Left: In 1986-87, the Netherlands' Yvonne van Gennip became the first woman ever to win both long-track event titles in a single ISU Speed Skating World Cup season.

THE WORLD CUP'S FIRST LONG TRACK STAR

While Bonnie Blair was tearing up the ice in the 500m and 1000m distances during the 1986–87 ISU Speed Skating World Cup season, Yvonne van Gennip was proving to be the star turn in the long-track disciplines. The Netherlands' star skater became the first woman in the event's history to win the overall season title for the 1500m and 3000m/5000m double (skaters contested the latter two distances as one discipline). Three other women – Germany's Gunde Niemann-Stirnemann (in 1991–92, 1992–93, 1994–95, 1995–96, 1997–98, 1998–99 and 1999–2000) and Anni Friesinger (in 2001–02) and Canada's Cindy Klassen (in 2005–06) – have since equalled van Gennip's feat.

Men's Short Track Speed Skating: Olympic Games

Short track speed skating, which takes place on an oval track with a circumference of 111.12 metres, differs from speed skating by virtue of the fact that instead of being contested by a pair of skaters a race begins with a mass start. A demonstration sport at the 1988 Winter Games in Calgary, it has been a full-medal event since Albertville 1992. Men contest four events: the 500m, 1000m, 1500m and 5000m Relay.

Above: South Korea's Kim Ki-Hoon won back-to-back 1000m gold medals at Albertville 1992 and Lillehammer 1994.

Right: South Korea's Lee Jung-Su dominated short track speed skating at Vancouver 2010.

TWO IN A ROW FOR KIM

The men's 1000m event at Albertville 1992 – the first short track speed skating event ever staged at the Winter Games – was expected to be a shootout between South Korea's Lee Jun-Ho (the 1990 world champion) and Kim Ki-Hoon and Britain's Wilf O'Reilly – all three of whom had "medalled" when the sport was staged as a demonstration event at Calgary 1988. O'Reilly fell in the semi-final and, in the final, Kim posted a new world record time to take gold (his country's first at the Winter Games). He made a successful defence of his title at Lillehammer 1994 and remains the only man in history to have claimed back-to-back 1000m short track speed skating gold medals at the Winter Games.

THE BEST OF TIMES FOR LEE JUNG-SU

The 2006 overall world junior champion, South Korea's Lee Jung-Su, had a Winter Games to remember at Vancouver, Canada, in 2010. He took his first gold medal in the men's 1500m and then, a week later, edged out compatriot Lee Ho-Suk on the back straight in the final of the men's 1000m to become the only man in short track speed skating history to win two individual gold medals at a single Winter Games. However, later in the year he was involved in a race-fixing scandal and was banned from the sport for three years.

LEE HO-SUK'S HAUL OF SILVER

South Korea's Lee Ho-Suk has once enjoyed the thrill of Olympic gold medal success as part of a team (he was a member of his country's gold-medal-winning relay team at the 2006 Winter Games in Turin), but as an individual he has had a record-breaking series of near misses. He picked up silver medals in the 1000m and 1500m at the Turin Games and four years later suffered the same fate in Vancouver, where he struck silver again both in the 1000m and as part of South Korea's relay team. His haul of four silver medals is a record for a male short track speed skater at the Winter Games.

MOST GOLD MEDALS WON

Three men hold the record for the most gold medals won in short track speed skating at the Winter Games (three): Canada's Marc Gagnon (in the 5000m Relay at Nagano 1998 and in the 500m and 5000m Relay at Salt Lake City 2002); South Korea's Kim Ki-Hoon (in the 1000m and 5000m Relay at Albertville 1992 and in the 1000m at Lillehammer 1994); and South Korea's Lee Jung-Su (in the 1000m, 1500m and 5000m Relay at Turin 2006).

BIZARRE BRONZE FOR GAGNON

Marc Gagnon now shares the record for the most gold medals won by a short track speed skater at the Winter Games (three, alongside South Korea's Kim Ki-Hoon and Lee Jung-Su), but his first medal win came in extraordinary circumstances. Having failed to make the final, he thought his chances of success were over and would have found little consolation in winning the B-final. In the final, however, strange things happened: while Kim Ki-Hoon and Chae Ji-Hoon completed a South Korean one-two, behind them Britain's Nicky Gooch and Canada's Derrick Campbell were both disqualified and Gagnon was promoted to the bronze medal position. He is the only speed skater in Olympic history to have won a medal without appearing in the final race.

AMERICA'S SHORT TRACK STAR

Born to a Japanese father and an American mother and raised in Seattle, Washington, Apolo Anton Ohno became his country's youngest national champion when he took the title in 1997 aged 14, won the world junior title two years later and, in 2001, became a world champion (in the 1500m) for the first time. He became the face of the 2002 Winter Games in Salt Lake City after winning gold in the 1500m (in controversial circumstances following the disqualification of South Korea's Kim Dong-Sung) and won a silver medal in the 1000m. Further success followed: he won his second career Olympic gold (in the 500m) at Turin 2006 and picked up bronze medals in the 1000m and 5000m Relay. He was among the medals at Vancouver 2010 too, claiming one silver medal (in the 1500m) and two bronzes (in the 1000m and 5000m Relay). His haul of eight Olympic medals is a record for a speed skater and also makes him the most decorated American athlete in Winter Games history.

Left: United States star Apolo Anton Ohno is the most decorated male short track speed skater in Olympic history.

SHORT TRACK'S STRANGEST GOLD MEDAL

When the men's 1000m short track speed skating final got under way at the 2002 Winter Games in Salt Lake City, Utah, Australia's Steven Bradbury was simply happy to be a part of the five-man field – a training accident in 2000 had left him with two broken vertebrae in his neck, causing him to miss the entire 2000–01 season, and he had battled back to fitness so that he could enjoy one last hurrah at the Games. Going into the final lap he lay in last place, some distance behind the other competitors, but then all hell broke loose in front of him; remarkably, every one of his rivals fell, leaving him the last man standing, and he crossed the line – arms spread in disbelief – to become Australia's first Winter Olympic champion and short track speed skating's only gold medallist to hail from the southern hemisphere.

Right: Australia's Steven Bradbury celebrates his shocking gold medal in the 1000m at the 2002 Winter Games in Salt Lake City.

MOST MEDALS WON (BY COUNTRY)

Pos	Medals	Country	G	S	B
1	19	South Korea	10	7	2
2	15	Canada	5	5	5
3	11	USA	2	3	6
4	6	China	-	3	3
5	3	Italy	1	2	-
=	3	Japan	1	-	2
7	2	Australia	1	-	1
8	1	Great Britain	-	-	1

Other Major Championships

Short track speed skaters contest two major international competitions beyond the Winter Games: the World Short Track Speed Skating Championships (which have been held every year since 1976); and the ISU Short Track Speed Skating World Cup (a season-long series of events to determine both overall discipline winners and an overall champion, which has been staged annually since 1997–98).

TWO-TIME 1500M SEASON CHAMPIONS

Three men have won the 1500m season title at the ISU Short Track Speed Skating World Cup on two occasions: South Korea's Kim Dong-Sung (in 1998–99 and 2001–02); the United States' Apolo Anton Ohno (in 2000–01 and 2004–05); and South Korea's Ahn Hyun-Soo (in 2003–04 and 2005–06).

THE WORLD CUP'S BEST

Apolo Anton Ohno of the USA is the most successful competitor in the history of the ISU Short Track Speed Skating World Cup. He won the overall title for the first time in 2000–01 (a year that saw him become the only skater ever to win all three discipline titles – the 500m, 1000m and 1500m), added a second overall title in 2002–03 and triumphed again in 2004–05 to become the only man to have won the overall title on three occasions. He also holds the record (with South Korea's Lee Ho-Suk) for the most 1000m season titles won (three).

Above: South Korea's Ahn Hyun-Soo is one of three men to have won the 1500m season title at the ISU Short Track Speed Skating World Cup on two occasions.

BOUCHER MAKES HIS MARK

Although he would go on to enjoy greater fame in speed skating, winning gold medals in the men's 1000m and 1500m at the 1984 Winter Games in Sarajevo, Bosnia, Canada's Gaetan Boucher also left his mark on the World Short Track Speed Skating Championships. After finishing as runner-up at the inaugural event in 1976, he took the overall title for the first time in 1977 in Grenoble, France, and won again in 1980, in Milan, Italy, to become the championships' first two-time winner.

Left: Following his success in 1977, Canada's Gaetan Boucher became the first-ever two-time ISU Short Track Speed Skating World Cup overall champion when he took the title for a second time in 1980.

THE WORLD CUP'S FIRST DOUBLE CHAMPION

Although his experiences at the Winter Olympics may have caused him to feel some frustration – in his four appearances at the Games he won five medals (two silver and three bronze), but failed in his quest to win gold – China's Li Jiajun enjoyed plenty of other successes in his lengthy career. He won 29 medals at the World Short Track Speed Skating Championships (14 of them gold) and will also go down in history as the first-ever overall champion in the ISU Short Track Speed Skating World Cup. Having won the overall title in 1997–98, he defended it successfully the following year. He is also the event's only two-time 500m overall season winner.

GAGNON HOLDS ON TO HIS TITLE

One of only three men in history to have won three gold medals in short track speed skating at the Winter Games (South Korea's Kim Ki-Hoon and Lee Jung-Su are the others), Canada's Marc Gagnon also put together some notable performances at the ISU World Short Track Speed Skating Championships. He won the overall title for the first time in 1993, in Beijing, China, retained it in Guildford, England, the following year (remarkably becoming the first skater in 19 editions of the event to make a successful defence) and after finishing runner-up in 1995, won again at The Hague, Netherlands, in 1996 to become the Championships' first three-time winner. He added a fourth title in Vienna, Austria, in 1998.

SOUTH KOREA IS THE TEAM TO BEAT

As in the Nations competition at the ISU Short Track Speed Skating World Cup (in which it won seven titles), South Korea has been the most successful nation in the ISU World Short Track Speed Skating Championships Team competition, winning eight titles: in 1992, 1994, 1997, 2004, 2006, 2009, 2010 and 2011.

Above: Canada's Marc Gagnon is a four-time World Championship gold medallist.

SHORT TRACK SPEED SKATING WORLD RECORDS

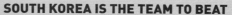

Event	Time	Name (country)	Date	Venue
500m	40.651	Sung Si-Bak (Korea)	14/11/2009	Marquette
1000m	1:23.454	Charles Hamelin (Canada)	18/01/2009	Montreal
1500m	2:09.041	Noh Jin-Kyu (Korea)	10/12/2011	Shanghai
3000m	4:31.891	Noh Jin-Kyu (Korea)	19/03/2011	Warsaw
5000m Relay	6:35.844	South Korea	09/12/2011	Shanghai

Above: South Korea's Sung Si-Bak set a new world-record mark in the 500m in Marquette, Canada, in November 2009.

Below: South Korea's Noh Jin-Kyu (No. 152) on his way to setting a new 1500m world record in Shanghai, China, in 2011.

FIVE IN A ROW FOR AHN

No one has enjoyed more success at the World Short Track Speed Skating Championships than Ahn Hyun-Soo. The South Korean star, who at Turin 2006 became the first, and to date only, short track speed skater in history to win two individual gold medals at a single Winter Games (in the 1000m and the 1500m – he added a third gold medal in the 5000m Relay), won five consecutive overall titles at the World Championships between 2003 and 2007. His record-breaking run came to an end when he fractured his kneecap in training and was forced to miss the 2008 Championships.

Women's Short Track Speed Skating: Olympic Games

Like the men's, women's short track speed skating made its first appearance at the Winter Games as a demonstration sport at Calgary 1988 and has been part of the full-medal programme since Albertville 1992. Women currently contest four disciplines: the 500m, 1000m, 1500m and the 3000m Relay.

YANG YANG AT THE DOUBLE

One of the most decorated female short track speed skaters in history, China's Yang Yang, known as Yang Yang (A) to differentiate her from her compatriot of the same name (the "A" denotes the month of her birth – August) made her first appearance at the Winter Games at Nagano in 1998 (picking up a silver medal in the 3000m Relay). By Salt Lake City 2002, however, she was the dominant force in her sport, and how she proved it. She took gold both in the 500m – to become her country's first-ever Winter Olympic champion – and a week later in the 1000m, to become the first woman in history to claim the 500m/1000m double. Her compatriot Wang Meng equalled her feat at Vancouver 2010.

Right: Yang Yang (A) (left) became China's first-ever Winter Olympic gold-medallist in the 500m at Salt Lake City 2002.

FROM VEGAS TO DOUBLE OLYMPIC GOLD

Cathy Turner's competitive career was as colourful as it was controversial. America's short track champion in 1979, she failed to win a place in the US team for the 1980 Winter Games and promptly left the sport to become a singer – working in a Las Vegas bar under the name Nikki Newland. She returned to training nine years later, aged 29, qualified for the US team for Albertville 1992, and duly won gold in the 500m, after which she announced her retirement from the sport. She wasn't finished there, however. She returned to competition a few months before Lillehammer 1994, qualified for the US team yet again and muscled her way to a second successive 500m gold medal. She is one of only two women in history (China's Wang Meng is the other) to make a successful defence of her Olympic 500m title.

Above: Cathy Turner's return to the sport resulted in two gold medals in the 500m at Albertville 1992 and Lillehammer 1994.

MOST MEDALS WON: TOP FIVE

Pos	Medals	Name (country)	G	S	B
1	6	Wang Meng (China)	4	1	1
2	5	Chun Lee-Kyung (South Korea)	4	–	1
=	5	Yang Yang (A) (China)*	2	2	1
=	5	Yang Yang (S) (China)†	–	4	1
5	4	Choi Eun-Gyeong (South Korea)	2	2	–
=	4	Cathy Turner (USA)	2	1	1
=	4	Tania Vincent (Canada)	–	2	2

* – (A) refers to the month of her birth – August
† – (S) refers to the month of her birth – September

WANG MENG: TOP OF THE CROP

No one has enjoyed more success in female short track speed skating at the Winter Games than China's Wang Meng. She opened her Olympic medal account at Turin 2006 with gold in the 500m, silver in the 1000m and bronze in the 1500m. She did even better in Vancouver four years later, emerging as the winner in the 500m, 1000m and as part of China's 3000m Relay team. Her haul of six medals makes her the most successful short track speed skater of all time (her four gold medals is also a record, shared with South Korea's Chun Lee-Kyung) and she is her country's most decorated Winter Olympian in history.

YOUNGEST-EVER GOLD MEDALLIST

South Korea's Kim Yun-Mi made history at the 1994 Winter Games in Lillehammer. When she took gold as part of her country's victorious 3000m Relay team, she became, aged 13 years 85 days, the youngest gold medallist (in any sport) in Winter Games history. She would go on to win a second career gold medal, again in the 3000m Relay, at Nagano four years later.

CHUN MAKES GOLD-MEDAL-WINNING MARK

South Korea's Chun Lee-Kyung first competed at the Winter Games as a 16-year-old at Albertville 1992 but, for the most part, her performance (she finished 12th in the 500m) slipped under the radar. There was no ignoring her at Lillehammer two years later, however: she won the 1000m (the first time the event had been contested at the Games) and then went on to form part of her country's gold-medal-winning 3000m Relay team. Her headline-grabbing exploits did not end there: at Nagano 1998 she took bronze in the 500m, made a successful defence of her 1000m title (she is still the only woman to achieve the feat) and added a further gold to her collection in the 3000m Relay. Her haul of four gold medals is a record for a female short track speed skater at the Winter Games (shared with China's Wang Meng).

Right: No woman has won more short track speed gold medals at the Winter Games than South Korea's Chun Lee-Kyung.

A GAMES TO REMEMBER FOR JIN SUN-YU

Jin Sun-Yu's first taste of Olympic competition at Turin 2006 may not have been altogether sweet (she finished 12th in the 500m), but what followed was the most commanding set of performances by a female short track speed skater in the history of the Games. The South Korean went on to win gold in the 1500m, then triumphed in the 3000m Relay and rounded out a truly memorable fortnight by winning gold in the 1000m to become the first female short track speed skater in history to win three gold medals at a single Winter Games.

Above: South Korea's Jin Sun-Yu won a record three women's short track speed skating gold medals at Vancouver 2010.

MOST MEDALS WON (BY COUNTRY)

Pos	Medals	Country	G	S	B
1	18	South Korea	9	4	5
=	18	China	7	7	4
3	10	Canada	2	5	3
4	7	USA	2	2	3
5	3	Bulgaria	-	2	1
6	2	Italy	-	-	2
7	1	North Korea	-	-	1
=	1	EUN	-	-	1

Other Major Championships

Although success at the Winter Games is rightly considered to be the pinnacle of a short track speed skater's career, women also contest two major championships on an individual basis – the ISU Short Track Speed Skating World Cup (held annually since the 1997–98 season) and the World Short Track Speed Skating Championships (staged on an annual basis since 1976) – and one as a team – the World Team Championships (which were held for the first time in 1991).

Above: China's Wang Meng won a record six straight ISU Short Track Speed Skating World Cup 500m titles.

YANG YANG SETS THE STANDARD

Yang Yang (A) reached the absolute zenith of her career at the 2002 Winter Games in Salt Lake City, at which she took gold in both the 500m and 1000m, but she had already shown her world-class potential at the ISU Short Track Speed Skating World Cup. She took the overall title for the first time in 1998–99 and was a model of consistency at the event as she claimed further overall titles in each of the next three years. She is still the only woman in history to have won the event on four occasions.

UNBEATABLE IN THE 500M

Wang Meng may not have surpassed her compatriot Yang Yang (A)'s achievement in terms of overall championship titles at the ISU Short Track Speed Skating World Cup (winning three titles to Yang Yang's four), but no one can question her absolute supremacy in the 500m discipline. The Chinese star, the most successful short track speed skater of all time at the Winter Games, claimed the 500m title a record six straight seasons between 2004–05 and 2009–10. It was Canada's Marianne St-Gelais who finally ended Wang Meng's spectacular run of success when she took the title in 2010–11.

UNFORGETTABLE SEASON FOR GOULET-NADON

The 2002–03 ISU Short Track Speed Skating World Cup season represented the unforgettable pinnacle of Amélie Goulet-Nadon's short career. Having come to prominence a year earlier at the 2002 Winter Games in Salt Lake City (at which she picked up a bronze medal as part of Canada's 3000m Relay team), she became the only woman in the competition's history to win all three discipline titles (in the 500m, 1000m and 1500m) and finished second in the overall standings. Shortly afterwards, however, she began to have difficulties with motor problems in her body and was forced to retire from the sport at the tender age of 23.

Above: Canada's Amélie Goulet-Nadon had a memorable 2002–03 season.

THE SPORT'S FIRST TRUE STAR

Although the best years of her career were almost certainly behind her by the time short track speed skating was elevated to full-medal status at the 1992 Winter Games in Albertville (by which stage she was 29 years old), Sylvie Daigle still enjoyed a gold-medal-winning moment as part of Canada's victorious 3000m Relay team. It was the least she deserved for, in the early part of her career, she was the best short track speed skater in the business. She became overall champion at the World Short Track Speed Skating Championships for the first time in 1979, won the title for a second time in 1983, and recorded a hat-trick of titles between 1988 and 1990 (to become the first woman to win three successive titles). Her haul of five titles has been equalled, by China's Yang Yang (A), but never beaten.

Above: China has been the team to beat in the Nations event at the ISU Short Track Speed Skating World Cup.

CHINESE DOMINATION

China enjoyed almost total domination of the Nations event at the ISU Short Track Speed Skating World Cup. Between 1998–99 (the first time it was contested) and 2009–10 (after which the event was discontinued) the country won ten of the 12 available titles – with South Korea (in 2003–04 and 2005–06) claiming the other two.

KATO THE FIRST TO RETAIN TITLE

Having taken a silver medal at the 1978 World Short Track Speed Skating Championships in Solihull, England, and a bronze medal a year later in Quebec, Canada, Japan's Miyoshi Kato became overall world champion for the first time in 1980, in Milan, Italy. She won again the following year in Meudon, France, to become the first of seven women in the history of the championships who have defended the title successfully.

THE TEAM CHAMPIONSHIPS TOP DOGS

While South Korea have been forced to play second fiddle to China in the Nations event at the ISU Short Track Speed Skating World Cup (claiming only two titles compared to China's ten), there is no doubt that the Koreans have been top dogs at the World Short Track Speed Skating Team Championships: they have claimed the gold medal on a record 12 occasions (six more than China).

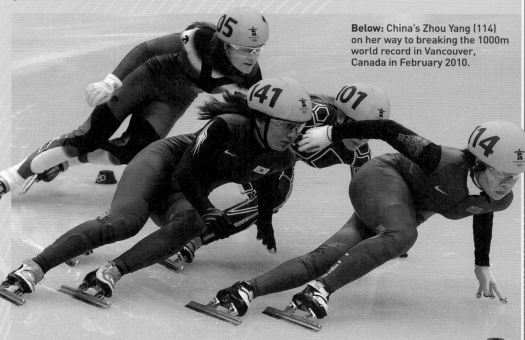

Below: China's Zhou Yang (114) on her way to breaking the 1000m world record in Vancouver, Canada in February 2010.

WOMEN'S SHORT TRACK SPEED SKATING WORLD RECORDS

Event	Time	Name (country)	Date	Venue
500m	42.609	Wang Meng (China)	29/11/2008	Beijing
1000m	1:29.049	Zhou Yang (China)	26/02/2010	Vancouver
1500m	2:16.729	Zhou Yang (China)	09/02/2008	Salt Lake City
3000m	4:46.983	Jung Eun-Ju (South Korea)	15/03/2008	Harbin
3000m Relay	4:06.610	China	24/02/2010	Vancouver

Chapter 3 TOBOGGANING

In ancient times a simple mode of transport, tobogganing is now a thrilling sport: an adrenaline-fuelled, seat-of-your-pants ride down man-made ice tracks. The term covers three disciplines: bobsleigh (two- or four-man), skeleton (an individual sport in which competitors slide head-first down the track on a small sled) – both of which are governed by the International Bobsleigh and Tobogganing Federation – and luge (a one- or two-man foot-first event that is governed by the International Luge Federation).

Above: Germany's Tatjana Hüfner on the first of her runs in the 2010–11 Luge World Cup women's singles at Sigulda, Latvia. Not only did she win this event but she also won the overall World Cup title for the fourth consecutive season.

Men's Bobsleigh: Olympic Games

Men's four-man bobsleigh was contested for the first time at the first-ever Winter Games in 1924 in Chamonix, France. It became a five-man event at St-Moritz 1928, but continued as a four-man event thereafter. The two-man event was added to the programme at Lake Placid 1932, and both competitions have appeared at every Games since, with the exception of Squaw Valley 1960.

MOST MEDALS WON: TOP TEN

Pos	Medals	Name (country)	G	S	B
1	7	Bogdan Musiol (East Germany/Germany)	1	5	1
2	6	Wolfgang Hoppe (East Germany/Germany)	2	3	1
=	6	Eugenio Monti (Italy)	2	2	2
4	5	Kevin Kuske (Germany)	4	1	0
=	5	André Lange (Germany)	4	1	0
=	5	Fritz Feierabend (Switzerland)	0	3	2
7	4	Bernhard Germeshausen (East Germany)	3	1	0
=	4	Meinhard Nehmer (East Germany)	3	0	1
=	4	Markus Zimmermann (Germany)	2	1	1
=	4	Donat Acklin (Switzerland)	2	1	1
=	4	Gustav Weder (Switzerland)	2	1	1
=	4	Christoph Langen (Germany)	2	0	2
=	4	Bernhard Lehmann (East Germany)	1	2	1
=	4	Sepp Benz (Switzerland)	1	2	1
=	4	Erich Schärer (Switzerland)	1	2	1
=	4	Wolfgang Zimmerer (West Germany)	1	1	2

Above: Bogdan Musiol (far left) celebrates gold at the 1980 Winter Games.

GERMANY'S GOLDEN DOUBLE ACT

Germany's André Lange and Kevin Kuske formed the most successful partnership in men's bobsleigh history at the Winter Games. Alongside Carsten Embach and Enrico Kühn, the pair struck gold for the first time (in the four-man event) at the 2002 Winter Games in Salt Lake City. They were unstoppable in Turin four years later, picking up both the two- and four-man titles (the latter with René Hoppe and Martin Putze) and made a successful defence of their two-man title in Vancouver four years later. They are the only athletes in history to have won four gold medals in bobsleigh at the Winter Games.

Right: André Lange (front) and Kevin Kuske won two-man gold at the 2010 Winter Games.

MOST MEDALS

A former shot putter who switched to pushing bobsleighs in 1977, Bogdan Musiol became a world champion for the first time in 1978 (with bob pilot Horst Bernhard) and went on to enjoy a hugely successful career as part of numerous East German and then German crews. He won the only Olympic gold medal of his career as part of East Germany's victorious four-man team at Lake Placid 1980, but remained a regular visitor to the Olympic podium, picking up a further five silver medals (in the two- and four-man events at both Sarajevo 1984 and Calgary 1988 and the four-man at Albertville 1992) and a bronze medal (in the two-man at Lake Placid 1980). His collection of seven Olympic medals is a record for a bobsledder at the Winter Games.

Above: Donat Acklin (left) and Gustav Weder won gold medals both in 1992 and 1994.

MOST MEDALS WITHOUT GOLD

Switzerland's Fritz Feierbrand enjoyed plenty of success throughout his impressive and lengthy career (he competed with the world's best from the mid-1930s to the mid-1950s), notably at the FIBT World Championships, at which he won five gold medals, but his experiences at the Winter Games probably left him feeling unfulfilled. He won two silver medals at Garmisch-Partenkirchen 1936, another silver at St-Moritz 1948 and two bronze medals at Oslo 1952. His haul of five medals is the most by any man in bobsleigh history who did not go on to win a gold medal at the Winter Games.

CLEAN SWEEP FOR OSTLER AND NIEBERL

Andreas Ostler and Lorenz Nieberl celebrated Germany's return to international competition for the first time since the Second World War in record-breaking fashion at the 1952 Winter Games in Oslo, Norway. First the pair combined to take gold in the two-man event; then, a week later, they formed part of the German quartet (alongside Friedrich Kuhn and Franz Kemser) that triumphed in the four-man event. In doing so, they became the first bobsledders in history to win both two- and four-man gold medals at a single Winter Games.

DOUBLE GOLDEN DELIGHT FOR SWISS DUO

Along with Swiss pairing Gustav Weder and Donat Acklin, German teams were widely expected to challenge for the gold medal in the two-man bobsleigh event at the 1992 Winter Games in Albertville – the first following Germany's reunification in 1990. It came as an enormous surprise, therefore, when British duo Mark Tout and Lenox Paul led the competition at the halfway stage. Then, however, the Swiss pair made its decisive move, posting the fastest time in the penultimate run to move from fifth to first in the standings, and holding off the challenge of the Germans in the final run to claim Switzerland's first two-man bobsleigh gold medal for 12 years. The Swiss took the title at Lillehammer in 1994 as well, to become the first two-man bobsleigh pair in Winter Games history to make a successful title defence.

ONLY SHARED GOLD MEDAL

The men's two-man bobsleigh event at the 1998 Winter Games in Nagano, Japan, was one of the most open in history, but the pattern for the event was set as early as the first run when Canada (Pierre Lueders and David MacEachern) and Italy (Günther Huber and Antonio Tartaglia) posted the fastest times. By the start of the final run, Canada trailed Italy by 0.02 seconds, but Lueders's run was slightly faster than Hüber's and, when the clock stopped, the two teams had posted identical times. As the tiebreaker rule that had decided the two-man event at the 1968 Winter Games was no longer in use, in meant that, for the first and only time in bobsleigh history, a gold medal was shared at the Winter Games.

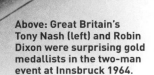

Above: Great Britain's Tony Nash (left) and Robin Dixon were surprising gold medallists in the two-man event at Innsbruck 1964.

NASH AND DIXON STRIKE BRITAIN'S ONLY GOLD

The two Italian teams – Sergio Zardini/Romano Bonagura and Eugenio Monti/Sergio Siorpaes – were firm favourites for two-man bobsleigh gold at the 1964 Winter Games in Innsbruck, but at the end of the first day, British duo Tony Nash and Robin Dixon held the surprise, albeit narrow, lead. The positions changed after the third run, with Zardini and Bonagura holding a slender 0.05-second lead over the British duo and, with one run remaining, the race for gold was on. Nash and Dixon went first, but made a crucial mistake on the Hexenkessel curve and, convinced that their chance of winning gold had gone, they retired to a café and listened to the rest of the runs via the on-course commentary. They would have liked what they heard: Zardini made a mistake on the same curve; Monti could not close the gap; and Nash and Dixon became the first British pair in history to win bobsleigh gold at the Winter Games.

OLDEST COMPETITOR

Hubert Menten did not win any medals when he formed part of the Dutch five-man bobsleigh team at the 1928 Winter Games in St-Moritz, Switzerland (the quintet would ultimately finish the event in 12th place), but his participation in the competition at the age of 54 years 158 days did earn him a place in the record books: he is the oldest man in history to have taken part in the bobsleigh at the Winter Games.

THE REMARKABLE EDDIE EAGEN

A former student of both Harvard and Oxford Universities, Eddie Eagen carved a remarkable niche for himself in the history of the Olympic Games. At the 1920 Summer Games in Antwerp, he won a gold medal in the light-heavyweight boxing competition and, although he lost his title four years later in Paris, he would go on to enjoy more time in the Olympic spotlight. He made his third Olympic appearance at the 1932 Winter Games in Lake Placid as part of the United States four-man bobsleigh crew and again took gold. He is the only athlete in history to have won gold medals at both the Summer and Winter Olympic Games.

Right: Victory in the four-man bobsleigh at Lake Placid 1932 earned Eddie Eagen a unique place in the Olympic record books.

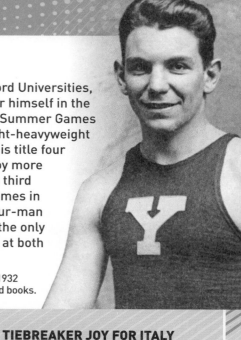

FIRST TWO-MAN CHAMPIONS

Bobsleigh proved to be the most popular event at the 1932 Winter Games in Lake Placid, New York: according to reports, a crowd of 14,000 assembled to watch the first day of the four-man event – keen, no doubt, to see the newly built Mount Van Hoevenberg track (the first permanent bob track in the United States). The two-man bobsleigh event was also contested for the first time at the Games, and the competition gave the home crowd much cause for cheer: Hubert and Curtis Stevens (two brothers from Lake Placid) took the gold medal to become the event's first-ever Olympic champions.

Right: Brothers Hubert (left) and Curtis Stevens won the inaugural two-man bobsleigh event at Lake Placid 1932.

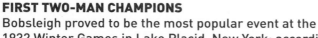

TIEBREAKER JOY FOR ITALY

When the Italian crew containing the legendary 40-year-old Eugenio Monti and Luciano de Paolis posted a new track record time in their first run over the Alpe d'Huez course in the two-man bob event at Grenoble 1968, there was genuine delight that Monti had recaptured his form of yesteryear, but no one knew how significant a moment it would turn out to be. For by the end of the competition's four runs, two crews (the Italians and the West Germans) had clocked identical times. Both teams started to celebrate, but then it was announced that, in accordance with the rules, the gold medal was to be awarded to the crew who had clocked the fastest time, and Italy were duly confirmed as champions. It is the only occasion in history that a bobsleigh event at the Winter Games has been decided by a tiebreaker.

THE FIRST TWO-MAN ONE-TWO FINISH

The race for the gold medal in the two-man bobsleigh event at the 1948 Winter Games in St-Moritz seemed to be over by the end of the first day when, after two runs, the Swiss duo of Felix Endrich and Friedrich Waller opened up an impregnable 2.5-second lead – and the pair duly hung on to take gold. But there was further delight for home fans as the race for silver provided a history-making moment: the second Swiss crew (Fritz Feierabend and Paul Eberhard) held off the challenge of the United States' Frederick Fortune and Schuyler Carron to secure the first one-two in the competition's history.

FULL MEDAL SET FOR MONTI

A 16-time medallist at the FIBT World Championships (a staggering 11 of those medals were gold), Italy's Eugenio Monti is regarded as one of the greatest bobsleigh pilots in history. He won his first Olympic medals at the 1956 Winter Games at Cortina d'Ampezzo, Italy (picking up a pair of silvers in the two- and four-man events). His next appearance on the Olympic podium came at Innsbrück 1964, when he collected two bronze medals. When he took double gold at Grenoble 1968 (aged 40), he became the first bobsledder in history to have won gold, silver and bronze medals at the Winter Games.

BOBSLEIGH'S ONLY ABSENCE FROM THE GAMES

Men's bobsleigh has been contested at every Winter Games since Chamonix 1924, with one exception: Squaw Valley 1960. Hosting the competition at the California venue meant constructing an entirely new course, and when the organizing committee at those Games discovered that only nine teams were planning on entering the event, they decided to reduce costs by abandoning the competition altogether. The FIBT were furious and appealed to the International Olympic Committee, but to no avail.

Right: Italy's Eugenio Monti confirmed his reputation as one of the greatest bobsleigh pilots in history with some memorable performances at the Winter Games.

MOST MEDALS WON (BY COUNTRY): TOP TEN

Pos	Medals	Country	G	S	B
1	30	Switzerland	9	10	11
2	18	Germany	9	4	5
3	17	United States	6	5	6
4	13	East Germany	5	5	3
5	11	Italy	4	4	3
6	6	West Germany	1	3	2
7	4	Canada	2	1	1
=	4	Great Britain	1	1	2
9	3	Austria	1	2	-
=	3	Soviet Union	1	-	2

MOST SUCCESSFUL NATION

Switzerland has enjoyed the most success in bobsleigh events at the Winter Games, winning a total of 30 medals (nine gold, ten silver and 11 bronze). It shares the record for the most gold medals won with Germany (both countries have claimed bobsleigh gold medals on nine occasions).

Below: Switzerland's four-man team edged to the gold medal at the 1988 Winter Games in Calgary.

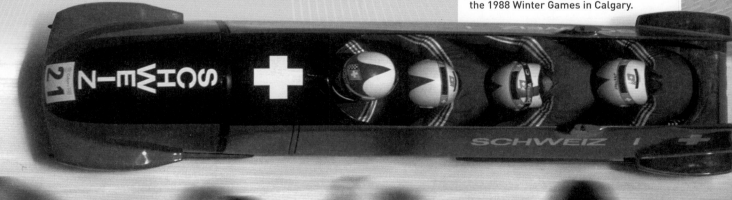

FIBT World Championships

The inaugural FIBT World Championships, an event for four-man crews, were staged at Caux-sur-Montreux, Switzerland, in 1930 (six years after the sport had made its first appearance at the Winter Games). A two-man event was contested a year later (albeit at a different venue from the four-man event). Both events have been staged annually (in non-Olympic years) and at a shared venue since 1947.

Above: Frederick McEvoy (left) drove Great Britain's two- and four-man teams to World Championships gold in 1937.

McEVOY AND BLACK AT THE DOUBLE

Great Britain's Frederick McEvoy and Bryan Black made FIBT World Championship history in 1937. First they combined to win gold in the two-man event at Cortina d'Ampezzo, Italy; later in the year, at St-Moritz, Switzerland, the pair (along with David Looker and Charles Green) also took gold in the four-man event. They are the first bobsledders in championship history to have won gold medals in both the two-man and four-man events in the same year.

MOST MEDALS WON: TOP TEN (BY BOB PILOTS)

Pos	Medals	Name (country)	G	S	B
1	19	Wolfgang Hoppe (East Germany/Germany)	8	5	6
2	16	Eugenio Monti (Italy)	11	3	2
=	16	Eric ccc v h Schärer (Switzerland)	6	5	5
4	15	Fritz Feierabend (Switzerland)	6	5	4
5	13	André Lange (Germany)	8	4	1
=	13	Wolfgang Zimmerer (East Germany/Germany)	5	4	4
7	12	Christoph Langen (Germany)	7	4	1
8	10	Gustav Weder (Swizerland)	5	4	1
=	10	Meinhard Nehmer (East Germany/Germany)	4	2	4
10	6	Andreas Ostler (West Germany)	4	2	-

Right: Germany's Wolfgang Hoppe (front) has won more medals (19) than any other bobsleigh driver in World Championships history.

HOPPE TOPS ALL-TIME MEDAL-WINNERS' LIST

Former army major Wolfgang Hoppe is the most successful bobsleigh pilot in the history of the FIBT World Championships. He picked up his first medal (a bronze) in the two-man event at Lake Placid, New York, in 1983, and continued to make regular visits to the podium. By the time he retired after the 1997 championships he had collected 19 medals (eight gold, five silver and six bronze) – an all-time record in the event. Perhaps his greatest claim to fame, however, came when he was selected to be Germany's flag-bearer at the 1992 Winter Games in Albertville – the first Olympic Games following his country's reunification in 1990.

BROTHERS IN ARMS

While the ultimate prize eluded them, the Austrian crew made history when it picked up a bronze medal in the four-man event at the 1962 World Championships in Garmisch-Partenkirchen, Germany. The quartet was made up of four brothers – Franz, Pepi, Heini and Fritz Isser – and it is the only instance in the event's history in which four brothers have combined to pick up a medal.

MOST FOUR-MAN GOLD MEDALS

A four-time Olympic gold medallist and regarded as one of the greatest bobsleigh pilots of all time, André Lange left his record-breaking mark on the FIBT World Championships. Coached by another German bobsledding great, Wolfgang Hoppe, he picked up his first gold medal at the championships in the four-man event at Altenberg, Germany, in 2000 and, although he would win six medals in the two-man event (three of them gold), he enjoyed his greatest successes in the four-man competition, Further gold medals followed in 2003, 2004, 2005 and 2008 – and his haul of five golds in the four-man is an all-time record at the championships.

Right: Another four-man gold medal for André Lange in 2008.

MAGICAL MONTI

No one has enjoyed more success in the two-man event at the FIBT World Championships than Eugene Monti. The Italian claimed his first world title (along with Renzo Alverà) in 1957 in St-Moritz, Switzerland; the pair successfully defended their title the following year in Garmisch-Partenkirchen, Germany (becoming the first duo to achieve the feat at the championships), and added further titles in 1959 and 1960. Monti then changed partners (he was joined by Sergio Siorpaes) – but not his winning ways. He added more gold medals to his collection in 1961, 1963 and 1966, and his overall haul of seven gold medals in the event is a record that is unlikely to be bettered. The Italian maestro's record-breaking exploits do not end there: along with Furio Nordio, Siorpaes and Alverà, he formed part of Italy's quartet that won back-to-back gold medals in the four-man event in 1960 and 1961 (the first crew to achieve the feat).

MOST SUCCESSFUL NATION

Switzerland has been the most successful nation at the FIBT World Championships. It has won a total of 83 medals in the two- and four-man competitions, of which 31 are gold, 26 silver and 26 bronze.

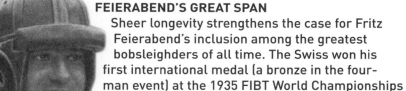

FEIERABEND'S GREAT SPAN

Sheer longevity strengthens the case for Fritz Feierabend's inclusion among the greatest bobsleighders of all time. The Swiss won his first international medal (a bronze in the four-man event) at the 1935 FIBT World Championships at St-Moritz, Switzerland, and struck gold in an international event for the first time at the 1939 Championships at Cortina d'Ampezzo, Italy. He would enjoy a highly successful association with the event, winning a total of 15 World Championship medals (to stand fourth on the all-time medal-winners' list), the last of which came in the four-man event at St-Moritz, Switzerland, in 1955 – a record 20 years after the first.

Left: Switzerland's Fritz Feierabend competed with the world's best for two decades.

FIBT World Cup

The FIBT World Cup, a season-long series of races to determine overall champions in both the two- and four-man disciplines (as well as a combined champion) was contested for the first time in 1984–85. FIBT-sanctioned races are awarded to either a country or a track through a bidding process, with each country allowed to field one sled per race; additional sleds must qualify.

(TWO-MAN) MOST OVERALL SEASON FINISHES: TOP FIVE PILOTS

Pos	Podiums	Name (country)	1st	2nd	3rd
1	12	Pierre Lueders (Canada)	6	5	1
2	6	Günther Huber (Italy)	2	2	2
=	6	André Lange (Germany)	1	1	4
4	4	Christoph Langen (Germany)	3	1	-
=	4	Gustav Weder (Switzerland)	1	3	-

(FOUR-MAN) MOST OVERALL SEASON FINISHES: TOP FIVE PILOTS

Pos	Podiums	Name (country)	1st	2nd	3rd
1	8	André Lange (Germany)	4	1	3
2	7	Alexandr Zubkov (Russia)	4	2	1
3	4	Marcel Rohner (Switzerland)	2	2	-
=	4	Wolfgang Hoppe (E. Germany/Germany)	1	2	1
=	4	Martin Annen (Switzerland)	1	1	2

LANGE LEAVES HIS MARK

A five-time medallist at the Winter Games (of which four were gold) and an eight-time gold medallist at the FIBT World Championships, Germany's André Lange, considered the dominant bobsleigh pilot of his generation, also left his talented mark on the FIBT World Cup. He shares the record (four) for the most combined titles (with Canada's Pierre Lueders), having taken the spoils in 2000–01, 2002–03, 2003–04 and 2007–08. He also took the four-man title in those same seasons to become that event's first four-time winner (a record since equalled by Russia's Alexandr Zubkov).

ONLY SHARED FOUR-MAN BOB TITLE

There has only been one instance in FIBT World Cup history when an end-of-season overall title has been shared. It occurred in the four-man competition in the 1987–88 season, which ended in a tie between Austrian bob sled pilots Ingo Appelt and Peter Kienast. Appelt went on to take the title the following year to become the event's first two-time winner.

PREPARATION PAYS FOR WEDER

Renowned for the intensity with which he would approach his craft (he spent hours studying video footage of his performances), Gustav Weder was proof that perfect preparation could make for perfect performance. A two-time gold medallist at the Winter Games (he piloted the Swiss two-man crew to victory at both Albertville 1992 and Lillehammer 1994), he was also one of the FIBT World Cup's early stars, claiming the two-man and combined titles in 1988–89 and the four-man and combined titles in 1990–91. He was the first man in the event's history to win the combined title on two occasions.

LUEDERS: THE TWO-MAN WORLD CUP KING

Nobody has enjoyed more success in the two-man event at the FIBT World Cup than Canada's most decorated bobsledder of all time, Edmonton-born Pierre Lueders. The five-time Olympian (who won gold in the two-man event at Nagano 1998), was an 85-time medallist in the World Cup, took the overall two-man title for the first time in 1993–94 and retained it the following year. By the time he retired following the 2010 Winter Games in Vancouver, he had added four further two-man titles (in 1996–97, 1997–98, 2002–03 and 2005–06). His haul of six overall two-man titles is a record for the event. He also shares the record (with Germany's André Lange) for the most combined titles (four).

Above: Six-time FIBT World Cup two-man champion Pierre Lueders.

ITALY'S BEST OF THE MODERN ERA

A bronze medallist in luge at the 1982 Junior World Championships, Günther Huber switched his attentions to bobsleigh shortly afterwards and went on to put together a hugely impressive career. Arguably Italy's greatest bobsleigh pilot since the legendary Eugenio Monti, he took the FIBT overall two-man bob title for the first time in 1991–92 and, the following season, became the first man in the competition's history to defend the title successfully. He also took the combined title in 1996–97, but the undoubted highlight of his career came when, alongside his long-time brakeman Antonio Tartaglia, he won two-man gold at the Winter Games of 1998 – the year of the shared gold medal.

ONLY CLEAN SWEEP

There has only ever been one clean sweep in the history of the FIBT World Cup, and it came in the two-man event in the 1999–2000 season, when three Swiss teams, piloted by Christian Reich, Reto Götschi and Marcel Rohner, finished first, second and third respectively.

Right: Günther Huber (front) is Italy's best bobsleigh driver since the legendary Eugenio Monti.

NEW FORCE FROM THE EAST

Russia's leading bobsleigh pilot in recent years, Alexandr Zubkov first started competing in 1999 and, by the middle of the following decade, had established himself as one of the best in the bobsledding business. He took his first overall four-man FIBT World Cup title in 2004–05, retained it in 2005–06, added a third crown in 2008–09 and claimed the spoils once again in 2011–12 to become only the second man in the competition's history (alongside Germany's André Lange) to have won the World Cup's four-man title on four occasions. He has also claimed the overall title in the two-man event (in 2010–11) and the combined title (in 2008–09).

Below: Russia's Alexandr Zubkov (far left) has been one of the dominant bobsleigh drivers of recent times.

MOST SUCCESSFUL NATION

Germany has been the most successful nation in the FIBT World Cup since the event's inception in 1984–85, claiming 22 titles (in combined, two-man and four-man), four more than second-placed Switzerland.

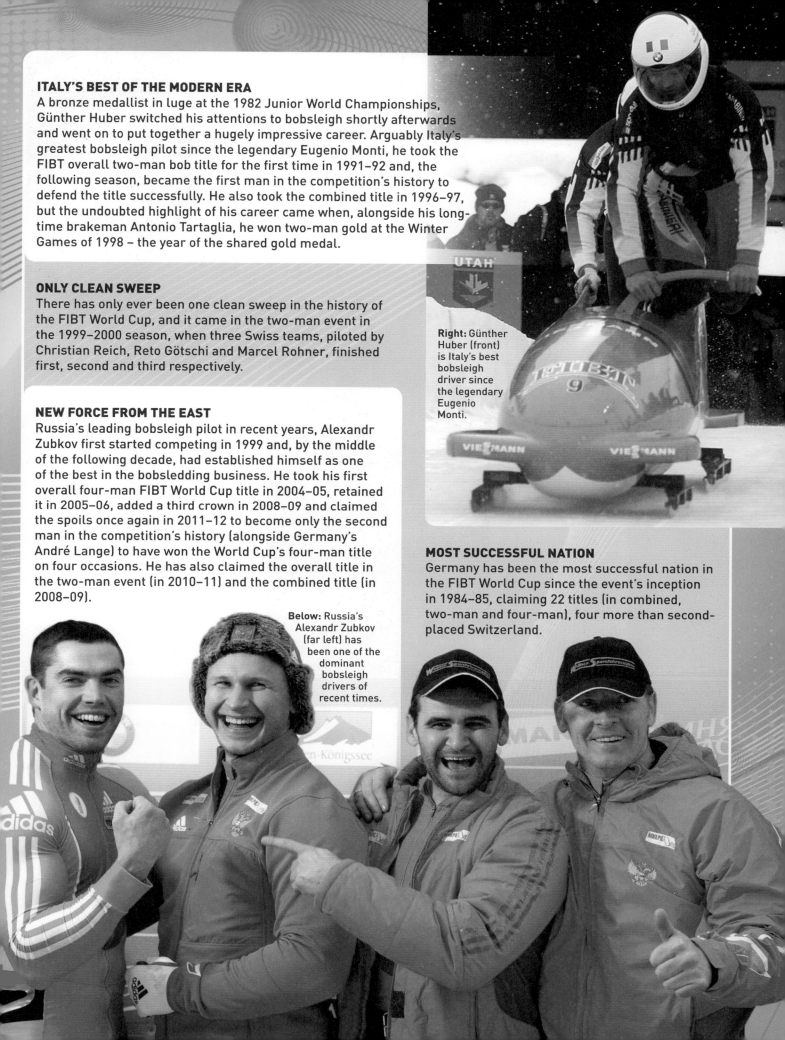

Women's Bobsleigh

Although women's bobsleigh has a long history (Katherine Dewey famously piloted her team to victory in the 1940 US Championships), it is a relatively new event on the international sporting calendar. Its first appearance on a global scale occurred when a women's event (two-women) was contested at the 1994–95 FIBT World Cup; it became part of the World Championships programme in 2000; and has been contested at the Winter Games since Salt Lake City 2002.

Above: United States duo Jill Bakken and Vonetta Flowers won the gold medal at Salt Lake City 2002.

Above: Canada won gold and silver on home ice at Vancouver 2010.

ONE-TWO JOY FOR CANADA

For the first time ever, the women's bobsleigh event at Vancouver 2010 comprised four runs held over two days, and the action proved electric from the event's opening run when defending champion Sandra Kiriasis and new partner Christin Senkel snatched the track record, posting a time of 53.41. The Germans pair's new record lasted barely five minutes: to the delight of the home crowd, Canada's Kaillie Humphreys and Heather Moyse went even faster, clocking 53.19 to establish a healthy lead. The Canadian pair was at it again in their second run, besting their first-run performance by 0.18 seconds to extend their lead, and when they posted their third successive track record time in their third run (52.85) the gold medal was theirs to lose. They duly held on and were joined on the podium by the second Canadian pairing of Helen Upperton and Shelley-Ann Brown, who pipped the US crew of Erin Pac and Elana Meyers for silver. Canada had recorded the first one-two finish in the event's history.

UP AND RUNNING

When two-women bobsleigh was introduced to the Winter Games in 2002, the two German crews were widely expected to be battling for the gold medal at Salt Lake City, Utah, but the headline-grabbing story after the first of the event's two runs was the performance of United States pair Jill Bakken and Vonetta Flowers (a relatively new combination), who stormed to the top of the time charts. They extended their lead in the second run to become (with a 0.3-second winning margin) the event's first-ever Olympic champions.

FIRST WORLD CHAMPIONS

Women's bobsleigh made its first appearance at the FIBT World Championships in 2000 at Altenberg, Germany, and the German pairing of Gabriele Kohlisch (a ten-time medallist at the Luge World Championships) and Kathleen Hering gave the home crowd plenty to cheer about. They beat off the challenges of Jean Racine and Jennifer Davidson of the USA and Françoise Burdet and Katharina Sutter of Switzerland to become women's bobsleigh's first-ever world champions.

Left: Sandra Kiriasis – the most successful female bobsleigh driver in history.

KIRIASIS LEADS THE WAY

Sandra Kiriasis (née Prokoff) is the only woman in history to have won two medals in bobsleigh at the Winter Games (she took silver at Salt Lake City 2002 and gold in Turin four years later), and given her performances at the FIBT World Championships, she may well be the best female bobsleigh pilot of all time. The German picked up back-to-back silver medals at the 2003 and 2004 Championships, struck gold for the first time in 2005 in Calgary and won again in both 2007 and 2008. She collected another silver medal at Lake Placid in 2012 and her haul of six medals in the event (three gold and three silver) is an all-time record at the championships.

FIBT WORLD CHAMPIONSHIPS (BOB DRIVERS): TOP FIVE

Pos	Medals	Name (country)	G	S	B
1	6	Sandra Kiriasis (Germany)	3	3	-
=	5	Cathleen Martini (Germany)	1	2	2
3	4	Shauna Rohbock (United States)	-	2	2
4	3	Susi Erdmann (Germany)	2	-	1
5	2	Nicola Minichiello (GB)	1	1	-
=	2	Françoise Burdet (Switzerland)	1	-	1

FIRST WORLD CUP CHAMPION

The first-ever women's bobsleigh FIBT World Cup season was staged in 1994–95, a decade after the debut of the men's event. Switzerland's Claudia Brühlmann took the spoils to enter the history books as the FIBT World Cup's first female champion.

THE WORLD CUP'S EARLY STAR

Switzerland's Françoise Burdet was the outstanding performer in women's bobsledding until Germany's Sandra Kiriasis arrived on the scene in the early part of the 21st century. Burdet took the FIBT World Cup title for the first time in 1995–96, retained it the following season, completed a hat-trick of titles in 1997–98 and made it four titles in a row in 1998–99. Her achievement stood as a record until 2007–08, when Kiriasis secured her fifth successive title – remarkably, the German would go on to claim the crown for eight years in succession between 2003–04 and 2010–11.

BACK-TO-BACK WORLD CHAMPIONSHIPS JOY FOR ERDMANN

A seven-time gold medallist at the Luge World Championships, Germany's Susi Erdmann switched to bobsleigh in 1998 and has gone on to enjoy supreme success in the discipline. In the FIBT World Championships she picked up a bronze medal (with Tanja Hess) in 2001 in Calgary, struck gold for the first time in 2003 in Winterberg, Germany (with Annegret Dietrich) and won again the following year in Königssee, Germany (with Kristina Bader), to become not only the event's first two-time champion but also the first woman in history to make a successful defence of her World Championship crown.

Above: Susi Erdmann (right) and Kristina Bader won gold at the 2004 FIBT World Championships.

Men's Luge: Olympic Games

Although male lugers had competed at the FIL (International Luge Federation) World Luge Championships since 1955, the sport had to wait until Innsbrück 1964 before it became part of the full-medal programme at the Winter Games. There are two disciplines: the singles and the doubles competition – the latter is officially an "open" event, but only men have ever contested it.

KING OF THE TRACK

After losing out to East Germany's Jens Müller in the battle for gold at the 1988 Winter Games in Calgary, West Germany's Georg Hackl went on to become the dominant force in men's luge singles, claiming two World Championship titles (in 1989 and 1990) and two overall World Cup titles (in 1988–89 and 1989–90). And the German army sergeant was relatively unchallenged in his bid for gold at Albertville 1992, cruising to victory with a 0.306-second winning margin over Austria's Markus Prock. It was a similar, albeit closer, story at Lillehammer two years later: Hackl held off Prock's challenge by just 0.013 seconds to become the first man in history to retain his title. And the German was still the class of the field at Nagano 1998, fending off the sport's new star, Italy's Armin Zöggeler, to claim his third successive Olympic crown. His winning run at the Games came to an end at Salt Lake City 2002, when he took silver behind Zöggeler, but he remains the event's only three-time champion and shares the record (with Zöggeler) for having won the most medals (five).

Above: Germany's Georg Hackl is the only man to win three successive luge gold medals at the Winter Games.

THE NEW KID ON THE BLOCK

Italy's Armin Zöggler – nicknamed "The Cannibal" because of his seemingly enormous appetite for titles – has been a genuine challenger for Olympic gold since his first appearance at the Games at Lillehammer in 1994, when he won bronze at the age of 20. He took the silver medal at Nagano four years later and struck gold for the first time at Salt Lake City in 2002 to become the first luger in history to win bronze, silver and gold medals at successive Games. He retained his title at Turin 2006 and won a silver medal at Vancouver 2010 to become one of two lugers (alongside Hackl) to have won medals at five separate editions of the Winter Games.

RINN AND HAHN AT THE OLYMPIC DOUBLE

East Germany's Hans Rinn and Norbert Hahn took full advantage of the mechanical problems suffered by compatriots and pre-event favourites Bernd and Ulli Hahn to take men's doubles gold at the 1976 Winter Games in Innsbrück. While luck may have played a part in that victory, it was talent alone that propelled them to the gold medal at Lake Placid four years later: the pair clocked the fastest time in the first run and the second fastest in the second to become the first pair in history to make a successful defence of their Olympic title.

Above: Hans Rinn (left) and Norbert Hahn took gold at Lake Placid 1980.

Above: Andreas and Wolfgang Linger are the only brothers ever to win the men's doubles luge Olympic gold medal, achieving the feat at the 2006 Winter Games.

BROTHERS IN ARMS

The leaderboard after the first run of the men's doubles luge competition at Salt Lake City, Utah, in 2002 was both an Austrian and a family affair. The names of brothers Andreas and Wolfgang Linger were at the top, with cousins Markus and Tobias Schiegl in second place. And the Lingers posted the second fastest time in the second and final run too to become the first brothers in the event's history to take gold. They won again at Vancouver 2010 to join Hans Rinn and Norbert Hahn as the only pairs in the competition's history to make a successful defence of their Olympic title.

MOST MEDALS WON (BY COUNTRY)

Pos	Medals	Country	G	S	B
1	17	Germany	8	5	4
2	15	East Germany	8	3	4
3	14	Italy	5	4	5
4	12	Austria	4	4	4
5	9	West Germany	3	3	3
6	4	United States	-	2	2
=	4	USSR	-	2	2
8	2	Latvia	-	1	1
9	1	Russia	-	1	-

MOST SUCCESSFUL NATION

Germany has enjoyed the most success in the men's luge competitions (singles and doubles) at the Winter Games, winning 17 medals (8 gold, 5 silver and 4 bronze). East Germany lies in second place (with 15 medals) and Italy third (with 14 medals).

MOST OLYMPIC APPEARANCES

The record for the most appearances in the luge competion at the Winter Games is six, a feat achieved by three men: Markus Prock (Austria, 1984–2002); Georg Hackl (West Germany/Germany, 1988–2006); and Wilfried Huber (Italy, 1988–2006).

Right: Austria's Marcus Prock competed at six Winter Games and medalled at three of them: Albertville 1992, Lillehammer 1994 (both silver) and Salt Lake City 2002 (bronze).

ONLY SHARED GOLD MEDAL

The men's doubles event at the 1972 Winter Games in Sapporo, Japan, was fraught with problems. First the starting gate malfunctioned, which meant that the results of the first run had to be cancelled. Then, on the second run, East Germany's Walter Hörnlein and Reinhard Bredow and Italy's Paul Hildgartner and Walter Plaikner clocked identical times (1:28.35). As no provision had been made for such an occurrence, it meant that the gold medal was shared for the only time in the event's history.

CLEAN SWEEPS

There have been two medal sweeps in the men's luge singles event at the Winter Games: at Innsbrück 1964, when Germany's Thomas Köhler, Klaus Bonsack and Hans Plenk took gold, silver and bronze respectively; and at Sapporo 1972, when East Germany's Wolfgang Scheidel, Harald Ehrig and Wolfram Fiedler matched their achievement. There has never been a medal sweep in the doubles competition at the Games.

FIL World Championships

The FIL World Championships (with both singles and doubles events) were staged for the first time in Oslo in 1955 and are currently staged in non-Olympic years. As is the case at the Winter Games, Germany has enjoyed the most success at the event, winning 55 medals (22 of them gold), four more than second-placed East Germany.

Below: Italy's Armin Zöggeler (centre) won his fifth World gold medal in 2005.

WOMEN MEDALLISTS

As is the case in the Winter Games, the doubles event at the FIL World Championships was always considered an "open" event – open to both men and women. Unlike the Winter Games, however, the World Championships have seen women competing successfully: Austria's Maria Isser won a silver medal in 1955 (with brother Josef); and Poland's Janina Suszczewska won silver in 1958 (with Jerzy Koszla), while her compatriot Halina Lacheta won bronze (with Ryszard Pedrak-Janowicz) in the same event.

FIRST TO RETAIN DOUBLES TITLE

After finishing in third place in the doubles competition at the inaugural FIL World Championships in 1955 in Oslo, West Germany's Fritz Nachmann and Josef Stillinger became world champions for the first time in 1957 in Davos, Switzerland. They won again the following year in Krynica, Poland, to become the first pair in history to retain the title: a feat since repeated on six occasions.

ONLY SIX-TIME CHAMPION

No one has enjoyed more success in the men's singles competition at the FIL World Championships than Italy's Armin Zöggeler, the Olympic champion of 2002 and 2006. A policeman by profession, Zöggeler took the title for the first time in 1995 in Lillehammer, Norway. A second title followed four years later; a third title followed in 2001, which he successfully defended in 2003 (becoming not only the second man in championships history to do so – alongside Georg Hackl – but also the event's first four-time winner. The Italian's fifth and sixth titles followed in 2005 and 2011 respectively.

MOST DOUBLES TITLES

Two crews hold the record for the most doubles titles (four) at the FIL World Championships: Germany's Stefan Krausse and Jan Behrendt (who triumphed in 1989, 1991, 1993 and 1995); and their compatriots Patric Leitner and Alexander Resch (who triumphed in 1999, 2000, 2004 and 2007).

Right: Germany's Jan Behrendt (left) and Stefan Krausse are four-time FIL World Championships gold-medallists.

MOST MEDALS WON (BY COUNTRY): TOP TEN

Pos	Medals	Country	G	S	B
1	55	Germany	22	23	10
2	51	East Germany	18	17	16
3	49	Austria	15	13	21
4	39	Italy	14	12	13
5	15	West Germany	5	2	8
6	9	Poland	3	5	1
=	9	United States	1	2	6
8	6	USSR	2	2	2
9	3	Latvia	-	1	2
10	1	Canada	1	-	-
=	1	Norway	1	-	-
=	1	Switzerland	-	1	-
=	1	Czechoslovakia	-	-	1

TRIPLE SUCCESS FOR HOFFMAN AND PIETZSCH

The ultimate highlight of their career may well have come when they took luge doubles gold at the 1988 Winter Games in Calgary, but East Germany's Jörg Hoffmann and Jochen Pietzsch had already made a record-breaking mark in the sport before their Olympic victory. They won the doubles titles at the FIL World Championships for the first time in 1983 at Lake Placid, New York; defended it successfully in Oberhof, Germany, two years later; and completed a hat-trick of titles in 1987 in Igls, Austria – becoming the first pair in the history of the championships to do so. Germany's Stefan Krausse and Jan Behrendt would equal their feat when they won three successive titles in 1991, 1993 and 1995.

FIRST WORLD CHAMPIONS

The FIL World Championships were begun at Oslo in 1955 – making it the first international luge competition in history. Norway's Anton Salvesen won gold in the men's singles and Austria's Hans Krausner and Josef Thaler in the doubles to become the sport's first world champions.

FIRST TWO-TIME SINGLES CHAMPION

Poland's Jerzy Wojnar's two appearances in the men's singles luge event at the Winter Games both ended in disappointment (his best result was an eighth-place finish at Grenoble 1968), but he enjoyed some headline-grabbing moments at the FIL World Championships. He took the title for the first time in front of his home crowd at Krynica in 1958 and won again in Girenbad, Switzerland, three years later to become the event's first three-time winner. He is still the only Pole to have won a men's singles gold medal.

UNIQUE PLACE IN THE RECORD BOOKS FOR KÖHLER

East Germany's Thomas Köhler holds some unique records at the FIL World Championships. He first came to international prominence when he took the men's singles gold medal for the first time at the 1962 Championships in Krynica, Poland. Three years later, in Davos, Switzerland, he became the only person in championships history to win two medals in the same event: taking doubles gold with Wolfgang Schneider and also picking up a silver medal in the same competition with Klaus Bonsack. His record-breaking feats did not end there: at the 1967 championships in Hammarstrand, Sweden, he became the first person in history to win gold medals in both the singles and doubles (the latter in partnership with Bonsack).

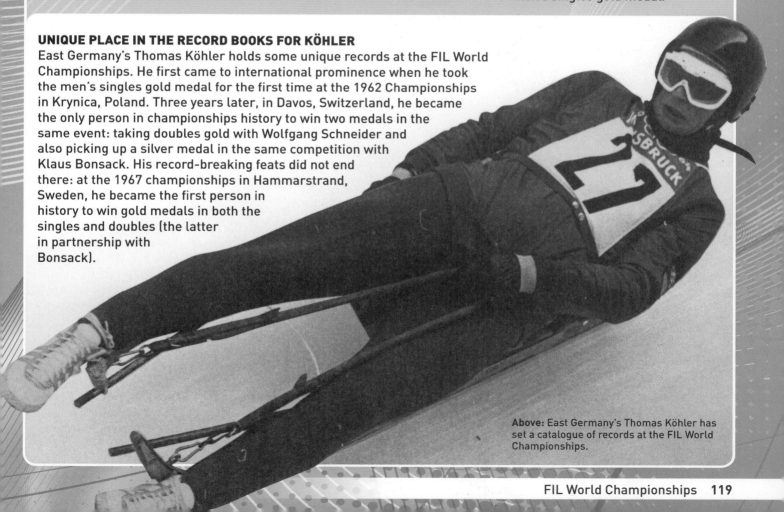

Above: East Germany's Thomas Köhler has set a catalogue of records at the FIL World Championships.

FIL World Cup

Organized by the International Luge Federation, the Luge World Cup is a season-long multi-race tournament to determine overall champions in both the singles and doubles disciplines. It was contested for the first time in the 1977–78 season.

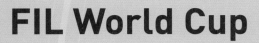

AUSTRIA'S WORLD CUP STAR

He may not have enjoyed the success at the Winter Games his success deserved (he picked up three medals in six Olympic appearances – two silver and one bronze), but few could match Markus Prock's performances in the FIL World Cup. Having finished second in 1984–85 and third in 1986–87, the Austrian took the overall singles title for the first time in 1987–88, finished second in 1989–90 and then embarked on a record-breaking run of success in the competition, claiming seven consecutive titles between 1990–91 and 1996–97. He won a record tenth title (since equalled by Italy's Armin Zöggeler) in 2001–02.

Above: Markus Prock is one of two ten-time winners of the FIL World Cup overall singles title.

Left: Italy's Norbert Huber and Hansjörg Raffl have won seven doubles events at the FIL World Cup.

SHARED SPOILS

Having won one title each in the previous two seasons, Italy's Paul Hildgartner (winner in 1978–79) and his compatriot Ernst Haspinger (1979–80) were widely expected to battle it out during the 1980–81 FIL World Cup season. As it transpired, nothing could separate the two Italians and the title was shared for the first, and to date only, time in the competition's history.

RAFFL AND HUBER TO THE FORE

Just as Markus Prock and Armin Zöggeler have been the outstanding performers in the singles event at the FIL World Cup, so Italy's Hansjörg Raffl and Norbert Huber have left a record-breaking mark on the doubles competition. The pair won the end-of-season overall title for the first time in 1984–85, held on to their title the following season and then went on to collect five consecutive titles between 1988–89 and 1992–93. Their haul of seven titles is an all-time competition record. Before their joint reign began, Raffl had already taken the title with Karl Brunner in 1982–83.

MOST END-OF-SEASON PODIUM FINISHES (SINGLES): TOP FIVE

Pos	Podiums	Name (country)	1st	2nd	3rd
1	14	Armin Zöggeler (Italy)	10	3	1
=	14	Markus Prock (Austria)	10	2	2
=	14	Georg Hackl (West Germany/Germany)	2	7	5
4	8	Jens Müller (East Germany/Germany)	-	3	5
5	5	Paul Hildgartner (Italy)	3	1	1
=	5	Alberto Demchenko (Russia)	1	2	2
=	5	David Möller (Germany)	-	4	1

MOST END-OF-SEASON PODIUM FINISHES (DOUBLES): TOP FIVE

Pos	Podiums	Name (country)	1st	2nd	3rd
1	12	Hansjörg Raffl (Italy)	8	1	3
2	11	Norbert Huber (Italy)	8	-	3
=	11	Patric Leitner (Germany)	6	3	2
=	11	Alexander Resch (Germany)	6	3	2
5	7	Jan Behrendt (Germany)	3	2	2
=	7	Stefan Krausse (Germany)	3	2	2
=	7	Patrick Gruber (Italy)	2	3	3
=	7	Christian Oberstolz (Italy)	2	3	3

Right: Armin Zöggeler of Italy shares the record of ten overall singles titles at the FIL World Cup.

WINKLER'S FINEST MOMENT

The 1977 European champion, whose best performance at the Winter Games was a bronze medal finish in the men's singles competition at Lake Placid 1980, Anton Winkler enjoyed his finest moment in the inaugural season of the FIL World Cup in 1977–78. The West German claimed the overall title that year to go down in history as being the competition's first-ever overall champion.

THE BEST OF THE HUBER BOYS

The most successful of four brothers (the others being Arnold, Günther and Wilfried), Italy's Norbert Huber participated at four Winter Games, picking up a bronze medal at Albertville 1992 and a silver at Lillehammer 1994 (both in the doubles), and as well as enjoying a unique run of success in the doubles competition at the FIL World Cup (he won a record seven titles with Hansjörg Raffl), he also left his mark on the singles competition. He won the singles overall season title for the first time in 1984–85 before twice defending it successfully to become the first man in the competition's history to win three titles in a row.

Below: Norbert Huber (second from right) was the first man to claim the FIL World Cup overall singles title on three occasions.

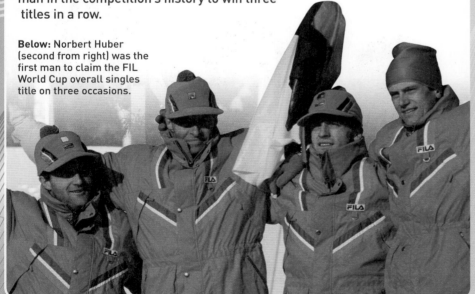

ZÖGGELER REIGNS SUPREME

Italy's Armin Zöggeler has been the man to beat in the FIL World Cup since 1994–95, when he finished the season in second place. Between then and the end of the 2011–12 season, the supremely talented Italian posted 14 top three finishes at the event, including an all-time record ten victories (shared with Austria's Markus Prock), six of which came in consecutive seasons between 2005–06 and 2010–11.

FIRST TWO-TIME DOUBLES CHAMPIONS

Nobody could match the consistency of Italian crew Peter Gschnitzer and Karl Brunner in the first two seasons of the doubles competition in the FIL World Cup. The duo won the title in both 1977–78 and 1978–79 to become not only the event's first champions, but also its first two-time winners and the first pair to defend their title. Their exploits were then surpassed by Austria's Günther Lemmerer and Reinhold Sulzbacher, who won successive titles in 1979–80, 1980–81 and 1981–82.

MOST SUCCESSFUL NATION

Italy has been the FIL World Cup's most successful nation, securing 64 end-of-season podium finishes (30 gold, 17 silver and 17 bronze) in the singles and doubles disciplines, ten more than second-placed Germany.

Women's Luge: Olympic Games

Women's luge made its Winter Games debut at Innsbruck in 1964 – nine years after it had first appeared at the FIL World Championships. Only a singles event is contested; although the doubles was always considered an "open" event in its early years, no women took part in it, and in modern times it has become the exclusive preserve of the men.

OLYMPIC MEDALS IN LUGE AND BOBSLEIGH

Two women have achieved the notable feat of having won medals in both luge and bobsleigh at the Winter Games. Italy's Gerda Weissensteiner took luge gold at Lillehammer 1994 and then won a bronze medal in the two-woman bobsleigh event at Turin 2006 (with Jennifer Isacco); and Germany's Susi Erdmann won a bronze medal in luge at Albertville 1992, as well as luge silver at Lillehammer 1994, and a bronze medal in the two-woman bobsleigh event at Salt Lake City 2002 (with Nicole Herschmann).

Right: Italy's Gerda Weissensteiner is one of only two women to have won medals in both luge and bobsleigh at the Winter Games.

KRAUSHAAR COMPLETES FULL MEDAL SET

It was a close run thing, but Silke Kraushaar's first-ever appearance at the Winter Games ended in the best moment of her career: she took the gold medal in the women's luge at Nagano 1998 by the slenderest of margins (by 0.002 seconds ahead of compatriot Barbara Niedernhuber). The medal success did not end there: she won a bronze medal at Salt Lake City 2002 and silver medal at Turin 2006 to become the only woman in history to win three Olympic medals in luge – and also the first to have won gold, silver and bronze medals at consecutive Games.

MOST SUCCESSFUL NATION

Germany has been the most successful nation in women's luge at the Winter Games, winning 14 medals in the competition (five gold, five silver and four bronze). East Germany lies in second place in the medal table (with nine medals) with Austria in third (with six medals).

SISTER ACT

The women's luge competition at Albertville 1992 was both controversial and a family affair. Austria's lugers had arrived at the Games with new, state-of-the-art bodysuits that gave them a distinct aerodynamic advantage – so much so that the American and Italian teams claimed they were illegal (only for the Jury of Appeal to reject their claim). Few were surprised, therefore, when Austrian lugers occupied the top two steps of the podium, with 20-year-old Doris Neuner claiming gold and, remarkably, her 22-year-sister Angelika taking silver. It is the only time in the competition's history that sisters have recorded a one-two finish.

Below: Doris Neuner (left) pipped her sister Angelika (centre) to singles gold at the 1992 Winter Games in Albertville.

ENDERLEIN UPSETS THE ODDS

Having taken gold at the FIL World Championships in both 1962 and 1963, East Germany's Ilse Geisler was the firm favourite to win the first-ever women's luge competition at the 1964 Winter Games at Innsbrück. The 23-year-old schoolteacher from Saxony expected challenges from the Polish and Austrian teams but, after the completion of the first run, she was left with only one serious rival: her 20-year-old team-mate Ortmun Enderlein – who was a member of the same club in East Germany. Enderlein took the lead after the second run and extended it in the third, leaving Geisler to make up a gap of 0.84 seconds on her final run. She failed, and Enderlein entered the history books as the first-ever Olympic champion in women's luge.

Left: Ortmun Enderlein won a surprise gold medal in the women's singles luge competition at the 1964 Winter Games in Innsbruck.

MOST GAMES PARTICIPATED IN

Two women hold the record for having taken part in the most luge competitions at the Winter Olympics. Gerda Weissensteiner of Italy (1988–2006) and Anne Abernathy of the US Virgin Islands (1988–2006) both competed at six editions of the Games.

MOST MEDALS WON (BY COUNTRY)

Pos	Medals	Country	G	S	B
1	14	Germany	5	5	4
2	9	East Germany	3	4	2
3	6	Austria	1	2	3
4	3	West Germany	-	1	2
5	2	Italy	2	-	-
=	2	USSR	1	-	1

BACK-TO-BACK JOY FOR MARTIN

East Germany's men may have lost their dominance in luge by the time of the 1984 Winter Games in Sarajevo, but the country's female lugers were as strong as ever. They had completed a clean sweep of the medals at the 1983 FIL World Championships, with Steffi Martin taking gold, Melitta Sollman silver and Ute Weiss bronze, and everyone expected these three to battle it out for the Olympic medals. As it transpired, Martin posted the fastest time in all four runs and eased to gold. By Calgary 1988, Martin (now Walter) had taken time out of the sport to marry and become a mother, but she was still the class act of the field, clocking the fastest time in two of the four runs to beat compatriot Ute Weiss to the gold medal by 0.132 seconds and become the first women in history to retain her Olympic luge title.

Above: Steffi Martin won women's singles luge gold at Calgary 1988.

HISTORY-MAKING DOUBLE FOR OTTO

Having claimed back-to-back titles at the FIL World Championships in 2000 and 2001, Germany's Sylke Otto was clearly the woman to beat in the luge competition at Salt Lake City 2002 and, to the surprise of no one, she stormed to the gold medal ahead of compatriot Barbara Niedernhuber with a 0.321-second winning margin. Otto took the title at Turin 2006 too, to become not only the second woman in history to retain her Olympic luge title (after Steffi Martin) but also, aged 36 years 222 days, the oldest woman in history to achieve that feat in any sport at the Winter Games.

FIL World Championships

The women's singles competition has been part of the FIL World Championships since the very first running of the event at Oslo in 1955 and is held in non-Olympic years. Germany has enjoyed the most success in the championships, winning 39 medals (14 gold, 15 silver and ten bronze).

MOST MEDALS WON: TOP TEN

Pos	Medals	Name (country)	G	S	B
1	6	Sylke Otto (Germany)	4	0	2
2	5	Susi Erdmann (East Germany/Germany)	3	2	0
=	5	Gabriele Kohlisch (East Germany/Germany)	2	3	0
=	5	Silke Kraushaar (Germany)	1	2	2
5	4	Tatjana Hüfner (Germany)	4	0	0
=	4	Margit Schumann (Germany)	4	0	0
=	4	Maria Isser (Austria)	2	2	0
=	4	Elisabeth Demleitner (East Germany)	1	2	1
=	4	Jana Bode (Germany)	1	1	2
=	4	Gerda Weissensteiner (Italy)	1	1	2

SUPERB OTTO FINALLY COMES GOOD

A European champion as early as 1990 and an overall Luge World Cup champion by 1994–95, Germany's Sylke Otto took a little longer to leave her indelible mark on the FIL World Championships, but when she finally did so, she did it with record-breaking success. She won her first medal (a bronze) at the 1999 championships in Königssee, Germany, and collected the first of three successive titles in 2000. She won another bronze medal at Nagano, Japan, in 2004 and picked up her fourth title in 2005 in Park City, Utah (to join Margit Schumann as the event's only four-time winners). Her overall tally of six medals (four gold and two bronze) is an all-time record at the championships.

Left: Germany's Sylke Otto is the most successful female slider in FIL World Championships history.

FULL MEDAL SET FOR DEMLEITNER

Elisabeth Demleitner first burst on to the international luge scene when she won a bronze medal at the 1970 FIL World Championships in Königssee in her native West Germany. She won gold in Olang, Italy, the following year (ahead of home favourite Erica Lechner), and when she picked up a silver medal in 1974, again in Königssee, she became the first woman in history to have collected a full set of medals at the event. She would go on to win a bronze medal at the 1976 Winter Games and won her fourth and final medal at the World Championships (a silver) in 1979.

Above: Elisabeth Demleitner won World Championships gold, silver and bronze.

HOME JOY FOR SEMCZYSZAK

The greatest moment of Maria Semczyszak's career was also a history-making one. When she took gold at the 1958 FIL World Championships in Krynica, Poland, she became not only the first, and to date only, Polish world champion, but also the first woman in history to enjoy her luge World Championships gold-medal-winning moment in front of her home crowd. The feat has been repeated on seven occasions.

UNBEATABLE SCHUMANN WINS FOUR IN A ROW

A three-time European champion and a gold medallist at the 1976 Winter Games in Innsbruck, East Germany's Margit Schumann also left her considerable mark on the FIL World Championships. She took the world title for the first time in Oberhof, West Germany, in 1973, defended it successfully in Königssee the following year, completed a hat-trick of world crowns in Hammarstrand, Sweden, in 1975 (becoming the first woman in championship history to achieve the feat), and made it four in a row in Igls, Austria, in 1977. She is still the only woman in championship history to have won four successive titles and one of only three women (Sylke Otto and Tatjana Hüfner being the others) to have won four gold medals at the World Championships.

HAMLIN BUCKS THE TREND

The first 39 editions of the FIL World Championships had produced 23 different champions, all of them European. That remarkable sequence was ended, however, at the 2009 Championships in Lake Placid, New York, when home favourite Erin Hamlin, who broke the track record on her second run, beat off the challenge of Germany's Natalie Geisenberger and Ukraine's Natalia Yakushenko to become the first, and to date only, non-European women's luge world champion.

MOST SILVER MEDALS

Germany's Gabriele Kohlisch won two gold medals at the FIL World Championships (in 1990 and 1995), but also endured her fair share of near misses in the competition. She finished as runner-up on three occasions (in 1987, 1991 and 1993) – an all-time record at the championships.

Right: Gabriele Kohlisch has won an all-time record three silver medals at the FIL World Championships.

Below: The United States' Erin Hamlin celebrates her gold-medal-winning performance at the 2009 FIL World Championships at Lake Placid.

THE NEW STAR OF THE SHOW

After Margit Schumann (East Germany), the leading women's luge competitor at the FIL World Championships in the mid-1970s, and Sylke Otto (Germany), the star turn in the early years of the 21st century, another German, Tatjana Hüfner, is the latest female luger to be acclaimed as the best of her generation. She took the title for the first time in 2007, retained it the following year in Oberhof, Germany, and added further titles in 2011 and 2012 to join Schumann and Otto as the event's only four-time winners.

FIRST TWO-TIME CHAMPION

Famed in the sport as being one of only three women to have medalled in the men's doubles event at the FIL World Championships (a silver with her brother Josef at Oslo in 1955), Austria's Maria Isser also left her mark on the women's singles event. In 1955 at Oslo she also picked up a silver medal in the women's singles. She won the title for the first time in 1957, picked up her second silver medal in the event in 1959 and, a year later, in Garmisch-Partenkirchen, Germany, took gold for a second time to become the event's first two-time winner.

FIL World Cup

Like the male lugers, women have been competing at the FIL World Cup – a season-long series of races in which athletes compete for points at each race to determine an overall season winner – since 1977–78. Germany has been the competition's standout nation, producing seven of the event's 19 champions.

Below: Silke Kraushaar is the FIL World Cup's most successful female luger with 11 top-three finishes.

CONSISTENCY THE KEY TO KRAUSHAAR'S SUCCESS

In the FIL World Cup, a competition in which success depends on maintaining the highest standard throughout the season, Germany's Silke Kraushaar was a model of consistency. After starting her career in 1984 at the age of 14, the German achieved her breakthrough in the 1997–98 season, when she finished second in the overall World Cup standings. It triggered a spectacular run of success: she took Olympic gold in Nagano the following year and ended that season as the overall World Cup champion for the first time. By the time she retired in 2008, she had added four further overall titles (in 2000–01, 2001–02, 2005–06 and 2006–07) and had finished runner-up on five further occasions (in 1999–2000, 2002–03, 2003–04, 2004–05 and 2007–08). Her haul of 11 World Cup medals is an all-time competition record.

MOST SUCCESSFUL NATION

German athletes lead the way in terms of success at the women's luge World Cup, having won an astonishing 54 medals in the competition (19 gold, 17 silver and 18 bronze), while athletes from Italy, the competition's second most successful nation, have only mustered a total of 16 medals.

NATALIE ALWAYS THE BRIDESMAID

One notable victim of Tatjana Hüfner's unprecedented run of success in the FIL World Cup in recent years (the German has claimed five successive titles between 2007–08 and 2011–12) has been her compatriot Natalie Geisenberger. The Munich-born star won bronze in 2007–08 and then recorded four consecutive runner-up finishes between 2008–09 and 2011–12. Her haul of four silver medals is an all-time record in the competition.

THE NEW WORLD CUP QUEEN

A four-time gold medallist at the FIL World Championships and the reigning Olympic champion (having taken the singles crown at Vancouver 2010), Germany's Tatjana Hüfner recorded her first race victory in the FIL World Cup in the 2005–06 season (in Altenberg, Germany) and won her first overall title in 2007–08. From that point on she has been unbeatable in the event, notching up five consecutive overall titles to equal Silke Kraushaar's all-time record.

Right: Tatjana Hüfner has been unbeatable in the FIL World Cup in recent years.

MOST MEDALS WON: TOP TEN

Pos	Medals	Name (country)	G	S	B
1	11	Silke Kraushaar (Germany)	5	6	0
2	9	Sylke Otto (Germany)	4	4	1
3	7	Tatjana Hüfner (Germany)	5	1	1
4	6	Gerda Weissensteiner (Italy)	2	4	0
=	6	Gabriele Kohlisch (East Germany/Germany)	1	2	3
=	6	Barbara Niedernhuber (Germany)	1	-	5
7	5	Ute Weiss (East Germany)	2	1	2
=	5	Marie-Luise Rainer (Italy)	1	3	2
=	5	Jana Bode (East Germany/Germany)	1	1	3
=	5	Natalie Geisenberger (Germany)	-	4	1

WOMEN OF BRONZE
The record for the most bronze medals won by an athlete at the FIL World Cup is five, a feat achieved by two women: Germany's Barbara Niedernhuber (in 1998–99, 1999–2000, 2001–02, 2002–03 and 2003–04) and her compatriot Anke Wischnewski (in 2006–07, 2008–09, 2009–10, 2010–11 and 2011–12).

WORLD CUP JOY FOR OTTO
Her record in the event may have since been eclipsed by others but, just as at the Winter Games (where she won back-to-back gold medals in 2002 and 2006) and at the FIL World Championships (where she won the singles gold medal on four occasions), Sylke Otto's considerable presence was also felt at the FIL World Cup. The German took the overall title in 1994–95, 1999–2000, 2002–03 and 2003–04 to become the event's first four-time winner – an achievement since surpassed by both Silke Kraushaar and Tatjana Hüfner.

Above: Germany's Sylke Otto was the first four-time winner of the FIL World Cup overall title.

THE WORLD CUP'S EARLY STAR
Angelika Schafferer never fulfilled her potential at either the Winter Games (her best performance coming at Lake Placid 1980, when she finished seventh) or at the FIL World Championships (at which she only won one medal, a bronze in 1978), but the Austrian enjoyed considerable success in the FIL World Cup. She finished third in the event's inaugural season in 1977–78, won the overall title for the first time the following year, defended it successfully in 1979–80 and completed a hat-trick of wins in 1980–81. Only one other woman (Tatjana Hüfner) has equalled Schafferer's feat of claiming three successive titles.

NOTHING BUT THE BEST
At the other end of the scale to 11-time medallist Silke Kraushaar, there are two women who have achieved the unusual feat of having won a solitary medal at the FIL World Cup, but they were both of the golden type. The first to achieve this was East Germany's Regina König, who won gold in the event's inaugural season, 1977–78, and she was followed by Vera Sozulia of the Soviet Union, who won it all in 1981–82.

Right: The Soviet Union's Vera Sozulia (front) made sure that her only FIL World Cup medal was special, winning gold in 1981–82.

Men's Skeleton: Olympic Games

Even though the sport can trace its roots back to Switzerland in 1882 and it made appearances at both the 1924 and 1948 Winter Olympics – principally, as both Games were staged in St-Moritz, to make use of the legendary Cresta Run – skeleton did not become a permanent fixture on the Winter Games programme until Salt Lake City 2002.

Right: Jim Shea won the men's skeleton gold medal in 2002.

IN THE NAME OF HIS GRANDFATHER

The third generation of his family to compete at the Winter Games – his father Jim Shea Sr had competed in cross-country skiing and Nordic combined at Innsbruck 1964 and his grandfather Jack had been a double gold medallist in speed skating at Lake Placid 1932 – Jim Shea Jr was the emotional favourite for skeleton gold at the 2002 Winter Games in Salt Lake City, Utah (the sport's first Olympic appearance for 54 years). Just a month before the start of the Games, his grandfather Jack had been killed by a drunk driver. And Shea Jr did his grandfather's memory proud, posting the fastest time in the first run and hanging on in the second to become America's second Olympic skeleton champion and the first to win the skeleton gold medal on home soil.

MOST SUCCESSFUL NATION

There have only been five editions of the men's skeleton event at the Winter Games, but North American neighbours the United States and Canada lead the way in terms of medal success. Both have produced two champions, but the US has won four medals (two gold, two silver) to Canada's three (two gold, one silver). Great Britain and Switzerland lie joint third in the medal table with two each (both bronze).

Below: Canada's Jon Montgomery slides to men's skeleton gold at the 2010 Winter Games in Vancouver.

MOST MEDALS WON (BY COUNTRY)

Pos	Medals	Country	G	S	B
1	4	United States	2	2	-
2	3	Canada	2	1	-
3	2	Great Britain	-	-	2
=	2	Switzerland	-	-	2
5	1	Italy	1	-	-
=	1	Austria	-	1	-
=	1	Latvia	-	1	-
=	1	Russia	-	-	1

CANADA SCRAPE TO GOLD

Sliding on their home track at Vancouver 2010 and having secured a one-two finish at the 2006 Winter Games in Turin, Canada expected to win gold at the Whistler Sliding Centre. But it was a Latvian, Martin Dukurs, who led after the home run, 0.28 seconds ahead of home favourite Jon Montgomery, with Russia's Aleksandr Tretyakov in third. And that is how the order remained until the final run, when Montgomery posted an outstanding time to beat Dukurs by a slender 0.07 seconds. Canada got the gold medal they wanted, but it was the closest finish in men's skeleton history at the Winter Games.

CLOSEST TO A CLEAN SWEEP

There has never been a medal sweep in the men's skeleton competition at the Winter Games, but Canada came mighty close to achieving the feat on the Cesana Pariol course at Turin 2006. Duff Gibson took gold (at 39 years of age he was the oldest gold medallist at the Games) and Jeff Pain took silver, but Paul Boehm's hopes of bronze ended when Switzerland's Gregor Stähli posted the third fastest time in the second and final run to edge the Canadian into fourth place and end Canada's hope of a clean sweep of the medals.

Right: Canada's Jeff Pain (left) and Duff Gibson celebrate their one-two finish in the men's skeleton at Turin 2006.

A GOLDEN FIRST FOR ITALY

The Cresta Run at St-Moritz, Switzerland, hosted skeleton's second appearance at the Winter Games, in 1948 – 20 years after the event has made its first Olympic appearance. And the event was wide open after the first three runs, with Great Britain's John Hammond posting the fastest time in the first, the USA's Jack Heaton (silver medallist in 1928) posting the fastest time in the second, and Italy's Nino Bibbia running fastest in the third. But it was the Italian, Bibbia, who dominated proceedings on the second day, clocking the fastest time in all three runs to take gold. In doing so, he became Italy's first-ever gold medallist at the Winter Games.

AMERICA'S YOUNG GUN

Although his older brother Jennison eventually beat him to the gold medal, Jack Heaton did remarkably well to compete at all at the 1928 Winter Games in St-Moritz. Just 19 years 161 days old at the time (making him the youngest participant in the competition's history) he took the silver medal despite being severely hampered with a broken wrist. And he was back at St-Moritz 20 years later (he was the only person to compete in the first two men's skeleton events at the Games) and took another silver medal. He is one of only two men (Switzerland's Gregor Stähli being the other) to have won two medals in men's skeleton at the Winter Games.

FIRST OLYMPIC CHAMPION

In the build-up to the Winter Games' inaugural skeleton competition in 1928, held on St-Moritz's famous Cresta Run course, the favourites for gold were expected to be two Brits: John Carnegie, the Earl of Northesk, who, the week before the event had broken the course record and claimed the spoils in the annual Grand National race held over the course; and John Cuthbert Moore. However, the latter broke his ribs falling off his sled two days before the Olympic event and did not start; and the former encountered problems with his sled on his opening run and lost valuable time. That left two Americans, Jennison Heaton and his younger brother Jack, to battle for the gold medal, with 23-year-old Jennison eventually winning out to become the sport's first Olympic champion.

Above: Jennison Heaton (right) won the inaugural men's skeleton bob gold medal at the St-Moritz Winter Games in 1928.

Other Major Championships

Men compete in two major skeleton competitions beyond the Winter Games: at the FIBT World Championships (the sport made its debut at the competition in 1982 and has been contested there on an annual basis since 1989); and at the Skeleton World Cup (a season-long series of races to determine an overall champion that was contested for the first time in 1986–87).

FIBT WORLD CHAMPIONSHIPS: MOST MEDALS (TOP FIVE)

Pos	Medals	Name (country)	G	S	B
1	9	Gregor Stähli (Switzerland)	3	3	3
2	5	Andi Schmid (Austria)	2	3	-
3	3	Jeff Pain (Canada)	2	1	-
=	3	Ryan Davenport (Canada)	2	-	1
=	3	Jim Shea (United States)	1	1	1

THE WORLD CUP'S BIGGEST STAR

Although he was some way past his best when he made his one and only appearance at the Winter Games at Salt Lake City in 2002 (aged 35 he finished in 12th place), by that stage Austria's Christian Auer had already made a considerable impact on the sport. A five-time medallist at the FIBT World Championships (including one gold in 1991), he finished third in his first two Skeleton World Cup seasons (in 1986–87 and 1987–88) and second in 1988–89 before claiming the overall title for the first time in 1989–90. He held on to his title the following year, completed a hat-trick of wins in 1991–92 (becoming the first person in the event's history to achieve the feat), and went on to win again in 1993–94 and 1994–95. His haul of five overall titles is an all-time record at the Skeleton World Cup.

Above: Christian Auer's five overall titles at the Skeleton World Cup is an all-time record.

MAGIC MOMENT FOR SANDFORD

New Zealand's Bruce Sandford launched his men's skeleton career in 1989 and enjoyed a career of limited success until his retirement in 2005 – with one notable exception. At the 1992 FIBT World Championships in Calgary, Canada, he held off the challenge of Switzerland's Gregor Stähli and Austria's Christian Auer (the defending champion) to become an unlikely world champion. He is still the only skeleton racer from the southern hemisphere to achieve the feat.

Below: Canada's Ryan Davenport won back-to-back world titles in 1996 and 1997.

BACK-TO-BACK JOY FOR DAVENPORT

The first nine editions of the men's skeleton event at the FIBT World Championships had produced nine different winners, but that peculiar statistic changed at Lake Placid, New York, in 1997. Ryan Davenport, who had won the event at Calgary in his native Canada the previous year, beat off the challenge of American duo Jim Shea and Chris Soule to become the first man in skeleton history to make a successful defence of his World Championship title. Only one man, Latvia's Martin Dukurs (in 2010 and 2011), has repeated his feat.

MOST OVERALL WORLD CUP TITLES: TOP FIVE

Pos	Medals	Name	(country, years)
1	5	Christian Auer	(Austria, 1989–90, 1990–91, 1991–92, 1993–94, 1994–95)
2	3	Martins Dukurs	(Latvia, 2009–10, 2010–11, 2011–12)
3	2	Andy Böhme	(Germany, 1998–99, 1999–2000)
=	2	Kristan Bromley	(Great Britain, 2003–04, 2007–08)
=	2	Jeff Pain	(Canada, 2004–05, 2005–06)
=	2	Andi Schmid	(Austria, 1986–87, 1987–88)

DR ICE STRIKES GOLD

Dubbed "Dr Ice" by the British media because, in 1999, he earned a PhD from the University of Nottingham with a thesis entitled "Factors affecting the performance of skeleton bobsleds", Kristan Bromley started competing on the international skeleton circuit in 1996 and won the overall title at the Skeleton World Cup for the first time in 2003–04. Further honours followed in the 2007–08 season and he ended that year by winning gold at the 2008 FIBT World Championships in Altenberg, Germany. He is the only Briton in men's skeleton history to have achieved either feat.

Right: Kristan Bromley is the only Briton to win a World Championship skeleton gold.

SUCCESS FOR STÄHLI

Disappointed though he may have been that the back-to-back medals he won at the 2002 and 2006 Winter Games were both bronze ones (and to have missed out on Vancouver 2010 through injury), Switzerland's Gregor Stähli has enjoyed plenty of highlights in his career, particularly at the FIBT World Championships. After picking up bronze medals in 1990 and 1993 and a silver medal in 1992, he took the title for the first time in 1994 in Altenberg, Germany, and remained a regular visitor to the podium from that point on. By 2012, he had won nine singles medals at the event (three gold, three silver and three bronze) – no man has won more.

Right: Switzerland's Gregor Stähli has enjoyed more success than any other slider at the FIBT World Championships, winning a total of nine medals (three each of gold, silver and bronze).

FIRST WORLD CHAMPION

The inaugural skeleton event at the FIBT World Championships took place in St-Moritz, Switzerland, in 1982 (although the second event was not contested until 1989) and was notable because it was not held on the town's legendary Cresta Run but on a bobsleigh track. Austria's Gert Elsässer held off the attentions of home favourites Nico Baracchi and Alain Wicki (who would go on to win the title in 1989) to become the sport's first-ever world champion.

THE WORLD CUP'S FIRST CHAMPION

One of the dominant skeleton racers on the international circuit in the sport's early years, and currently the performance director for the British skeleton team, Austria's Andi Schmid won the Skeleton World Cup's first-ever overall title in 1986–87 and made a successful defence of the title the following year – he was the first of four men to achieve the feat.

Women's Skeleton

Although women's skeleton is only a relatively new addition to the full-medal programme at the Winter Games (it made its Olympic debut at Salt Lake City 2002), international competitions in the sport have been around for some time. Women have competed at the FIBT World Championships since 2000 and have contested the Skeleton World Cup since the 1996–97 season.

YOUNGEST PARTICIPANT

While Marinela Mazilu's performance in the women's skeleton competition at the 2010 Winter Games in Vancouver ended in disappointment (she finished in 19th and last place, some 14.28 seconds behind gold-medallist Amy Williams), her presence in the competition earned her a place in the record books: aged 18 years 313 days at the time, she is the youngest athlete to compete in the women's skeleton competition at the Winter Games.

Right: Marinela Mazilu is the youngest woman ever to participate in the women's skeleton bob competition at the Winter Games.

RULE BRITANNIA

No country has enjoyed more medal success in the women's skeleton competition at the Winter Games than Great Britain. The country has produced three medallists: Alex Coomber (bronze medal at Salt Lake City 2002), Shelley Rudman (silver at Turin 2006) and Amy Williams (gold at Vancouver 2010).

Above: Amy Williams celebrates her 2010 gold-medal-winning performance.

FIRST WORLD CHAMPION

Women's skeleton was included on the programme of the FIBT World Championships for the first time at Igls, Austria, in 2000 – some 18 years after the men's skeleton had made its debut. And the result raised few eyebrows: Germany's Steffi Hanzlik (who had won the overall World Cup title in both 1996–97 and 1998–99) held off Canada's Mellisa Hollingsworth and the USA's Tricia Stumpf to become the first-ever world champion in women's skeleton.

SILVER PUTS PARSLEY IN THE RECORD BOOKS

The United States' Lea Ann Parsley came tantalizingly close to winning the women's skeleton gold medal at the 2002 Winter Games in Salt Lake City – she lost out to compatriot Tristan Gale by a mere tenth of a second – but her silver-medal-winning performance was also a record-breaking one: aged 33 years 253 days at the time, she remains the oldest medallist in women's skeleton in Winter Games history.

WINTER GAMES MEDAL TABLE

Pos	Medals	Name (country)	G	S	B
1	1	Tristan Gale (United States)	1	-	-
=	1	Maya Pedersen (Switzerland)	1	-	-
=	1	Amy Williams (Great Britain)	1	-	-
4	1	Lea Ann Parsley (United States)	-	1	-
=	1	Shelley Rudman (Great Britain)	-	1	-
=	1	Kerstin Szymkowiak (Germany)	-	1	-
7	1	Alex Coomber (Great Britain)	-	-	1
=	1	Mellisa Hollingsworth (Canada)	-	-	1
=	1	Anja Huber (Germany)	-	-	1

GALE UPSETS THE ODDS

When women's skeleton made its first-ever appearance at the Winter Games in Salt Lake City in 2002, the battle for the gold medal was expected to be between Germany's Steffi Hanzlik (the 2000 world champion), Switzerland's Maya Pedersen (the 2001 world champion) and Great Britain's Alex Coomber (the 2001 and 2002 World Cup winner). Instead, it was Salt Lake City native Tristan Gale who stole the show. The young American, who had only taken up the sport a year earlier, posted the fastest time in the first run and the second fastest time in the second to become not only the sport's first female Olympic champion but also the only woman to win the skeleton gold medal on home soil. Aged 21 years 194 days at the time, she also holds the honour of being the youngest female medallist in skeleton in Winter Games history.

Right: Tristan Gale was a surprise gold medallist at Salt Lake City 2002.

WILLIAMS HAS MAIDEN WIN ON PERFECT STAGE

When the three pre-race favourites at Vancouver 2010 – Germany's Marion Trott, Canada's Mellisa Hollingsworth and Britain's Shelley Rudman – ended up in ninth, fifth and 11th position respectively after the first run, all bets were off. Instead, leading after the first run was 27-year-old Briton Amy Williams, who had never won a World Cup race. Williams held on in the second run to become Great Britain's first individual medallist at the Games since Robin Cousins in 1980 and the country's first female gold medallist since Jeannette Altweg took figure skating gold in 1952.

OLDEST PARTICIPANT

Experience appeared to count for little for Norway's Desirée Bjerke in the women's skeleton event at Vancouver 2010, as she finished 17th out of the 19 competitors, but she still made history: aged 38 years 334 days at the time, she is the oldest-ever woman to compete in skeleton at the Winter Games.

WOMEN'S FIBT WORLD CHAMPIONSHIPS: MOST MEDALS (TOP FIVE)

Pos	Medals	Name (country)	G	S	B
1	3	Maya Pedersen (Switzerland)	2	–	1
2	2	Marion Trott (Germany)	2	–	–
=	2	Anja Huber (Germany)	1	1	–
=	2	Noelle Pikus-Pace (United States)	1	1	–
=	2	Michelle Kelly (Canada)	1	–	1

PEDERSEN MAKES AMENDS

Having been ranked firmly among the favourites for women's skeleton gold at Salt Lake City in 2002, Maya Pedersen would have been disappointed with a fifth-place finish – despite having posted the fastest time in the second run. But the Swiss star more than made amends at the 2006 Winter Games in Turin: she established a huge lead after the first run (0.65 seconds) and extended it in the second to take gold with a massive 1.23-second winning margin. Aged 33 years 88 days at the time, she remains women's skeleton's oldest Olympic champion.

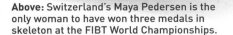

Above: Switzerland's Maya Pedersen is the only woman to have won three medals in skeleton at the FIBT World Championships.

UHLAENDER COMPLETES THE SET

A native of Vail, Colorado, US skeleton racer Katie Uhlaender has competed on the international circuit since 2003. She won her first medal (a bronze) at the 2007 FIBT World Championships at St-Moritz, Switzerland, claimed a silver the following year in Altenberg, Germany, and finally became champion for the first time in 2012 in front of her home crowd at Lake Placid, New York. In doing so, she became the first woman in the event's history to have won a full set of medals (gold, silver and bronze).

Above: Katie Uhlaender has won World Championship gold, silver and bronze.

TWO IN A ROW FOR TROTT

The first eight editions of the women's skeleton event at the FIBT World Championships had produced seven different champions, none of whom had made a successful defence of her title. And, following her eighth-place finish at the 2010 Winter Games in Vancouver, few thought that the 2009 champion Marion Trott (née Thees) would be the one to buck that trend at the 2011 World Championships in Königssee. But the German thrilled the home crowd when she posted the fastest time in three of the competition's four runs to become women's skeleton's first back-to-back world champion.

Below: In 2011 Marion Trott was the first woman to successfully defend her world title.

FIRST TWO-TIME CHAMPION

The women's Skeleton World Cup kicked off in 1986–87, some ten years after the men's equivalent event had made its debut, and Germany's Steffi Hanzlik proved the star turn, becoming the event's inaugural champion. She finished second in 1997–98, behind Switzerland's Maya Pedersen, before claiming the title for a second time the following year – thus becoming the event's first two-time champion.

MOST WORLD CHAMPIONSHIP MEDALS FOR MAYA

Regarded as one of the greatest performers in women's skeleton history, Maya Pedersen took the world title for the first time in 2001 at Calgary, Canada. Favourite to win the gold medal at the 2002 Winter Games in Salt Lake City, she finished fifth and the disappointment she suffered appeared to check her progress. But the Swiss star bounced back, winning her second world title in 2005, again in Calgary, and finally getting her hands on an Olympic gold medal at Turin 2006. She took silver at the 2007 FIBT World Championships in St-Moritz, Switzerland. Her haul of three World Championship medals is an all-time record.

WOMEN'S SKELETON WORLD CUP: MOST SEASON TITLES

Pos	Titles	Name (country, season)
1	3	Alex Coomber (Great Britain, 1999–2000, 2000–01, 2001–02)
2	2	Steffi Hanzlik (Germany, 1996–97, 1998–99)
=	2	Mellisa Hollingsworth (Canada, 2005–06, 2009–10)
=	2	Katie Uhlaender (United States, 2006–07, 2007–08)
5	1	Maya Pedersen (Switzerland, 1997–98)
=	1	Michelle Kelly (Canada, 2002–03)
=	1	Lindsay Alcock (Canada, 2003–04)
=	1	Noelle Pikus-Pace (United States, 2004–05)
=	1	Marion Trott (Germany, 2008–09)
=	1	Anja Huber (Germany, 2010–11)
=	1	Shelley Rudman (Great Britain, 2011–12)

THE WORLD CUP QUEEN

A former officer in Britain's Royal Air Force, Alex Coomber was virtually unbeatable in the Skeleton World Cup in the early years of the 21st century. She took the overall title for the first time in 1999–2000 (competing under her maiden name, Hamilton), retained it the following year (becoming the first woman in the event's history to achieve the feat) and made it three in a row in 2001–02 (she is still the only woman to have completed a hat-trick of successes). Favourite for gold at the 2002 Winter Games in Salt Lake City, she broke her wrist ten days before the start of the race, but defied her injury to pick up a bronze medal.

Left: Alex Coomber of Great Britain is the only woman to win the Skeleton World Cup overall title on three occasions.

RUDMAN SHOWS HER CLASS

A surprise silver medallist at the 2006 Winter Games in Turin (given that her stated ambition before the event was to achieve a top ten finish), Britain's Shelley Rudman went on to show her world-class ability in the Skeleton World Cup. She finished second on a record three successive occasions (in 2008–09, 2009–10 and 2010–11) before finally claiming the overall title for the first time in 2011–12.

Above: Britain's Shelley Rudman celebrates her Skeleton World Cup overall title in 2011–12.

ONLY OTHER BACK-TO-BACK CHAMPION

Women's skeleton's reigning world champion (after she took the title at Lake Placid in 2012), the USA's Katie Uhlaender first displayed her talent at the Skeleton World Cup. She took the title for the first time in 2006–07 (becoming the second American, after Noelle Pikus-Pace in 2004–05, to do so) and successfully defended her title the following year (becoming only the second women in the event's history, after Alex Coomber, to achieve that feat).

Other Sledging Events: The Cresta Run

The most famous tobogganing track in the world, the Cresta Run, located in the Swiss Alps and first constructed in 1884, is a 1,323-yard ice shute that drops 514 feet to the village of Celerina, near St-Moritz, through a series of ten heart-arresting configurations negotiated headfirst at speeds of up to 90mph.

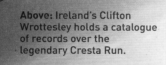

Above: Ireland's Clifton Wrottesley holds a catalogue of records over the legendary Cresta Run.

THE MODERN CRESTA KING

Ireland's Lord Clifton Wrottesley has been the King of the Cresta Run in recent times. He achieved his first victory in 1997, has won the Curzon Cup (the blue riband event from the Junction) eight times, equalling Franco Gansser and Nino Bibbia's record, the Morgan Cup eight times, the Brabazon Trophy a record 11 times and the Grand National (the blue riband event from the Top) eight times, equalling Gansser and Bibbia's record. He has also won the Grand Slam (all four Classic races in one season) on four occasions (in 2003, 2005, 2006 and 2010). And the records do not stop there: Wrottesley also holds the record for the number of Classic races won (35) and the Flying Junction record (ridden from the Top and timed from the Junction), with 31.44 seconds.

SHUTTLECOCK CLUB

If riders are out of control, they are certain to be thrown off the Run at Shuttlecock, Cresta's most famous corner. But with the inevitable pain comes some consolation: fallers at Shuttlecock automatically become members of the Shuttlecock Club and are entitled to wear the Shuttlecock tie.

THE START OF AN INSTITUTION

W.H. Bulpetts, a major in the British Army (who would eventually go on to found the world-famous St-Moritz Tobogganing Club), and Caspar Badrutt, the owner of the Kulm Hotel in St-Moritz, came up with the concept of the Cresta Run in 1884 – principally to provide an arena dedicated to skeleton racing, but also to protect visitors to the St-Moritz slopes from the ever-increasing number of toboggans. The first Run was completed in January 1885 and took nearly nine weeks to build, with only the first three corners of the course receiving any detailed work. The course – the oldest and steepest in the world – continues to be built from scratch each year, although it still follows much of the original layout.

Right: There is little room for error in the first few turns of the Cresta Run, which starts by the church (top).

COURSE RECORDS

The Cresta Run has two starting points: one from the top of the course, which is located under a geographical formation known as the Leaning Tower, and one from the Junction, which is located about one-third of the way down the track, opposite to the clubhouse. The course record from the top is 50.09 seconds, set by James B. Sunley at the 1999 Grand National – at an average speed of 54.13mph. The record from the Junction is 41.02 seconds, set by Johannes Badrutt, also in 1999.

RUN GRAND NATIONAL WINNERS – LAST TEN YEARS

Year	Winner	Total time
2011	Lord Wrottesley (Ireland)	154.49
2010	Lord Wrottesley (Ireland)	151.60
2009	Lord Wrottesley (Ireland)	156.81
2008	Lord Wrottesley (Ireland)	154.91
2007	Count L.L. Marenzi (United States)	154.65
2006	Lord Wrottesley (Ireland)	156.78
2005	Lord Wrottesley (Ireland)	152.99
2004	Christian Bertschinger (Switzerland)	153.07
2003	Lord Wrottesley (Ireland)	153.58
2002	Johannes Badrutt (Switzerland)	168.94

BONE-BREAKING

It is claimed that, at various stages in the Run's illustrious history, every bone in the human body has been broken by riders who fail to complete the run successfully. Evidence of this is displayed as a composite picture of the human body made up of X-rays of the fallen, which is shown in the introductory lecture all newcomers must attend before completing a run on the track. Remarkably, however, given the inherent dangers of descending the course, there have been only five fatalities in the Run's 126-year history.

A CRESTA RUN LEGEND

Born in Lombardy, Italy, on 15 March 1922, but a resident of St-Moritz, Nino Bibbia was a fruit and vegetable seller by trade who devoted his spare time to practising winter sports – the bob, luge and skeleton – and became not only a legendary figure in Italian winter sports circles but also a significant figure in the history of the Cresta Run. In an illustrious career that yielded a skeleton gold medal at the 1948 Winter Games (the event was staged on the Cresta and as a result of his victory he became Italy's first-ever Winter Olympic champion), Bibbia recorded over 200 race wins on the Run, including eight victories in the Grand National – a joint record.

A MEN-ONLY AFFAIR

Owing to the inherent dangers of riding the course, women were banned from the Cresta Run on 6 January 1929 – the last woman credited with riding the Cresta before the ban was a Mrs J.M. Baguley on 13 January 1925. However, today there is an annual invitation-only women's event, which is held from the Junction only.

WINTER OLYMPIC GAMES VENUE

The historic Cresta has twice been used as a venue for the tobogganing (skeleton) event at the Winter Olympic Games – in 1928 and 1948, when the Games came to St-Moritz. Jennison Heaton of the United States claimed gold in the former (which was contested over three runs) and Italy's Nino Bibbia (one of Cresta's most famous riders) came out on top in the latter (which was contested over six runs). These were tobogganing's only two appearances at the Winter Olympic Games before it was permanently added to the programme for the 2002 Games in Salt Lake City.

Right: Nino Bibbia won the gold medal when the men's skeleton event at the 1948 Winter Games was contested over the course.

Chapter 4 SNOWBOARDING

Right: Shaun White, who at Vancouver 2010 would become the first man to win consecutive snowboarding halfpipe Winter Olympic Games gold medals, soars through the air in another spellbinding exhibition, this time in the 2009 US Championships at Copper Mountain, Colorado.

A recent addition to winter sports international competition (it did not make its first appearance at the Winter Olympic Games until Nagano 1998), snowboarding took its inspiration from skateboarding, surfing and skiing and was developed in the United States in the 1960s and '70s. The International Snowboarding Federation was created in 1990 to govern the sport, and disciplines contested in competition are slopestyle, big air, halfpipe, snowboard cross (also known as boardercross), superpipe, street and a number of slalom events.

Men's Snowboarding: Olympic Games

Men's snowboarding made its debut at the Winter Games in 1998 at Nagano with two events: the halfpipe and the giant slalom. Two further events have since been added to the programme: the parallel giant slalom at Salt Lake City 2002 (which replaced the giant slalom) and snowboard cross at Turin 2006. The United States has enjoyed the most success in Olympic snowboarding, winning 11 medals (five of them gold).

Above: Switzerland's Philipp Schoch was a surprise gold-medal winner in the men's parallel slalom at Turin 2006.

THE PARALLEL GIANT SLALOM KING

Having never before produced a podium finish at a major international competition and after scraping through the elimination round as the 15th qualifier (of 16), Switzerland's Philipp Schoch would have been both surprised and delighted to have made it through to the gold-medal race in the inaugural men's parallel giant slalom competition at the 2002 Winter Games in Salt Lake City. And when pre-event favourite Richard Richardsson (Sweden) led by 0.24 seconds after the first of the two final runs, it seemed as though the 22-year-old would have to settle for silver. Instead, the Swede fell in the second run and Schoch became the shock champion. There were no such surprises four years later: by the time Schoch arrived at Turin for the 2006 Winter Games, he was considered the best in the sport and he showed his class, moving effortlessly into the final in which he beat his older brother Simon to become the first snowboarder in history to win two Olympic gold medals.

SURPRISE GOLD FOR SIMMEN

When the world's best halfpiper, Norway's Terje Hakonsen (the three-time International Snowboarding Federation champion), refused to compete at Nagano 1998 (the sport's first appearance at the Winter Games) in protest at the IOC's decision to recognize the International Skiing Federation as the sport's governing body rather than the International Snowboarding Federation, it left the competition wide open. In the end, Switzerland's Gian Simmen (then 38th in the world rankings) came out on top of the 36-strong field – taking the lead in the first run and holding on in the second – to become the first-ever men's halfpipe Olympic champion.

MOST SUCCESSFUL NATION

No country has enjoyed more success in snowboarding at the Winter Games than the United States: the country has claimed 11 medals in the sport (five gold, two silver and four bronze), while second-placed Switzerland has five (three gold, one silver and one bronze).

ONLY MEDAL SWEEP

There has only been one medal sweep in men's snowboarding at the Winter Games: by the USA in the men's halfpipe event at Salt Lake City 2002, when Ross Powers took gold, Danny Kass took silver and Jarrett Thomas took bronze.

Below: (from left) Danny Kass, Ross Powers and Jarrett Thomas.

SOLE SNOWBOARD CROSS CHAMPION

An event that has achieved enormous popularity at the Winter X Games, snowboard cross (a race over a course for four contestants) made its long-awaited debut at the Winter Games at Turin in 2006. And America's Seth Wescott, a former parallel giant slalom racer and sometime halfpiper, took the spoils, beating Slovakia's Radoslav Zidek to the gold medal. The American was the star of the show at Vancouver 2010 too, breaking Canada's collective heart when he overtook home favourite Mike Robertson on the home stretch to retain his title. He is still the only man in history to win snowboard cross gold at the Winter Games.

MEDALS WON (BY COUNTRY): TOP TEN

Pos	Medals	Country	G	S	B
1	11	United States	5	2	4
2	5	Switzerland	3	1	1
3	3	Canada	2	1	-
=	3	France	-	-	3
5	2	Finland	-	1	1
=	2	Austria	-	1	1
7	1	Italy	-	1	-
=	1	Norway	-	1	-
=	1	Slovakia	-	1	-
=	1	Sweden	-	1	-

REBAGLIATI'S CONTROVERSIAL NAGANO 1998 GOLD MEDAL

Whereas the men's halfpipe competition at Nagano 1998 had been tinged with controversy before the action had even got underway, when it came to the men's giant slalom the shenanigans only started after the race. But what a race it was: after the first run, eight racers – led by Canada's Jasey Jay Anderson – remained in contention; after the second, which was marred by bad weather, Ross Rebagliati (who lay in eighth after his first run) stood on top of the pile. And then came the controversy: Rebagliati tested positive for marijuana, but because the drug was labelled as a restricted rather than a prohibited substance, he was allowed to keep his gold medal and thus became the first-ever men's snowboarding giant slalom Olympic champion – and to date the only one. The event has not been contested again at the Winter Games.

WHITE MAKES HIS MARK

A supremely talented skateboarder (so good, in fact, that he caught the eye of the legendary Tony Hawk, who mentored him), American Shaun White has also made a considerable mark in the sport of snowboarding. He made his first appearance at the Winter Games in the men's halfpipe competition at Turin 2006 and, although he struggled in qualifying (finishing in a lowly seventh place), he produced a stunning performance in the first of his final two runs to take gold. Considered the best in the business by Vancouver 2010, he was the class of the field and cemented the gold medal with an electrifying first run (that earned him a colossal 45.8 points) to become the first snowboarder in history to make a successful defence of his Olympic halfpipe title.

MOST SILVER MEDALS

America's Danny Kass took halfpipe gold at the 2001 Winter X Games, but twice at the Winter Olympics he narrowly failed to reach the top step of the podium. He took a silver medal at both Salt Lake City in 2002 (behind Ross Powers) and Turin in 2006 (behind Shaun White) and is the only snowboarder in history to have won two silver medals at the Winter Games.

MOST MEDALS

The record for the most medals won in snowboarding at the Winter Games is two, held by five men: Philipp Schoch (Switzerland, two parallel giant slalom golds – in 2002 and 2006); Shaun White (United States, two halfpipe golds – in 2006 and 2010); Seth Wescott (United States, two snowboard cross golds – in 2006 and 2010); Danny Kass (two halfpipe silvers – in 2002 and 2006); and Ross Powers (halfpipe bronze in 1998 and gold in the same event in 2002).

Above: Shaun White is probably the best snowboarder of modern times.

FIS Snowboarding World Championships

Staged for the first time in 1996 in Lienz, Austria, the FIS Snowboard World Championships are currently staged in odd-numbered years. Competitors contest six disciplines: parallel slalom, halfpipe, snowboard cross, parallel giant slalom, big air and slopestyle. Austria and France have been the event's most successful nations, winning 17 medals each.

Left: Benjamin Karl roared to parallel slalom gold at the 2011 FIS Snowboard World Championships.

MOST MEDALS WON (BY COUNTRY): TOP TEN

Pos	Medals	Country	G	S	B
1	17	Austria	6	1	10
=	17	France	6	8	3
3	15	United States	5	1	9
4	13	Switzerland	5	6	2
=	13	Finland	5	2	6
6	10	Canada	4	3	3
=	10	Sweden	2	6	2
8	7	Germany	2	3	2
=	7	Slovakia	2	3	2
10	5	Italy	2	1	2

DE LA RUE MAKES HISTORY

A three-time overall World Cup winner in snowboard cross, France's Xavier de la Rue has also made his mark at the FIS Snowboard World Championships. The Bayonne-born star took snowboard cross gold for the first time at the 2003 championships in Kreischberg, Austria, and then made history when, in 2007 at Arosa, Switzerland, he won the event for the second time to become the discipline's only two-time world champion.

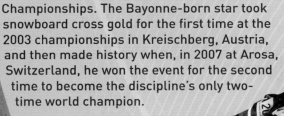

Right: Belgium's Seppe Smits, the 2011 slopestyle world champion.

KARL BUCKS THE TREND

At the 2011 FIS Snowboard World Championships at La Molina, Spain, history was against Benjamin Karl mounting a successful defence of the parallel slalom title he had won in Gangwon, South Korea, in 2009: in the eight previous editions of the event, no defending champion had managed to achieve the feat. But the 26-year-old Austrian bucked the trend, narrowly defeating Switzerland's Simon Schoch to take gold and rewrite the record books. He won the parallel giant slalom too, to become only the second person in the championships' history (after Canada's Jasey Jay Anderson in 2005) to win the parallel slalom/parallel giant slalom double.

SMITS SHINES FOR BELGIUM

The best snowboarder Belgium has ever produced, Seppe Smits won back-to-back silver medals in the big air competition at the 2009 and 2011 FIS Snowboard World Championships, but his greatest moment came at the latter of those two championships when he won the gold medal in the slopestyle competition (the first time the event had been staged at the championships). He is still the only Belgian snowboarder in history to have won a World Championship medal.

A COUPLE OF FIRSTS FOR ASIA

Japan's Kazuhiro Kokubo made history at the 2007 FIS Snowboard World Championships in Arosa, Switzerland, when he took silver in the men's halfpipe (behind France's Mathieu Crepel) to become the first Asian to medal at the championships. But compatriot Ryo Aono went one better two years later in Gangwon, South Korea. The Japanese halfpiper saw off the challenges of Canada's Jeff Batchelor and defending champion Crepel to become the first, and to date only, Asian snowboarding world champion.

AUTTI ANNOUNCES HIS ARRIVAL ON THE WORLD STAGE

Antti Autti of Finland, who went on to become one of the leading snowboarders of his generation, was still relatively unknown when he arrived at the 2005 FIS Snowboard World Championships in Whistler, Canada. There, however, aged just 19, he took gold in both the halfpipe and big air events to become the first person in history to land that particular golden double. France's Mathieu Crepel equalled his feat at the 2007 Championships in Arosa, Switzerland.

YEAR OF THE AUSTRALIANS

Following the 2009 FIS Snowboard World Championships in Gangwon, South Korea, the eighth edition of the event, 114 medals had been won in seven disciplines and every one of those medals had been awarded to a snowboarder from the northern hemisphere. That peculiar quirk changed at La Molina, Spain, in 2011, when Australia's Nathan Johnstone took halfpipe gold and his compatriot Alex Pullin took the spoils in the snowboard cross event to become the southern hemisphere's first-ever snowboarding world champions.

MOST SUCCESSFUL NATION

Two countries share the record for the most medals won at the FIS Snowboard World Championships (17): Austria (with six gold medals, one silver and ten bronze) and France (with six gold medals, eight silvers and three bronze).

ONLY SLALOM WORLD CHAMPION

The slalom has only ever been contested once at the FIS Snowboard World Championships: at Innichen, Italy, in 1997. Germany's Bernd Kroschewski took the spoils ahead of compatriot Dieter Moherndl and America's Anton Pogue and thus remains the discipline's only world champion.

Left: Canada's Jasey Jay Anderson has set numerous records at the FIS Snowboard World Championships.

MAGIC MOMENTS FOR JASEY JAY

The true highlight of Jasey Jay Anderson's career came when he won parallel giant slalom gold in front of an adoring home crowd at the 2010 Winter Games in Vancouver, but the most decorated Canadian snowboarder in history first showed his immense talent at the 2005 FIS Snowboard World Championships at Whistler, when he became the first snowboarder in the championships' history to win the parallel slalom/parallel giant slalom double. He carved out another space for himself in the record books at the 2009 championships in Gangwon, South Korea, when he took parallel giant slalom gold for the second time in his career: he is the discipline's only two-time winner.

Other Major Championships

Launched by the International Ski Federation (FIS) in the 1994–95 season, the FIS Snowboard World Cup is a season-long series of events around the world to establish both individual discipline champions and an overall champion. The Winter X Games, devised by the television channel ESPN, were contested for the first time in 1997 and are staged on an annual basis in Aspen, Colorado, USA.

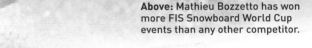

Above: Mathieu Bozzetto has won more FIS Snowboard World Cup events than any other competitor.

THE WORLD CUP'S BIG AIR KING

There has been no greater exponent of big air snowboarding – an event that sees competitors perform tricks after launching themselves off a man-made jump – at the FIS Snowboard World Cup than Stefan Gimpl. The Austrian has enjoyed unparalleled success in the competition, claiming the discipline title a record four times: in 2005–06, 2007–08, 2008–09 and 2009–10.

Below: Austria's Stefan Gimpl has won four World Cup big air overall titles.

THE BEST IN WORLD CUP HISTORY

His performances in one-off competitions have never reflected his true talent – in four appearances at the Winter Games he only ever picked up one medal (a bronze in the parallel giant slalom at Vancouver 2010) – but when it came to producing a consistent run of performances over the course of an FIS Snowboard World Cup season, France's Mathieu Bozzetto was the unrivalled master. He was the competition's first two-time overall champion (taking the spoils in 1998–99 and 1999–2000) and holds the record for the most parallel slalom discipline titles (four, shared with Austria's Benjamin Karl), the most podium finishes (64) and the most race victories (35).

KORPI HITS THE HEIGHTS

After winning halfpipe gold at the 2005 Junior World Championships in Zermatt, Switzerland, Janne Korpi confirmed his status as one of snowboarding's next big stars when he won his first FIS Snowboard World Cup event the following year. Five further victories by the end of the 2009–10 season supported that claim, but the Finn's real breakthrough season came in 2011–12: he won both the halfpipe and big air discipline titles at the World Cup – the first time in history anyone had achieved the feat.

HALFPIPE TITLE GOES EAST

The record for the most World Cup halfpipe discipline titles is two, shared by two men: the USA's Ross Powers, who took the title in 1995–96 and 1998–99, and Japan's Ryoh Aono, who took the title in 2006–07 and 2008–09 and is the only Asian to have won a World Cup discipline crown.

MOST WORLD CUP RACE WINS: TOP TEN

Pos	Wins	Name (country, span)
1	35	Mathieu Bozzetto (France, 1998–2009)
2	27	Jasey Jay Anderson (Canada, 1996–2010)
3	15	Philipp Schoch (Switzerland, 2002–06)
4	14	Siegfried Grabner (Austria, 2001–12)
=	14	Pierre Vaultier (France, 2005–12)
=	14	Benjamin Karl (Austria, 2004–12)
7	13	Nicolas Huet (France, 1996–2007)
8	11	Stefan Kaltschuetz (Austria, 1994–2005)
=	11	Dejan Kosir (Slovenia, 1996–2006)
=	11	Xavier de la Rue (France, 1997–2011)

Above: Xavier de la Rue won three straight overall World Cup snowboard cross titles between 2002–03 and 2004–05.

THREE IN A ROW FOR DE LA RUE

Although he won two gold medals in snowboard cross at the FIS Snowboard World Championships (in 2003 and 2007), arguably Xavier de la Rue's greatest achievements have been in the FIS Snowboard World Cup. The Frenchman won the snowboard cross discipline title for the first time in 2002–03, retained it in 2003–04 and completed a hat-trick of titles in 2004–05. He is the only man in the competition's history to have achieved the feat.

THE BEST IN HISTORY

Shaun White of the USA is the greatest snowboarder in history. If his back-to-back halfpipe triumphs at the Winter Games are not enough to prove it (he took gold at both Turin 2006 and Vancouver 2010), one need look no further than at his performances at the Winter X Games. The Californian has been virtually unbeatable at the event, picking up a staggering 17 medals, 12 of them gold (five in slopestyle and seven in superpipe) – a record that will surely never be beaten.

FIRST OVERALL WORLD CUP CHAMPION:

Although the inaugural FIS Snowboard World Cup was held in 1994–95, an overall title wasn't awarded until the 1995–96 season. The United States' Mike Jacoby, who took the first-ever parallel slalom discipline in 1994–95, was the first to receive the honour. He went on to compete at the 1998 Winter Games in Nagano (the first time snowboarding was contested at the Olympics), finishing 17th in the giant slalom.

THE X GAMES' BOARDERCROSS KING

Ultimate success may be said to have eluded Nate Holland at both the Winter Games (his best finish was fourth at Vancouver 2010) and at the FIS Snowboard World Championships (at which he picked up bronze medals in 2007 and 2011), but there is no doubt that Holland has been the man to beat in the snowboard cross event at the Winter X Games over the last seven years. During that time, the Idaho-born star has taken the gold medal on an astonishing six occasions; his only "failure" came in 2011 when he had to settle for bronze.

MOST OVERALL WORLD CUP TITLES FOR JASEY JAY

Winning the parallel giant slalom gold medal in front of an adoring home crowd at the 2010 Winter Games in Vancouver may well be the highlight of his career, and justifiably so, but Canada's Jasey Jay Anderson also enjoyed plenty of memorable moments at the FIS Snowboard World Cup. He holds the competition's all-time record for the most overall titles (four in succession from 2000–01 to 2003–04) and also won two snowboard cross discipline titles (in 2001–02 and 2005–06) – only France's Xavier de la Rue (with three) has won more.

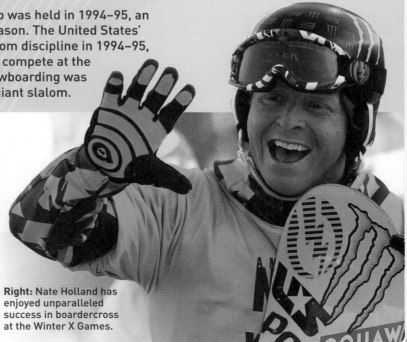

Right: Nate Holland has enjoyed unparalleled success in boardercross at the Winter X Games.

Women's Snowboarding: Olympic Games

Women's snowboarding, like the men's, made its first appearance at the Winter Games in 1998 at Nagano with two events, the halfpipe and the giant slalom. Parallel giant slalom replaced giant slalom at Salt Lake City 2002, and snowboard cross was added to the programme at Turin 2006.

Below: Hannah Teter was a Winter Games sensation at Turin 2006.

MEDALS WON (BY COUNTRY)

Pos	Medals	Country	G	S	B
1	8	United States	2	3	3
2	5	France	2	3	-
3	4	Switzerland	2	-	2
4	3	Germany	1	2	-
5	2	Canada	1	-	1
=	2	Norway	-	1	1
=	2	Austria	-	-	2
8	1	Australia	1	-	-
=	1	Netherlands	1	-	-
=	1	Russia	-	1	-
=	1	Italy	-	-	1

TETER SHOWS HER CLASS

Having become world junior halfpipe champion in 2002 at the age of 15, Hannah Teter made her debut at the Winter Games in 2006 in Turin. And what a debut: she posted the highest score in each of the final two runs to take gold. She came mighty close to retaining her title at Vancouver 2010, only to lose out to Australia's Torah Bright, but in claiming the silver medal she had become one of only three women (alongside compatriot Kelly Clark and France's Karine Ruby) to have won two medals in snowboarding at the Winter Games.

CONSISTENCY PAYS FOR THOST

The surprises in the inaugural women's halfpipe competition at the 1998 Winter Games in Nagano started as early as the qualifying round, when Switzerland's 1997 world champion Anita Schwaler failed to make it through to the final (placing 11th). Of the eight who made it through, America's Shannon Dunn led after the first run with Germany's Nicola Thost, a former gymnast, placing second. Norway's Stine Brun Kjeldaas produced the best performance in the second run, with Dunn back in seventh position, but it was Thost, again placing second, who took gold to become the event's first Olympic champion.

Right: Nicola Thost won women's halfpipe gold at Nagano 1998.

A FIRST FOR THE NETHERLANDS

She may well have benefited from the mistakes of others to get there, but the Netherlands' Nicolien Sauerbreij produced the performance of her life in the women's parallel giant slalom at the 2010 Winter Games in Vancouver. Trailing Russia's Yekaterina Ilyukhina by 0.02 seconds after the first run, she powered past the Russian in the second to claim gold by 0.23 seconds. It was the first medal of any kind the Netherlands had won in a "snow" event at the Winter Games – all their previous medals had come in "ice" sports.

GOLDEN REDEMPTION FOR BLANC

A former alpine skier who switched to snowboarding at the age of 18, Isabelle Blanc's first taste of competition at the Winter Games, in Nagano in 1998, was a bitter one: heading for the silver medal in the giant slalom, the Frenchwoman missed the final gate and failed to finish. But what a difference four years can make: at Salt Lake City 2002, having made it through to the parallel giant slalom final, she then opened up a massive 1.89-second lead over compatriot Karine Ruby in the first run and held on in the second to become the discipline's first Olympic champion. Incidentally, the event also saw the first one-two finish in women's snowboarding at the Winter Games.

Below: France's Isabelle Blanc celebrates winning the parallel giant slalom gold medal at Salt Lake City in 2002.

BRILLIANT BRIGHT SHINES IN VANCOUVER

After turning professional at the tender age of 14 and having finished fifth in her first appearance at the Winter Games (at Turin 2006 at the age of 19), Australia's Torah Bright was ready to challenge for halfpipe honours at Vancouver 2010. But, after qualifying comfortably for the final, her chances of success seemed to go up in smoke when she fell in the first of her two runs. However, the 23-year-old lifted her game when it mattered, posting the highest score of the competition in her second run (45.0) to take gold and become women's snowboarding's first-ever champion from the southern hemisphere.

THE FIRST WOMEN'S SNOWBOARDING STAR

The most decorated female snowboarder of her generation, who claimed 67 World Cup victories in her glittering career, Karine Ruby first came to international prominence when she won the women's giant slalom event as a 20-year-old at the 1998 Winter Games in Nagano (the only time the event was contested at the Olympics). The Frenchwoman's mark on the Winter Games did not end there; when she came second behind compatriot Isabelle Blanc to claim the silver medal in the parallel giant slalom at Salt Lake City 2002, she became the first, and to date only, woman snowboarder in history to win medals in two separate events at the Winter Games. Tragically, she was killed in a climbing accident on Mont Blanc in May 2009, aged just 31.

Right: France's Karine Ruby won two medals in two Winter Games: gold at Nagano 1998 and silver at Salt Lake City 2002.

CLARK MAKES RECORD-BREAKING MARK

Of the 23 competitors in the women's halfpipe competition at Salt Lake City 2002 the youngest was 18-year-old American Kelly Clark, who proceeded to throw down an early gauntlet when she posted the highest score in the qualifying round. She produced the best run in the final too (47.9) to become, aged 18 years 219 days, the youngest women's snowboarding Olympic champion in history. The Vermont-born star's record-breaking achievements did not end there; when she took halfpipe bronze at Vancouver 2010, she became one of only three women (alongside compatriot Hannah Teter and France's Karine Ruby) to have won two medals in snowboarding at the Winter Games.

FRIEDEN TRIUMPHS AS JACOBELLIS FALLS

Although women's snowboard cross had been contested at the FIS Snowboard World Championships since 1997, it did not make it on to the Olympic programme until the 2006 Winter Games, but the dynamic nature of the competition in Turin left few in doubt that the wait had been worthwhile. The final was between America's Lindsey Jacobellis (a three-time X Games winner in the event), two Canadians – Dominique Maltais and Maëlle Ricker – and Switzerland's Tanja Frieden. Jacobellis, the heavy favourite, dominated most of the race, but fell dramatically on the final jump and could only slide over the line to claim silver. It was the 30-year-old Frieden, to her great surprise, who had the honour of becoming the event's first-ever Olympic champion.

FIS Snowboarding World Championships

Women have been competing at the FIS Snowboard World Championships since the inaugural event was staged at Lienz, Austria, in 1996. Medals are contested in five disciplines: halfpipe, parallel slalom, parallel giant slalom, snowboard cross and slopestyle; former events include slalom and giant slalom. France has enjoyed the most success in the competition, winning 26 medals (12 of them gold).

Above: Ursula Bruhin won parallel giant slalom gold medals at the 2001 and 2003 World Championships.

THE WORLD CHAMPIONSHIPS' BEST HALFPIPER

Doriane Vidal's performances at the Winter Games did scant justice to her talent (she only picked up one medal – a silver in the halfpipe at Salt Lake City 2002 – in three Olympic appearances), but the Frenchwoman's achievements at the FIS Snowboard World Championships mark her out as one of the leading halfpipers of her generation. The Limoges-born star picked up her first medal at the championships in 1999 (a silver), became world champion for the first time in 2001, retained her title in 2003 (she is still the only woman in the event's history to achieve the feat) and completed a hat-trick of titles at Whistler, Canada, in 2005. She retired after the 2006 Winter Games to become an analyst on French television.

BRILLIANT BRUHIN MAKES WAVES

A 12-time race-winner and two-time overall champion (in 2002 and 2003) in parallel slalom in the World Cup, Switzerland's Ursula Bruhin also made waves at the FIS Snowboard World Championships. She took parallel giant slalom gold in Madonna di Campiglio, Italy, in 2001 and defended her title two years later in Kreischberg, Austria. She is the event's only two-time champion and remains the only woman in the event's history to have made a successful defence of her world title.

MOST MEDALS WON (BY COUNTRY): TOP TEN

Pos	Medals	Country	G	S	B
1	26	France	12	11	3
2	19	Austria	4	8	7
3	14	Switzerland	6	4	4
4	13	United States	5	4	4
5	9	Italy	4	2	3
6	5	Norway	2	2	1
=	5	Russia	2	2	1
=	5	Germany	1	1	3
9	4	Sweden	-	-	4
10	3	Netherlands	1	2	-
=	3	Canada	-	-	3

Above: Holly Crawford made history at the 2011 World Championships in La Molina.

FIRST CHAMPION FROM THE SOUTHERN HEMISPHERE

A two-time competitor in halfpipe at the Winter Games (with a best finish of eighth at Vancouver 2010), Holly Crawford made history at the 2009 FIS Snowboard World Championships when she finished second behind China's Jiayu Liu to become Australia's first-ever medallist at the competition. Two years later, in La Molina, Spain, she went one better, winning gold to become the southern hemisphere's first-ever snowboarding world champion.

RUBY'S STAR TURNS

To gauge Karine Ruby's credentials as the best female snowboarder of her generation, one only has to look at her performances at the FIS Snowboard World Championships. The French star won the snowboard cross event for the first time in 1997, collected her second title in the event in 2001 and made it three gold medals in the event in 2003, to become the first woman in the event's history to make a successful defence of her title (the feat was equalled by the USA's Lindsey Jacobellis, who won in 2005 and 2007). Ruby's record-breaking achievements at the championships did not end there; she was the first to win two gold medals at a single championships (winning the parallel slalom and snowboard cross events in 2001) and is the only two-time giant slalom champion (taking gold in 1996 and 2001).

LIU STRIKES GOLD FOR ASIA

China's Jiayu Liu was a relatively late starter to snowboarding – she only switched her focus to the sport at the age of 11, having previously practised martial arts – but she didn't take long to establish her credentials as a halfpiper of immense talent. She made her competitive international debut aged 17 at the 2007 FIS Snowboard World Championships, finishing 23rd in the halfpipe, and later that year finished third in her first-ever appearance at the World Cup. The best was still to come: she took halfpipe gold at the 2009 World Championships in Gangwon, South Korea, to become the sport's first-ever female Asian world champion.

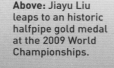

Above: Jiayu Liu leaps to an historic halfpipe gold medal at the 2009 World Championships.

UP AND RUNNING

Slopestyle, a popular snowboarding event in which competitors aim to perform a series of difficult tricks while achieving the maximum possible height in their jumps, was contested for the first time at the FIS Snowboard World Championships in 2011 at La Molina, Spain. Twenty-year-old Finn Enni Rukajärvi took the gold medal, ahead of Sarka Pancochova (Czech Republic) and Shelley Gotlieb (New Zealand) to become the event's first-ever female world champion.

MOST SUCCESSFUL NATION

No country has enjoyed more success at the FIS Snowboard World Championships than France: the country has won 26 medals in the competition (12 gold, 11 silver and three bronze), while second-placed Austria has 19 (four gold, eight silver and seven bronze).

ONLY DOUBLE PARALLEL SLALOM CHAMPION

Marion Posch may not have enjoyed huge success at the Winter Games (in two Olympic appearances her best performance was a sixth-place finish in the giant slalom at Nagano 1998), but it was a different story at the FIS Snowboard World Championships. The Italian won the first-ever parallel slalom competition at the event, at Lienz in 1996, and took the title for a second time at Berchtesgaden, Germany, in 1999. She is still the event's only two-time winner.

Right: Marion Posch is the most successful women's parallel slalom competitor in the World Championships.

SLALOM JOY FOR RENOTH

A five-time race-winner at the World Cup, the highlight of Heidi Renoth's career came at the 1997 FIS Snowboard World Championships at Innichen, Italy, when she beat off the challenge of home favourite Dagmar Mair Unter Der Eggen and France's Dorothée Fournier to win gold in the slalom – the only time the event was contested at the championships. She is still the only female German snowboarder to win a gold medal at the championships.

Other Major Championships

The women's FIS Snowboard World Cup was launched in the 1994–95 season, with parallel slalom (and giant parallel slalom) and halfpipe events. A snowboard cross event and an award for an overall winner were added to the programme the following year, and slopestyle was contested for the first time in 2011–12. Women snowboarders have competed at the annual Winter X Games since 1997.

MOST HALFPIPE DISCIPLINE TITLES

The FIS Snowboard World Cup record for the most halfpipe discipline titles is three, held by two women: Switzerland's Manuela Pesko (who took the crown in 2005–06, 2006–07 and 2007–08) and China's Cai Xuetong (who won in 2009–10, 2010–11 and 2011–12).

Above: Three-time champion Cai Xuetong has been dominant in the women's World Cup halfpipe.

JACOBELLIS MAKES AMENDS

Lindsey Jacobellis will always be remembered for her premature "showboating" celebration which led her to crash on the second to last jump while leading the snowboard cross final at the 2006 Winter Games in Turin. On that occasion she had to settle for the silver medal, but she has more than made amends for one of the most shocking capitulations in Olympic history with a string of stunning performances at the Winter X Games. The Connecticut-born star has been almost unbeatable at the event, claiming snowboard cross gold on seven occasions between 2003 and 2011.

Above: Lindsey Jacobellis has taken seven gold medals in the snowboard cross event at the Winter X Games.

THE SUPERPIPE QUEEN

A silver medallist in halfpipe at the 2006 Winter Games in Turin and one of the pin-up girls of the US snowboarding team, Gretchen Bleiler has left an indelible mark on the Winter X Games. She won the superpipe competition for the first time in 2003 and added further titles in 2005, 2008 and 2010 to become the event's first four-time winner.

CLARK'S MAGIC MOMENT

A gold medal winner in the halfpipe at her first-ever appearance at the Winter Games, at Salt Lake City in 2002, Kelly Clark has also enjoyed considerable success at the Winter X Games, claiming superpipe gold on three occasions — in 2006, 2011 and 2012. But what really captured the imagination of the public was the moment during her 2011 superpipe performance when she became the first woman in history to land a "1080" in competition (a move involving three revolutions in mid-air that is considered the hardest in the sport).

MEULI: THE PARALLEL SLALOM MASTER

Gold medal winner in the parallel slalom at the 2001 Junior World Championships, Daniela Meuli did not take long to confirm her potential in senior competition. After recording her first FIS Snowboard World Cup victory (in parallel giant slalom) on 8 January 2002, she took the parallel slalom (including parallel giant slalom) discipline title for the first time in 2003–04 (a season that saw her record seven race wins), defended it successfully the following season and completed a hat-trick of triumphs in 2005–06. She is the only woman in the competition's history to have won the parallel slalom discipline title on three occasions.

Below: Daniela Meuli is the World Cup's parallel slalom queen.

REGAL RUBY TOP OF THE CLASS

Karine Ruby's debut at the FIS Snowboard World Cup, at Zell am See, Austria, on 24 November 1994, was a sign of things to come: aged just 16 years 237 days she won the parallel slalom event to signal the start of a glittering career. By the time the Frenchwoman retired following the 2005–06 season she was considered the greatest female snowboarder of her generation and held several all-time competition records: for the most race wins (67); the most podium finishes (122 in 205 starts); as well as the most overall titles (six) and the most snowboard cross discipline titles (four), all achieved between 1995–96 and 2003–04.

YOUNGEST AND OLDEST

The youngest event winner in the women's FIS Snowboard World Cup France's Sophie Rodriguez, who was 15 years 200 days old when she won the halfpipe event at Kreischberg, Austria, on 23 January 2004. The oldest event winner is the USA's Sondra van Ert, who was 35 years 316 days old when she won the giant slalom event at Schoenried, Switzerland, on 19 January 2000.

MOST WORLD CUP RACE WINS: TOP TEN

Pos	Wins	Name (country, span)
1	67	Karine Ruby (France, 1994–2006)
2	22	Daniela Meuli (Austria, 2000–07)
3	16	Marion Posch (Italy, 1995–2006)
=	16	Lindsey Jacobellis (USA, 2000–12)
5	15	Tricia Byrnes (USA, 1996–2008)
6	13	Isabelle Blanc (France, 1996–2006)
=	13	Manuela Laura Pesko (Switzerland, 1997–2010)
8	12	Manuela Riegler (Austria, 1994–2010)
=	12	Ursula Bruhin (Switzerland, 2001–06)
10	11	Amelie Kober (Germany, 2002–12)
=	11	Ursula Fingerlos (Austria, 1995–2004)
=	11	Doresia Krings (Austria, 1997–2010)

EMERGING FROM RUBY'S SHADOW

A gold medal at the 2005 World Championships apart (in the parallel giant slalom), Manuela Riegler spent the majority of her career living in the considerable shadow of Karine Ruby, but the snowboard cross/parallel giant slalom specialist did manage to make her mark on the FIS Snowboard World Cup. She finished third in the overall standings in 1996–97, second the following year and first in 1998–99 to become the first woman in the competition's history to win overall bronze, silver and gold medals. When the Austrian went on to retain her title in 1999–2000, she became the only woman, other than Ruby, to achieve the feat.

Right: Austria's Manuela Riegler won a full set of FIS Snowboard World Cup medals; her gold came in 1998–99.

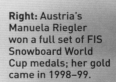

Chapter 5 ICE HOCKEY

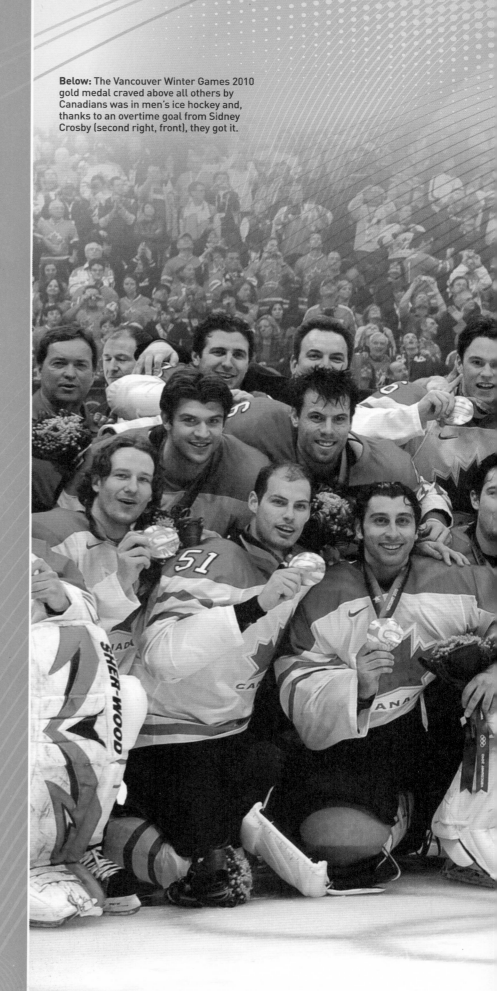

Below: The Vancouver Winter Games 2010 gold medal craved above all others by Canadians was in men's ice hockey and, thanks to an overtime goal from Sidney Crosby (second right, front), they got it.

One of the world's most popular sports, ice hockey is among the most eagerly anticipated competitions at the Winter Olympic Games. International competition does not end there, however, as the International Ice Hockey Federation (IIHF) also organizes an annual World Championships. Meanwhile the sport's diehard fans are to be found in the many domestic competitions around the world: North America's National Hockey League (the NHL) is the most famous, but other leagues (notably in Europe) have also attracted a huge following.

vancouver 2010

Men's Ice Hockey: Olympic Games

Considered as one of the blue riband events of the Winter Olympics, ice hockey was contested for the first time at Antwerp 1920 and has been an ever-present feature of the Games since. Canada have been the competition's most successful team, winning the gold medal on a record eight occasions.

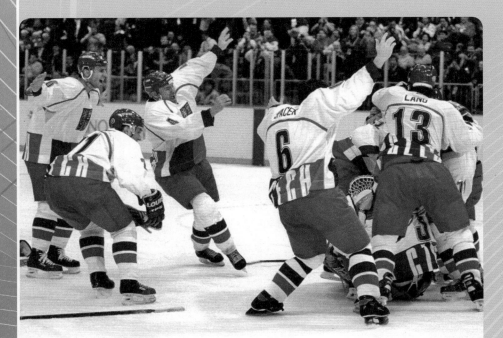

Above: The Czech Republic celebrate gold at Nagano 1998.

UP AND RUNNING

Ice hockey made its first appearance at the Olympics at the 1920 Summer Games in Antwerp, with all the matches (which were seven a side instead of the normal six) played at the Palais de Glace d'Anvers, a smaller than usual rink. The Winnipeg Falcons (representing Canada) took gold, the United States silver and Czechoslovakia bronze. The sport was part of the programme when the first Winter Olympic Games were held in Chamonix in 1924, with Canada defending their title; they would go on to win six of the first seven titles, five of them consecutively.

TOO OFTEN THE BRIDESMAIDS

Although US teams won the ice hockey gold medal both in 1960 (at Squaw Valley) and in 1980 (at Lake Placid), the tournament has frequently ended in disappointment for the United States. They have finished as runners-up on eight occasions (in 1920, 1924, 1932, 1952, 1956, 1972, 2002 and 2010) – an unwanted tournament record.

TURNING PRO

From its inception in 1920, the Olympic Games ice hockey competition had been a wholly amateur affair, but that all changed in 1995 when the International Olympic Committee, the International Ice Hockey Federation, the National Hockey League (NHL) and the NHL Players' Association reached an agreement to allow NHL players to participate at the Winter Games from 1998. The Czech Republic won the tournament's first professional gold medal when they beat Russia 1–0 in the final.

NOT TO BE FOR UNCLE SAM

The United States team had history to live up to at the 2002 Winter Olympic Games at Salt Lake City. On the previous two occasions in which the event had been staged in the country (at Squaw Valley in 1960 and at Lake Placid 20 years later), the team had thrilled the home nation by walking away with the gold medal. It wasn't to be on this occasion, however: they made it to the final, but lost 5–2 to Canada in the highest-scoring gold medal match in Olympic history.

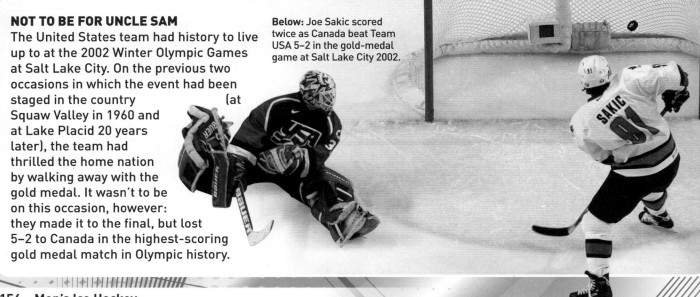

Below: Joe Sakic scored twice as Canada beat Team USA 5–2 in the gold-medal game at Salt Lake City 2002.

Below: The United States celebrate their gold medal at Lake Placid in 1980.

MIRACLE ON ICE

The United States ice hockey team had the advantage of playing in front of a partisan home crowd at the 1980 Winter Games at Lake Placid, but nobody fancied their chances of taking gold. The general perception was that the team, coached by Herb Brooks and made up largely of college players, lacked the firepower to end the Soviet Union's grip on the gold medal that stretched back to 1964 – and that perception seemed to be confirmed when the two countries met in an exhibition match three days before the start of the tournament and the Soviets won 10–3. However, after tying their opening game with Sweden (2–2) the US recorded wins over Czechoslovakia (7–3), Norway (5–1), Romania (7–2) and West Germany (4–2) to progress to the final round. And then came the big one: the match against the Soviet Union (who had eased through the preliminary round with five comfortable wins). After trailing three times, the US took a 4–3 lead with ten minutes left on the clock and held on for perhaps the most famous victory in the tournament's history – and one that prompted ABC commentator Al Michaels to proclaim: "Do you believe in miracles? Yes!" The US secured gold two days later with a 4–2 victory over Finland.

MOST MEDALS WON (BY COUNTRY): TOP TEN

Pos	Medals	Country	G	S	B
1	14	Canada	8	4	2
2	11	United States	2	8	1
3	9	Soviet Union	7	1	1
=	9	Czechoslovakia	-	4	5
5	8	Sweden	2	2	4
6	4	Finland	-	2	2
7	2	Great Britain	1	-	1
=	2	Czech Republic	1	-	1
=	2	Russia	-	1	1
10	1	Unified Team	1	-	-

FIRST GOLD MEDAL MATCH

The format for the first 16 Winter Olympic Games ice hockey competitions saw a preliminary round followed by a final round, with the gold medal awarded to the country that finished on top of the league table following a series of round-robin matches. That changed in 1992, when a knockout format was introduced after the preliminary round for the first time; as a result, the Unified Team (made up of countries from the former Soviet Union) hold the distinction of winning the Winter Games' first-ever gold medal match when they beat Canada 3–1.

SHOOTOUT SUCCESS FOR SWEDEN

The 1994 Winter Olympic Games ice hockey gold medal match between Sweden and Canada had spectators on the edge of their seats. At the end of regulation and overtime play the scores were locked at 2–2, producing a Winter Games first: a penalty shootout. Both nations scored with their first two attempts, which resulted in a sudden-death penalty shootout. Sweden's Peter Forsberg scored with his attempt, Canada's Paul Kariya missed and the whole of Sweden celebrated.

Below: Tommy Salo (right) denies Canada's Paul Kariya as Sweden wins gold in 1994.

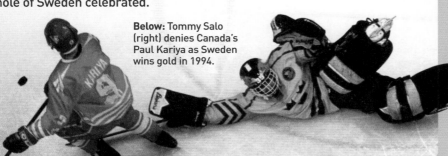

GREAT BRITAIN'S GOLD WITH HELP FROM CANADA

Canada's monopoly on the Olympic ice hockey crown (they had won the first four titles) finally came to an end in 1936, although Great Britain's 13-man squad had a distinctively Canadian flavour: one of their players had been born in Canada and nine others had been brought up in the country. It remains Great Britain's only victory in the competition.

LONGEST INTERVAL BETWEEN MEDALS

The record for the greatest number of years between winning medals in ice hockey at the Winter Games is 20, held by Switzerland's Richard Torriani. Having won a bronze medal at St Moritz 1928 he won another bronze at the same venue in 1948.

SERIAL MEDAL WINNERS AT THE GAMES

Three men have won medals in ice hockey competition at four editions of the Winter Games: Vladislav Tretyak (Soviet Union, three gold medals and one silver between 1972 and 1984); Jiri Holik (Czechoslovakia, two silver and two bronze between 1964 and 1976); and Igor Kravchuk (Soviet Union/Unified Team/Russia, two gold, one silver and one bronze between 1988 and 2002).

FASTEST GOAL

The United States team could not have got off to a worse start in the last of their final-round matches at the 1960 Winter Games in Squaw Valley – a game they had to win to ensure their country's first-ever ice hockey gold medal. To the shock of the home crowd, Czechoslovakia's Miroslav Vlack handed his country the lead after a mere eight seconds – the fastest goal in ice hockey history at the Winter Games. The United States recovered, however, ultimately winning the game 7–4 to become Olympic ice hockey champions for the first time.

DOWEY SHUTS THE DOOR

One of the principal reasons behind Canada's nail-biting success at the 1948 Winter Games at St Moritz (they secured their fifth gold medal in the event on goal difference ahead of Czechoslovakia) was the performance of their goaltender, Murray Dowey. The Ottawa star conceded just five goals during the competition, including an all-time high five shutouts.

Left: Finland's Raimo Helminen appeared at a record six Winter Games.

SIX IN A ROW FOR HELMINEN

The most capped player in international ice hockey history (he made an astonishing 331 appearances for his country), Finland's Raimo Helminen also left his mark on the sport at the Winter Games. No player has appeared in as many tournaments (six between 1984 and 2002) or played in as many matches (39). His incredible stamina earned him three medals – one silver (in 1988) and two bronze (in 1994 and 1998).

WATSON'S GOAL-SCORING BLITZ

Harry Watson was in the goal-scoring form of his life for his country during Canada's march to the gold medal at the 1924 Winter Games in Chamonix. The Newfoundland-born star, who turned down several lucrative offers to play in the NHL during the course of his amateur career, scored an astonishing 13 goals in Canada's thumping 33–0 victory over Switzerland (a record in a single match at the Winter Games), repeated the feat in Canada's 30–0 thrashing of Czechoslovakia, and ended the tournament with 36 goals (out of his country's 110) to his name – a record tally for the tournament that seems certain to stand the test of time.

ASSISTS RECORDS

The record for the most assists in a Winter Games career is 21, held by the Soviet Union's Valeri Kharlamov (in 17 matches between 1972 and 1980) and Viacheslav Fetisov (in 22 matches between 1980 and 1988). The record for the most assists in a single tournament is 12, held by Canada's Bob Attersley and Fred Etcher (who both achieved the feat in seven matches in 1960).

MOST MEDALS

The record for the most medals won in ice hockey at the Winter Games is four, held by six men: Vladislav Tretyak (Soviet Union, three gold, one silver); Jiri Holik (Czechoslovakia, two silver and two bronze); Igor Kravchuk (Soviet Union/Unified Team/Russia, two gold, one silver and one bronze); Ville Peltonen (Finland, one silver and three bronze); Jere Lehtinen (Finland, one silver and three bronze); and Saku Koivu (Finland, one silver and three bronze).

ZABRODSKY'S EFFORTS NOT ENOUGH FOR GOLD

The headline-grabbing performances of Vladimir Zabrodsky may not have been enough to win his country the gold medal at the 1948 Winter Games at St Moritz (Czechoslovakia ultimately finished in second place behind Canada), but he still had a tournament to remember. The centre-forward, revered as the greatest goalscorer in his country's history, found the back of the net on 22 occasions (in eight matches) – a record in the modern era at the Winter Games.

Left: Igor Kravchuk (left) of the Soviet Union won a record four Winter Games ice hockey medals, three of them gold.

GREATEST NUMBER OF VICTORIES IN THE SAME EVENT

The record for the greatest number of gold medals won in ice hockey at the Winter Games is three, set by five players: Aleksandr Ragulin, Viktor Kousine, Andrei Komutov, Vitali Davidov and Anatoli Firsov. They were all part of the USSR's victorious teams in 1964, 1968 and 1972. They are the only ice hockey players in Winter Games history to have won three consecutive gold medals.

Right: Anatoli Firsov (right), one of five men to win three Winter Games ice hockey gold medals.

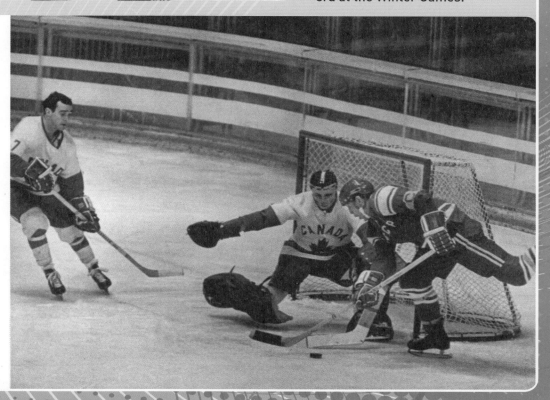

IIHF World Championships

Organized by the International Ice Hockey Federation (IIHF), the Ice Hockey World Championships are the sport's highest-profile annual competition. The tournament held at the 1920 Olympic Games is generally considered to be the first; and, until 1968, the Olympic ice hockey tournament was also considered the World Championship competition for that year.

THE SOVIET UNION'S SHINING STAR

Wounded three times fighting against the Germans during the Second World War (the last of the injuries was so bad that doctors feared they would have to amputate his leg), the Soviet Union's Nikolai Solugubov bounced back from his bitter wartime experiences to enjoy a glittering ice hockey career. A two-time world champion (in 1956 and 1963), and a distinctive figure on the ice with his trademark gold tooth, he was named the IIHF World Championships' best defenceman on three occasions, in 1956, 1957 and 1960, to become the accolade's first three-time winner.

Right: Nikolai Solugubov (centre) was a two-time world champion.

THE FIRST GREAT GOALTENDER

A former NHL star with the St Louis Blues (for whom he appeared in the Stanley Cup finals in 1967–68), goaltender Seth Martin was a star of Canada's team – known as the "Trail Smoke Eaters" – that won the 1961 IIHF World Championships in Switzerland (becoming the last amateur team to win the event), and he was voted the tournament's best goaltender. It wasn't the only time he shone at the championships: he received the accolade on three further occasions (in 1963, 1964 and 1968) to become the first four-time winner of the award.

THE SOVIET UNION REIGN SUPREME

The Soviet Union were serial challengers for IIHF World Championship honours from the moment they made their debut in the tournament in 1954. From 1963 until the nation's break-up in 1991, they claimed the gold medal on 20 occasions, including a tournament-best nine straight gold medals between 1963 and 1971.

MOST AWARDS TO FORWARDS

Only two men have received the honour of being voted the best forward at the IIHF World Championships on three occasions, both of them from the Soviet Union: Anatoli Firsov (in 1967, 1968 and 1971) and Aleksandr Maltsev (in 1970, 1972 and 1981).

FLUCTUATING FORTUNES FOR CANADA

Canada's status as the most successful team in IIHF World Championships history is based on the country's early domination of the event, for while the tournament was still in its infancy, the Canadians were virtually unbeatable, winning 19 of the first 28 championships (including six triumphs at the Winter Games). But the emergence of the Soviet Union changed all that: between 1963 and 1991 (the last time the Soviet Union competed at the event), Canada did not win a single title. They have collected five more titles since 1994, however, and their haul of 24 gold medals is an all-time best in the tournament.

Below: Rick Nash (61) scores for Canada in the final of the 2007 World Championships.

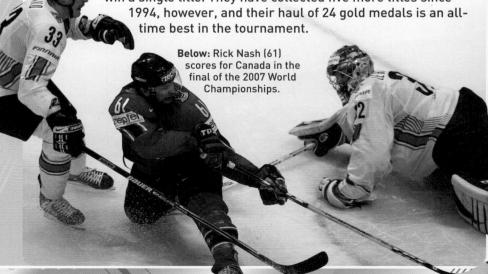

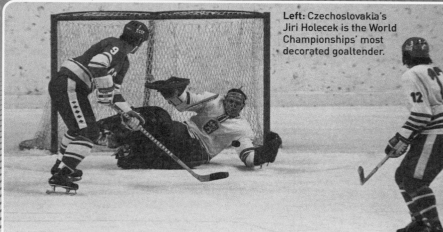

Left: Czechoslovakia's Jiri Holecek is the World Championships' most decorated goaltender.

HOLECEK OUTSHINES HIS HERO

Jiri Holecek of Czechoslovakia was known as "The Magician" in his homeland for the wonders he frequently performed, and was widely considered to be the first of the Eastern Bloc's great goaltenders (some even think of him as *the* best). Holecek's idol as a child was Canada's Seth Martin, so it was ironic that Holecek should go on to surpass Martin's achievements at the IIHF World Championships, both in terms of gold medals won – three (in 1972, 1976 and 1977) to Martin's one (in 1961) – and goaltender of the tournament awards: Holecek collected the accolade on a record five occasions, in 1971, 1973, 1975, 1976 and 1978.

FANTASTIC FETISOV

A hugely instrumental figure in breaking down the political barriers that had previously prevented Soviet Union players from playing in the NHL, Viacheslav Fetisov was granted permission to play for the New Jersey Devils (and subsequently the Detroit Red Wings) only on condition that he continued to turn out for the Soviet Union's national team. He fulfilled his end of the bargain and continued to play at the same sparkling level that had first caught the attention of the NHL's scouts. Before he joined the Devils in 1989, he had won two gold medals at the Winter Games (in 1984 and 1988) and had also been a standout performer at the IIHF World Championships, picking up seven gold medals and winning the defenceman of the tournament award on a record five occasions – in 1978, 1982, 1985, 1986 and 1989.

ONLY TWO-TIME MVP

Canada's all-time leading goalscorer (with 44 goals), Dany Heatley has been forced to overcome serious tragedy in his life – in September 2003, the car he was driving was involved in an accident that resulted in the death of one of his Atlanta Thrashers team-mates and he was subsequently charged with vehicular homicide. But he has found both solace and redemption on the ice rink, particularly at the IIHF World Championships, at which he is the only player in the tournament's history to have won the MVP award on two occasions (in 2004 and 2008).

A FIRST FOR SUNDIN

Although history will ultimately remember him as the NHL's longest-serving non-American captain (he led the Toronto Maple Leafs for 11 seasons between 1997–98 and 2007–08), Swedish star Mats Sundin also made his mark at the IIHF World Championships: at the 2003 tournament, at which Sweden won the silver medal, he became the first player in the competition's history to be awarded both the best forward and MVP (Most Valuable Player) awards.

Above: Sweden's Mats Sundin (in yellow) made history at the 2003 World Championships.

NHL – Stanley Cup

Without doubt the premier professional league in ice hockey, the National Hockey League (NHL) was founded in November 1917 in Montreal, Canada. It started with four teams, known as franchises, and has expanded over the years to its current count of 30, seven of which are located in Canada and 23 in the United States. Teams vie for the Stanley Cup, one of the most iconic trophies in all sport.

HENRI "POCKET ROCKET" RICHARD LEADS THE WAY

If Henri Richard's older brother Maurice (nicknamed "The Rocket") was the game's undoubted goalscoring king from the early 1940s through to his retirement in 1960 (in 1944–45 he became the first player in history to score 50 goals in 50 matches), then Henri, a.k.a. "The Pocket Rocket", was the lord of the assist (leading the league twice in the category in 1957–58 and 1962–63). The younger Richard was also a key member of the hugely successful Montreal Canadiens side of the era and holds the all-time record for the most Stanley Cup wins by a single player (11 from 1956 to 1973).

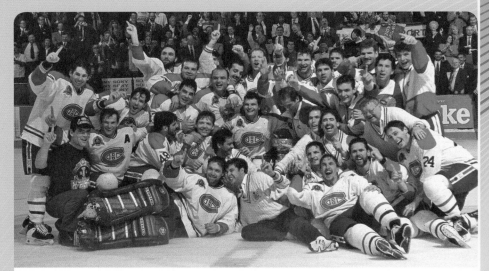

MAGICAL MONTREAL TOP STANLEY CUP CHARTS

Even though 18 long years have passed since they last took the spoils (in 1993, when they beat the Los Angeles Kings 4–1 in the best of seven finals), the Montreal Canadiens have been the most successful franchise in NHL history, winning the Stanley Cup 23 times in the NHL era. The Canadiens have set numerous all-time Stanley Cup records along the way: for the most consecutive appearances in the finals (ten between 1951 and 1960); for the most consecutive victories (five between 1956 and 1960); for the most appearances in the finals (32); for the most match wins in the finals (387); and for the most appearances in the playoffs (75).

Above: The Montreal Canadiens celebrate their 1993 Stanley Cup success.

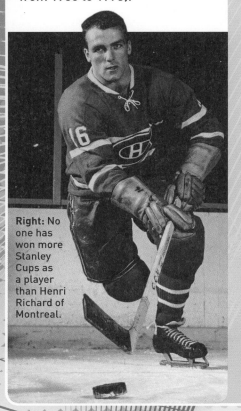

Right: No one has won more Stanley Cups as a player than Henri Richard of Montreal.

CURRENT NHL TEAMS NEVER TO HAVE WON STANLEY CUP

Team (first season)
Los Angeles Kings (1967–68)
St Louis Blues (1967–68)
Buffalo Sabres (1970–71)
Vancouver Canucks (1970–71)
Washington Capitals (1974–75)
Winnipeg Jets/Phoenix Coyotes (1979–80/1996–97)
San Jose Sharks (1991–92)
Florida Panthers (1993–94)
Nashville Predators (1998–99)
Atlanta Thrashers/Winnipeg Jets (1999–2000/2011–12)
Minnesota Wild (2000–01)
Columbus Blue Jackets (2000–01)

NOT ALL GOOD NEWS FOR THE RED WINGS

The Detroit Red Wings have enjoyed Stanley Cup success on 11 occasions (most recently in 2008) to become the most successful American franchise in NHL history (only Canada's Montreal Canadiens and the Toronto Maple Leafs have won the Stanley Cup on more occasions), but they have also suffered their fair share of near misses. They have lost in the finals a record 13 times between 1934 and 2009.

MOST SUCCESSFUL COACH

Although a fractured skull suffered while playing in the minor leagues may have scuppered any aspirations he had of making an impact on the game as a player, Scotty Bowman switched to coaching and went on to become the most successful coach in NHL history. He holds the all-time records for the most wins (1,244 wins in the regular season and 223 in the playoffs) and for the most Stanley Cup wins (nine) – five with the Montreal Canadiens (in 1973, 1976, 1977, 1978 and 1979), one with the Pittsburgh Penguins (in 1992) and three with the Detroit Red Wings (in 1997, 1998 and 2002).

Right: Scotty Bowman won nine Stanley Cups as a coach.

FIRST 4–0 WHITEWASH

Their path to the 1941 Stanley Cup finals was far from straightforward (they needed all seven games to edge past the Toronto Maple Leafs in the playoffs), but once they got there the Boston Bruins were simply too good for the Detroit Red Wings. The Bruins kicked off with two victories at Boston Garden (3–2 and 2–1), won game three at Detroit Olympia 4–2 and became the first team in history to win a best-of-seven finals series 4–0 when they triumphed 3–1 in game four. Surprisingly, the feat is not as unusual as one might think: it has since been repeated on 19 occasions.

MOST STANLEY CUP WINS: TOP TEN

Pos	Wins	Team
1	23	Montreal Canadiens
2	13	Toronto Maple Leafs
3	11	Detroit Red Wings
4	6	Boston Bruins
5	5	Edmonton Oilers
6	4	Chicago Blackhawks
=	4	New York Rangers
=	4	New York Islanders
9	3	New Jersey Devils
=	3	Pittsburgh Penguins

Note: this list is for post-1918 NHL winners

BABANDO PICKS HIS MOMENT

His six seasons and 351 regular-season games in the NHL (playing for the Boston Bruins, Detroit Red Wings, Chicago Blackhawks and New York Rangers) may not have yielded particularly remarkable figures (he registered 86 goals and 73 assists), but Pete Babando chose a sensational time to write his name in the game's record books. On 23 April 1950, playing for the Detroit Red Wings in game seven of the Stanley Cup finals against the New York Rangers, he became the first player in history to score a sudden-death (and game-clinching) goal in overtime to win the Stanley Cup. Tony Leswick (playing for the Red Wings in 1954) is the only other player to have achieved the feat.

THE GREATEST COMEBACK IN FINALS HISTORY

Having slipped to defeat in the first three of a possible seven matches in the 1942 Stanley Cup finals against the Detroit Red Wings (3–2 and 4–2 at home and 5–2 in Detroit), the Toronto Maple Leafs were on the verge of being whitewashed. Needing to stir things up, the Maple Leafs' coach Hap Day benched several of the team's regulars and inserted rookies in their place. The move may have been borne out of desperation, but it proved to one of the most inspirational decisions in ice hockey history: the Maple Leafs won a nail-biting game four 4–3 to keep their hopes alive and kick-start of one of the greatest comebacks in sporting history. They won the next two games (9–3 and 3–0) to level the series and then won the deciding game in front of an ecstatic home crowd to become the only team in history to win the Stanley Cup having trailed 3–0 in a seven-game series.

Left: The Toronto Maple Leafs enjoyed an unlikely comeback success in the 1942 Stanley Cup finals.

NHL – Team Records

MOST ALL-TIME WINS (BY TEAM): TOP TEN

Pos	Wins	Team (span)
1	3,132	Montreal Canadiens (1918–2012)
2	2,849	Boston Bruins (1925–2012)
3	2,707	Detroit Red Wings (1927–2012)
4	2,668	Toronto Maple Leafs (1918–2012)
5	2,530	New York Rangers (1927–2012)
6	2,457	Chicago Blackhawks (1927–2012)
7	1,752	Philadelphia Flyers (1968–2012)
8	1,565	Buffalo Sabres (1971–2012)
9	1,541	St Louis Blues (1968–2012)
10	1,508	Dallas Stars (1968–2012)

WINS: HIGHS AND LOWS

There was little doubt as to which team was the star performer in the 1995–96 regular season, with the Detroit Red Wings posting an all-time NHL record 62 wins during the campaign. But regular-season success does not always equate to Stanley Cup glory: the Red Wings' season came to an abrupt, and surprising, end when they lost 4–2 to eventual champions Colorado Avalanche in the playoffs. The record for the fewest wins recorded in a single NHL regular season is eight, set by the Washington Capitals during their miserable 1974–75 season.

Right: Colorado Avalanche center Joe Sakic shoots at Chris Osgood's goal during his team's playoff upset of Detroit in 1996.

GOALS: HIGHS AND LOWS

Helped in no small part by Wayne Gretzky's personal haul of 87 goals, the Edmonton Oilers were a goalscoring machine in the 1983–84 regular season – a year that ended in the franchise's first Stanley Cup triumph. The Oilers scored 466 goals – an all-time record in the NHL. The NHL record for the fewest goals in a season is 133, set by the 1953–54 Chicago Blackhawks.

Above: Wayne Gretzky's performances helped the Edmonton Oilers to the Stanley Cup in 1984.

GOALS DIFFERENTIAL: HIGHS AND LOWS

The all-time record for the best goal differential (the total of goals scored minus the number of goals conceded) in a single NHL season is +216, set by the Stanley Cup-winning Montreal Canadiens in the 1976–77 season. The worst goal differential ever recorded in a single NHL season is –265, posted by the Washington Capitals in their first-ever season in the NHL in 1974–75.

WORST AWAY RECORD

A famous name in the NHL, the Ottawa Senators had enjoyed enormous success in the past, winning the Stanley Cup on 11 occasions (the last of those triumphs came in 1927) before the franchise left the NHL and moved to St Louis in 1934. But a new Ottawa Senators team was back in the NHL in the 1992–93 season. Unfortunately, it turned out to be a campaign to forget: the Senators posted the worst away record in NHL history, with one win, 41 losses and no ties.

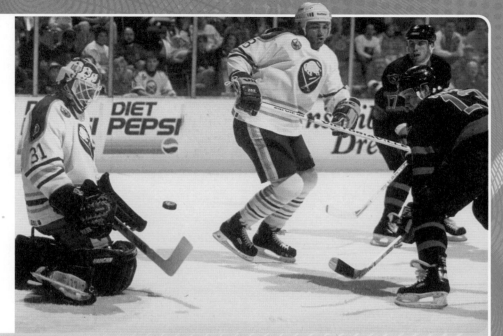

Right: The Ottawa Senators (in blue) had a miserable debut season in 1992–93.

DEFEATS: HIGHS AND LOWS

If the San Jose Sharks needed any reminder that life was going to be tough for them in the NHL, it came in their inaugural season in 1991–92 when they won only 17 games and lost 58 to finish the regular season bottom of the Smythe Division in the Campbell Conference. And things went from bad to worse for the Sharks in 1992–93: they posted only 11 wins and suffered 71 defeats – an all-time NHL regular-season record. The record for the fewest regular-season defeats is eight, set by the all-conquering Montreal Canadiens in 1976–77.

TIES: HIGHS AND LOWS

The all-time NHL record for the most ties in a single season is 24, set by the Philadelphia Flyers in the 1969–70 season (a year that saw them post a 17-35-24 record). The all-time NHL record for the fewest ties in a single season is two, set by the San Jose Sharks in 1992–93 (the franchise's second season in the NHL).

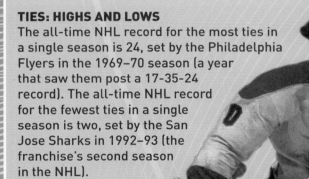

Right: Guy Lafleur (left) in action for the Montreal Canadiens during the 1977–78 season.

POINTS: HIGHS AND LOWS

The Montreal Canadiens' march to Stanley Cup victory in 1977 was as imperious as it was serene. The NHL's most successful franchise showed their form in the regular season, posting a win-loss-tie record of 60-8-12, and scoring an all-time NHL record 132 points along the way, before sweeping the Boston Bruins 4–0 in the finals to win the Stanley Cup for the 20th time in their history (and for the 19th time in the NHL era). The record for the fewest points in a single NHL season (21) was set by the Washington Capitals in the 1974–75 season – the franchise's first in the NHL.

POWER PLAY PERCENTAGES

The best power play percentage (calculated by dividing the number of power play goals by power play opportunities) ever recorded in an NHL regular season is 31.88 percent, set by the Montreal Canadiens in 1977–78 (a year that climaxed in the Canadiens' 20th Stanley Cup success of the NHL era). The worst power play percentage in a season is a miserable 9.35 percent, set by Tampa Bay Lightning in 1997–98.

MOST ALL-TIME POINTS (BY TEAM): TOP TEN

Pos	Points	Team (span)
1	7,194	Montreal Canadiens (1918–2012)
2	6,594	Boston Bruins (1925–2012)
3	6,312	Detroit Red Wings (1927–2012)
4	6,213	Toronto Maple Leafs (1918–2012)
5	5,955	New York Rangers (1927–2012)
6	5,817	Chicago Blackhawks (1927–2012)
7	4,051	Philadelphia Flyers (1968–2012)
8	3,621	Buffalo Sabres (1971–2012)
9	3,613	St Louis Blues (1968–2012)
10	3,555	Dallas Stars (1968–2012)

LONGEST LOSING STREAK

Overall: 17 games Washington Capitals in 1974–75
  San Jose Sharks in 1992–93
Home: 14 games Pittsburgh Penguins in 2003–04
Away: 38 games Ottawa Senators in 1992–93

OILERS OFF TO A FLIER

As statements of intent go, this was the most impressive in NHL history. Defending Stanley Cup champions Edmonton Oilers opened their 1984–85 campaign by winning 12 and tying three of their opening 15 games – the longest undefeated streak to start the season in NHL history. They ended up posting a 49-20-11 record in the regular season and beat the Los Angeles Kings (3–0), Winnipeg Jets (4–0) and Chicago Blackhawks (4–2) in the playoffs before overcoming the Philadelphia Flyers 4–1 in the finals to retain their Stanley Cup crown.

Above: Wayne Gretzky (C) with the Stanley Cup in 1985.

LONGEST WINLESS STREAK

Overall: 30 games
  Winnipeg Jets in 1980–81
Home: 17 games
  Ottawa Senators in 1995–96
  Atlanta Thrashers in 1999–2000
Away: 38 games
  Ottawa Senators in 1992–93

LONGEST STREAK WITHOUT FAILING TO GAIN A POINT

Overall: 35 games
  Philadelphia Flyers in 1979–80
Home: 34 games
  Montreal Canadiens in 1976–77
Away: 23 games
  Montreal Canadiens in 1974–75

Note: Teams get one point from ties, overtime losses and shootout losses.

BEST SEASON-ENDING UNDEFEATED STREAK

Even though the Pittsburgh Penguins ended the 1992–93 regular season in record-breaking fashion, winning 17 and tying one of their last 18 games (an NHL record) to post a 56-21-7 regular-season record, it still wasn't a springboard to Stanley Cup success; they ended up losing 4–3 to the New York Islanders in the division finals. Instead, Stanley Cup honours that year went to the Montreal Canadiens – the last time the NHL's most successful franchise has had its hand on the iconic trophy.

Above: The Pittsburgh Penguins' Mario Lemieux in full flow during the 1992–93 season.

DUCKS FAST OUT OF THE BLOCKS

A good start is crucial to an NHL team's hopes of success, and there's no better illustration than the way the Anaheim Ducks began their 2006–07 campaign. The Ducks recorded 12 wins in their first 16 matches (the only losses coming in overtime – their streak of 16 matches without a loss in regulation time is an NHL record), posted a 48-20-14 regular-season record and beat Minnesota Wild 4–1, Vancouver Canucks (4–1) and Detroit Red Wings (4–2) in the playoffs before triumphing over the Ottawa Senators 4–1 in the finals to win the Stanley Cup for the first time in their history and to become the first Californian franchise to achieve the feat.

Above: Anaheim started 2006-07 with a record-breaking streak and ended it with the Stanley Cup.

11 IN A ROW FOR THE DEVILS

The New Jersey Devils completed the 2005–06 regular season in spectacular fashion, winning all 11 of their final games – an all-time NHL record – and then beat local rivals New York Rangers 4–0 in the Conference quarter-finals. But then their campaign finally ran out of steam: they lost 4–1 to eventual champions Carolina Hurricanes in the Conference semi-finals.

Left: New Jersey's Brian Gionta in action during the Devils' first round series sweep of the New York Rangers.

NHL – Player Records (Career)

MOST REGULAR SEASON CAREER POINTS: TOP TEN

Pos	Points	Player (span)
1	2,857	Wayne Gretzky (1979–99)
2	1,887	Mark Messier (1979–2004)
3	1,850	Gordie Howe (1946–80)
4	1,798	Ron Francis (1981–2004)
5	1,771	Marcel Dionne (1971–89)
6	1,755	Steve Yzerman (1983–2006)
7	1,723	Mario Lemieux (1984–2006)
8	1,646	Jaromir Jagr (1990–2012)
9	1,641	Joe Sakic (1988–2009)
10	1,590	Phil Esposito (1963–81)

MR HOCKEY

Gordie Howe made his debut for the Detroit Red Wings in 1946 at the age of 18 – and scored a goal; it was a memorable start for a player who would go on to become one of the greatest legends in NHL history. During a sensational career that spanned five decades with the Red Wings and the Hartford Whalers (he finally retired in 1980 at the age of 52), the man known as "Mr Hockey" held numerous all-time records – including those for the most goals (1,071), the most assists (1,518) and the most points (2,589). Most of his records have since been broken, but one of them seems sure to stand the test of time: the number of matches he played in (1,767). It will be a worthy testament for one of the sport's genuine nice guys.

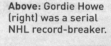

Above: Gordie Howe (right) was a serial NHL record-breaker.

Above: Martin Brodeur – goaltender supreme.

BRILLIANT BRODEUR SETS NEW BENCHMARKS

The son of Canadian international goaltender David Brodeur (who won a bronze medal at the 1956 Winter Games and went on to become one of ice hockey's leading photographers), Martin Brodeur has followed in his father's footsteps with distinction. In his 19-year career with the New Jersey Devils, for whom he made his debut in the 1991–92 season aged 19, his lightning-sharp reflexes and puck-handling abilities have marked him out as one of the outstanding goaltenders of his generation. A two-time Olympic gold medallist (in 2002 and 2010) and three-time Stanley Cup champion (in 1995, 2000 and 2003), he has set numerous all-time NHL regular-season records for a goaltender: for the most games played (1,184); the most career wins (651); the most career losses (370); the most career shutouts (118); and the most career saves (29,882).

SCORING WHEN IT MATTERS

One of the highest scoring left-wingers in NHL history, with a tally of 640 goals in 1,639 matches from a 29-year, six-team career (with the Buffalo Sabres, Toronto Maple Leafs, New York Devils, Boston Bruins, Colorado Avalanche and Tampa Bay Lightning between 1982–83 and 2005–06), Dave Andreychuk had a habit of scoring goals when it really mattered: his career haul of 274 regular-season powerplay goals and 17 game-tying goals are both all-time NHL records.

BIG BIRD FLIES HIGH

A strong defenceman who, despite his 6ft 4in frame, was extremely mobile, Larry Robinson enjoyed a stellar 17-season career with the Montreal Canadiens (during which they won six Stanley Cups) and spent three seasons with the Los Angeles Kings. The man they called "Big Bird" ended his career having scored 208 goals, 750 assists and 958 regular-season points – a remarkable achievement for a defender – and also holds the NHL's all-time record for the highest plus/minus score (an award devised to rate a player's contribution to offence and defence), with +730.

Left: All-round excellence was the hallmark of Larry Robinson's distinguished career.

JAGR HUNTS WITH THE PENGUINS

Europe's most successful export to the NHL (no other European player can match his career haul of 664 goals, 982 assists and 1,646 points), Czech-born Jaromir Jagr made a sensational start to his NHL career with the Pittsburgh Penguins, winning two Stanley Cups in his first two seasons (in 1991 and 1992). One of a small band of players to have triumphed in the Stanley Cup, the IIHF World Championships (in 2005 and 2010) and the Olympic Games (in 1998), the right-winger also has the knack of scoring goals at crucial times: no player in NHL history has scored more regular-season game-winning goals (114) or overtime goals (16).

RECORD-BREAKING BOURQUE

Although he became near-synonymous with the Boston Bruins (for whom he played 21 seasons between 1979–80 and 1998–99, becoming the team's longest-serving captain), Ray Bourque enjoyed a fairytale end to his career with Colorado Avalanche, winning the Stanley Cup in 2000–01 in his last-ever NHL game at the age of 40. It brought down the curtain on a stellar career: Bourque holds the all-time NHL records for a defenceman for the most goals (410), assists (1,169) and points (1,579) and also holds the record, for any player, for the most shots taken in a career – 6,206.

THE GREAT ONE

Wayne Gretzky was a child prodigy who transferred the genius he displayed as an infant into the adult game and left a bigger mark on the NHL than any other player in history. After two seasons playing in the World Hockey Association league (principally because NHL teams were not allowed to sign players under the age of 20), he made his NHL debut for the Edmonton Oilers in 1979–80 and at the end of the season was voted the league's MVP (the first of eight consecutive wins) after setting the record for the most points scored by a player in his rookie season (137). It was a sign of things to come: by the time he retired following the 1998–99 season he was being hailed as the greatest player in history and held all-time NHL career records for the most goals (894); the most assists (1,963); the most points (2,857); and the most short-handed goals (73).

Above: Wayne Gretzky – the greatest.

TIGER OVERSTEPS THE LEGAL LINE

Given his role as an enforcer, the frequency with which Dave "Tiger" Williams scored goals during his 14-year career in the NHL was surprising (he scored 241 goals in 962 matches). The amount of time he spent in the sin bin was less so – he always used to tread a fine line with the on-ice officials. In fact the 3,996 penalty minutes he collected during the course of his career is an all-time NHL high.

NHL – Player Records (Single Season)

MORE GRETZKY RECORDS

The litany of records Wayne Gretzky set during his unparalleled NHL career also extends to the single-season records list. He set all-time highs for the most goals in a single season (92 in 1981–82) – and he has three other single-season totals in the top ten; for the most assists (163 in 1985–86) – a category in which he set nine of the all-time top ten marks; and for the most points (215 in 1985–86) – another category in which he set nine of the all-time top ten marks.

THE BATTLER

A gifted playmaker, Mario Lemieux battled through numerous ailments – including a spinal disc herniation, Hodgkin's lymphoma and chronic back pain – to carve out one of the most successful careers in NHL history and earn a reputation as one of the game's all-time greats. A one-club man (he played for the Pittsburgh Penguins between 1984–85 and 2005–06), he was the NHL's seventh highest ranked scorer of all time (with 690 goals and 1,033 assists), won Stanley Cup honours in 1991 and 1992 and holds the NHL all-time single-season record for the most short-hand goals (13 in the 1988–89 season).

Above: Mario Lemieux scored a record 13 short-handed goals for the Pittsburgh Penguins in 1988–89.

MOST WINS AND MOST LOSSES

The all-time NHL record for the most wins by a goaltender in a single season is 48, set by Martin Brodeur for the New Jersey Devils in the 2006–07 season. The record for the most losses suffered by a goaltender in a single season is also 48, set by Gary Smith for the California Golden Seals in the 1970–71 season.

KERR FIGHTS BACK

Before he started the 1985–86 season, Tim Kerr's career was at a particularly low ebb: he had just been re-signed by the Philadelphia Flyers as an undrafted free agent (in other words nobody wanted him) and, in September 1985, he was hospitalized with aseptic meningitis. But adversity can produce untold strength and, having recovered from his illness, Kerr's performances that season earned him a place in the history books: he scored 34 powerplay goals – an all-time NHL single-season record.

THE HAMMER STRIKES

Nicknamed "The Hammer" for his aggressive style of play, Canadian Dave Schultz enjoyed a 13-year career in the NHL, during which time he played in two Stanley Cup-winning teams (in 1974 and 1975) with the Philadelphia Flyers and earned a reputation as being one of the game's great enforcers. He more than lived up to his name in the 1974–75 season, spending 472 minutes in the sin bin – an all-time NHL single-season record.

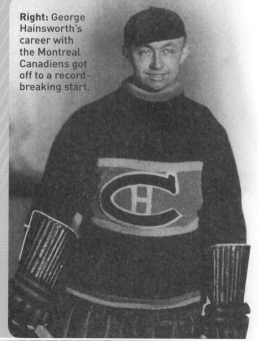

Right: George Hainsworth's career with the Montreal Canadiens got off to a record-breaking start.

HAINSWORTH STEPS UP

Signed by the Montreal Canadiens in 1926 to fill the gaping void created by the sudden death of the club's legendary goaltender Georges Vezina (who had played every game in the club's history between the 1910–11 and 1925–26 seasons), George Hainsworth rose to the mighty challenge with aplomb. He won the Vezina Trophy (for the most valuable keeper in the NHL) in his first three seasons (in 1926–27, 1927–28 and 1928–29) and in the latter of those seasons set an all-time NHL single-season record when he completed 22 shutouts.

MOST SINGLE SEASON GOALS: TOP TEN

Pos	Goals	Player	Season
1	92	Wayne Gretzky	1981–82
2	87	Wayne Gretzky	1983–84
3	86	Brett Hull	1990–91
4	85	Mario Lemieux	1988–89
5	76	Phil Esposito	1970–71
=	76	Teemu Selanne	1992–93
=	76	Alexander Mogilny	1992–93
8	73	Wayne Gretzky	1984–85
9	72	Brett Hull	1989–90
10	71	Wayne Gretzky	1982–83
=	71	Jari Kurri	1984–85

GOALS AND SHOTS

Two men hold the NHL's all-time record for the most game-winning goals in a single season (16): the Boston Bruins' Phil Esposito (who achieved the feat in both the 1970–71 and 1971–72 seasons); and Michel Goulet (who did it playing for the Quebec Nordiques in the 1983–84 season). Esposito also holds the record for the most shots taken in a single season – 550 in 1970–71.

THE REVOLUTIONARY

A defenceman who used his speed over the ice and his scoring and playmaking abilities to revolutionize the way in which future players in his position approached the game, Bobby Orr is widely considered to be one of the greatest NHL players of all time. Still the only defenceman in history to have won the league's scoring title (a feat he achieved twice), he also holds the all-time single-season records for a defenceman for the most points (135 in 1974–75) and the most assists (102 in 1970–71), as well as the all-time NHL single-season record (for any player) for the highest plus/minus rating: +124 in the 1970–71 season.

Right: Bobby Orr is considered the best attacking defenceman in NHL history.

NHL – Player Records (Playoffs)

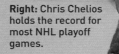

ST PATRICK SHINES

A four-time Stanley Cup winner (twice with the Montreal Canadiens and twice with Colorado Avalanche), Patrick Roy is the only player in history to have won the Conn Smythe Trophy (awarded to the MVP in the Stanley Cup playoffs) on three occasions; and in 2004 he was selected as the greatest goaltender in NHL history by a panel of 41 writers and a fan poll. The Quebec native, nicknamed "St Patrick", has set numerous all-time playoff records for a goaltender: for the most wins (151); for the most losses (94); for the most shutouts (23); for the most playoff saves (6,561); for the most shots faced (7,145) and for the most games played (247).

Right: Chris Chelios holds the record for most NHL playoff games.

MR PLAYOFF

His path into the NHL may read like that of a journeyman (he played five years in the junior leagues before eventually being drafted by the Montreal Canadiens), but when he finally made it into the NHL, Chris Chelios forged a long and successful career that stretched over a staggering 28 seasons and brought him three Stanley Cup wins (in 1985–86, 2001–02 and 2007–08). He has the distinction of having played more games (1,651) than any other defenceman in NHL history (while standing fifth on the all-time appearances list for players of any position), and he also holds the all-time record for having featured in more playoff matches (266) than any other player in NHL history.

MOST CAREER PLAYOFF POINTS: TOP TEN

Pos	Points	Player (span)
1	382	Wayne Gretzky (1979–99)
2	295	Mark Messier (1979–2004)
3	233	Jari Kurri (1980–98)
4	214	Glenn Anderson (1980–96)
5	196	Paul Coffey (1980–2001)
6	190	Brett Hull (1985–2006)
7	188	Joe Sakic (1988–2009)
=	188	Doug Gilmour (1983–2003)
9	185	Steve Yzerman (1983–2006)
10	184	Bryan Trottier (1975–94)

THE RED WINGS' SUPER SWEDE

Revered in his homeland for scoring the goal against Finland that won the gold medal for Sweden in the 2006 Olympic ice hockey final, such has been Niklas Lindstrom's impact on the NHL that many consider him to be the league's best-ever European-born player. During his 19 years with the Detroit Red Wings (between 1991–92 and 2011–12), the Swede has won four Stanley Cups, seven Norris Trophies (awarded to the league's best defenceman) and, in 2009, was *Sports Illustrated*'s pick as the player of the decade. His impact hasn't been confined to his defensive duties, however: he has also posted the best plus/minus score (+61) in playoffs of any player in NHL history.

Right: Sweden's Niklas Lindstrom starred in the NHL for 20 years.

THOMAS'S STAR TURN FOR THE BRUINS

In 2011, as the Boston Bruins celebrated their first Stanley Cup triumph for 39 years, their goaltender Tim Thomas could reflect on some of the finest moments of his career – his performances in the playoffs had been nothing short of sensational. During the Bruins' playoff run, he set the record for the most saves in a single postseason (798), for the most saves in a Stanley Cup series (238) and also for conceding the fewest goals in a seven-game Stanley Cup finals (eight, including a match-winning shutout in game seven). His performances earned him the Conn Smythe Trophy (for the playoffs' MVP) and, aged 37 years 62 days, he became not only the award's oldest recipient but also the first American-born goaltender to win it.

Left: Tim Thomas had a postseason to remember in 2011.

SHUTOUT SUCCESS FOR BRODEUR

New Jersey Devils' march to Stanley Cup glory in 2003 (the franchise's third success in the competition) had much to do with the performances of their goaltender Martin Brodeur. The four-time winner of the Vezina Trophy (awarded to the NHL's best goaltender) produced seven shutouts in the playoffs that season – an all-time NHL record.

RICHARDS IGNITES THE LIGHTNING

Tampa Bay Lightning owed a huge debt to Brad Richards as they marched to a first-ever Stanley Cup triumph in 2004. Lightning had won every one of the 31 matches in which Richards had scored during the course of that season, and the centre continued to exert his influence on the team during the playoffs: he netted seven game-winning goals – a single-season playoffs record.

PLAYOFF PRINCES

Two players hold the record for the most playoff goals in a single season (19): Jarri Kurri (for the Edmonton Oilers in the 1984–85 season); and Reggie Leach (for the Philadelphia Flyers in the 1975–76 season). Kurri's Oilers went on to win Stanley Cup honours that season, while Leach's Flyers would go on to lose out to the Montreal Canadiens.

GRETZKY IMPERIOUS IN PLAYOFFS

Wayne Gretzky's massive impact on the NHL's record books does not end with his dominating presence in the career and single-season lists. The Great One also enjoyed stunning success in the playoffs, setting records for the most career goals (122); the most career assists (260); the most career points (382); the most playoff points in a single season (47 in the 1984–85 season), and the most playoff assists in a single season (31 in 1987–88).

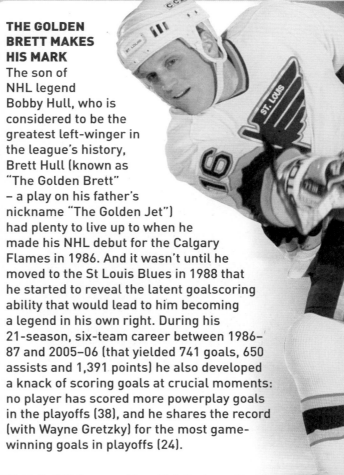

THE GOLDEN BRETT MAKES HIS MARK

The son of NHL legend Bobby Hull, who is considered to be the greatest left-winger in the league's history, Brett Hull (known as "The Golden Brett" – a play on his father's nickname "The Golden Jet") had plenty to live up to when he made his NHL debut for the Calgary Flames in 1986. And it wasn't until he moved to the St Louis Blues in 1988 that he started to reveal the latent goalscoring ability that would lead to him becoming a legend in his own right. During his 21-season, six-team career between 1986–87 and 2005–06 (that yielded 741 goals, 650 assists and 1,391 points) he also developed a knack of scoring goals at crucial moments: no player has scored more powerplay goals in the playoffs (38), and he shares the record (with Wayne Gretzky) for the most game-winning goals in playoffs (24).

Right: Brett Hull emerged from his father's considerable shadow to become an NHL legend in his own right.

Other Domestic Competitions

A testament to ice hockey's enormous popularity is the astonishing number of professional hockey leagues around the world. The following pages focus on the seven strongest of those leagues (as ranked by the International Ice Hockey Federation in 2008), some of those league's most famous exports and two, albeit short-lived, international club competitions.

SLOVAK EXTRALIGA

Ranked as the fifth strongest league in the world by the IIHF in 2009, Slovakia's Extraliga – which currently consists of 11 teams – is rooted in Czechoslovakia's former league of the same name and kicked off in the 1993–94 season following Czechoslovakia's split into two countries – the Czech Republic and Slovakia. HC Slovan Bratislava have been the most successful team in the competition's history, claiming the championship on seven occasions, most recently in 2008.

Right: Slovakia's Andrei Meszaros went on to enjoy considerable success in the NHL.

MESZAROS MAKES NHL MARK FOR SLOVAKIA

Slovakia's most famous ice hockey export of recent times, defenceman Andrej Meszaros first caught the eye when he captained his country to a surprise silver medal at the 2003 World Under-18 Championships. He had made his debut in the Slovak Extraliga for Dukla Trencan earlier that season and, after another promising season, was drafted 23rd in the 2004 NHL Entry Draft by the Ottawa Senators. Meszaros made his NHL debut in 2005 and shone in his first year, earning selection for the NHL's All-Rookie Team. He currently plays for the Philadelphia Flyers.

Right: Sergei Mozyakhin is the leading goalscorer in KHL history

THE KHL'S ALL-TIME LEADING GOALSCORER

A two-time gold medallist with Russia at the IIHF World Championships (in 2008 and 2009), Sergei Mozyakhin was drafted in the ninth round of the 2002 NHL Entry Draft by the Columbus Blue Jackets, but never made an appearance in the NHL. He has made an enormous impact on the KHL, though: in 219 matches in the competition (for Atlant Moskow Oblast and Metallurg Magnitogorsk between 2008 and 2012) he has scored 108 goals – an all-time record in the KHL.

MAJOR EUROPEAN LEAGUES' PAST FIVE CHAMPIONS

Year	Russia	Sweden	Czech Republic	Finland	Switzerland	Slovakia	Germany
2011	Salavat Yulaev Ufa	Farjestad BK	Ocelari Trinec	HIFK	HC Davos	Kosice	Eisbären Berlin
2010	Ak Bars Kazan	HV71	Pardubice	TPS	SC Bern	Kosice	Eisbären Berlin
2009	Ak Bars Kazan	Farjestad BK	Energie Karlovy Vary	JYP	HC Davos	Kosice	Hannover Scorpions
2008	-	HV71	Slavia Praha	Karpat	ZSC Lions	Slovan Bratislava	Eisbären Berlin
2007	-	Modo Hockey	Sparta Praha	Karpat	HC Davos	Slovan Bratislava	Adler Mannheim

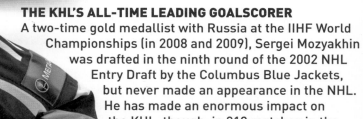

RUSSIA'S FINEST

In July 2008, at a time when Russia's Alexander Radulov was still under contract with the NHL's Nashville Panthers (for whom he signed in 2006), it was announced that he would be returning to Russia to play for Salavat Yulaev Ufa in the KHL's inaugural season. And he has been a huge hit in the league, winning the golden stick award (for the league's MVP) in 2010, helping his team to its first Gagarin Cup win in 2011, while setting single-season records for the most points (80) and assists (60), and setting the league's all-time career records for the most points (254) and for the most assists (163).

Right: Salavat Yulaev Ufa, 2011 KHL champions.

VICTORIA CUP

Devised by the IIHF to pit Europe's leading club against a representative of the NHL (the initial intention was for the reigning Stanley Cup champions to play in the event, a request the NHL rejected), the Victoria Cup was staged on two occasions: in 2008, when the New York Rangers beat Russia's reigning European Champions Cup champions Metallurg Magnitogorsk 4–3 in a seven-game series; and in 2009, when Switzerland's ZSC Lions (the 2009 Champions Hockey League winners) beat the Chicago Blackhawks 2–1 in the three-game series. The collapse of the Champions Hockey League led to the event's cancellation in 2010 and it has not been staged since.

THE ELITSERIEN'S MOST SUCCESSFUL TEAM

The Elitserien originated in 1975 (to replace the Swedish ice hockey championships, which had been contested on an annual basis since 1922 – with the exception of 1939, 1949 and 1952) and currently consists of 12 teams. Farjestad, who have played every year in the competition since its inception, have been the event's most successful team, winning the competition on nine occasions, most recently in 2011.

KONTINENTAL HOCKEY LEAGUE

The successor to the Soviet Championship League (which ran from 1947 to 1992), the International Hockey League (1993 to 1996) and the Russian Superleague (1997 to 2008), the Kontinental Hockey League (the KHL) was founded in 2008 and currently features 23 teams – 19 from Russia and one each from Belarus, Kazakhstan, Latvia and Slovakia. In what is generally considered to be the strongest league outside the NHL, teams vie for the Gagarin Cup. Ak Bars Kazan, a franchise based in the Republic of Tatarstan (a subject of the Russian Federation) have been the competition's most successful team, winning the Gagarin Cup on two occasions (in 2008–09 and 2009–10).

CHAMPIONS HOCKEY LEAGUE

Launched in 2008 by the IIHF to replace the European Champions Cup (which had been staged under various guises between 1965 and 2008), the Champions Hockey League was only contested once, in the 2008–09 season. Fourteen teams from seven countries took part in the competition, with Switzerland's ZSC Lions eventually beating Russia's Metallurg Magnitogorsk 7–2 on aggregate in the two-leg final. However, on 15 June 2009, the IIHF announced the cancellation of the 2009–10 competition and, despite efforts to revive it, the event has not been staged since.

Below: Switzerland's ZSC Lions celebrate Champions Hockey League glory in 2008–09.

NATIONALLIGA A

In terms of attendance figures, Switzerland's Nationalliga A is the second most popular ice hockey league in Europe (only Sweden's Elitserien attracts more spectators). The 12-team league has been staged under various guises on an annual basis since 1916 and HC Davos have been the most successful team, winning 30 titles, most recently in 2011.

GERMANY'S MOST FAMOUS EXPORT

After catching the eye with some impressive performances in the Deutsche Eishockey Liga for EV Landshut between 1995 and 1997, Marco Sturm signed for the San Jose Sharks in July 1997 and has gone on to enjoy a 14-year, six-team career in the NHL to establish his credentials as Germany's most famous ice hockey export. By 2012, his NHL career numbers read: 931 games, 241 goals, 244 assists and 485 points.

Above: New York Islander Mark Streit was the first Swiss-born player to be captain of an NHL team.

Above: Marco Sturm has enjoyed a 14-year NHL career.

SWISS SUPERSTAR

Switzerland's most famous ice hockey player, Mark Streit made his debut in the Nationalliga A as an 18-year-old in 1995–96 with HC Fribourg-Gottéron and moved to HC Davos, the country's most successful club, the following season. A brief, albeit unsuccessful, stint in North America followed in 1999–2000 before he moved back to the Nationalliga A with ZSC Lions, helping them to the title in 2001. Drafted by the Montreal Canadiens in 2004, he finally made his NHL debut in 2005–06 and soon established his credentials as a defenceman of the highest quality (in 2007–08 he finished third in league scoring for defencemen). He joined the New York Islanders in 2008 and became the club's captain in 2011 to become the first Swiss-born player in history to captain an NHL club.

AN EYE FOR A GOAL

Famed for being the first European draft pick made by the Pittsburgh Penguins, Arto Javanainen only played one season in the NHL (in 1984–85), but his exploits in the SM-liiga mark him out as one of the greatest players in the history of Finnish ice hockey. During his 14-year career in the league (playing for Ässät Pori and TPS Turku) between 1975–76 and 1993–94, he scored 462 goals (an all-time league record) and won the Aarne Honkavaara trophy (awarded to the player who scores the most goals during the regular season) on a record five occasions: in 1980–81, 1983–84, 1985–86, 1987–88 and 1990–91.

CZECH EXTRALIGA

Ranked the third strongest league in Europe by the IIHF in 2009 and with its roots in the Czechoslovak Extraliga (an annual competition that ran between 1931 and 1993), the Czech Extraliga, like that of Slovakia, was contested for the first time in 1993 – the year Czechoslovakia split into two countries (the Czech Republic and Slovakia). HC Vsetin have been the competition's most successful team, claiming the title on six occasions – most recently in 2001.

THE DOMINATOR

The youngest player in history to appear in the Czechoslovak Extraliga – he was only 16 when he made his debut for Pardubice in 1980 – Dominik Hasek played for ten seasons in his homeland before moving to North America and enjoying one of the finest careers in NHL history. In 16 seasons in the NHL (with the Chicago Blackhawks, Buffalo Sabres, Detroit Red Wings and Ottawa Senators), during which he earned the nickname "The Dominator", he established a fearsome reputation as being one of the finest goaltenders in the game – and still holds two all-time NHL records: for the highest career save percentage (.922) and for the most games played by a European goaltender (735). When Hasek announced his retirement in June 2008 following his second career Stanley Cup win (with the Red Wings), everyone thought that would be that. Ten months later, however, he was back on the ice, playing for his childhood club Pardubice in the Czech Extraliga, and he played one more season in the KHL (for HC Spartak Moscow) before finally hanging up his gloves for good.

Above: Dominik Hasek – a legendary NHL goaltender.

FROM PARDUBICE TO EDMONTON

Although several Czech-born players have gone on to star in the NHL – Jaromir Jagr and Jiri Slegr (both members of the sport's exclusive Triple Gold Club) to name but two – the Czech Extraliga's most successful export to the NHL in recent years has been Ales Hemsky. He first came to wider attention when he made his professional debut as a 16-year-old for HC Moeller Pardubice in 1999–2000, after which he opted to move to Canada to further his prospects of playing in the NHL. After two seasons with the Hull Olympiques in the Quebec Junior League he moved to the Edmonton Oilers in 2002–03 and started to make his mark. During the NHL lockout season of 2004–05 he returned to Pardubice and showed his class by helping his childhood club to win its first championship in 16 years (and was named playoff MVP for his exploits). A Stanley Cup finalist with the Oilers in 2005–06, by 2011 he had racked up 490 career games in the NHL, with 395 points, 114 goals and 281 assists.

HAGMAN HITS THE HEIGHTS

The first Finnish-born and Finnish-trained player to play in the NHL, and to appear in the Stanley Cup finals (both for the Boston Bruins in 1976–77), Matti Hagman first made a name for himself playing in the SM-liiga for HIFK (between 1972 and 1976). After his NHL experiences (which also included a two-season spell with the Edmonton Oilers), he returned to the Finnish league in 1982 to see out the rest of his career with HIFK and Reipas before his retirement at the end of the 1991–92 season. He is the only player in the league's history to have won the Veli Pekka Ketola trophy (awarded to the player who scores the most points during the regular season) on four occasions: in 1979–80, 1982–83, 1983–84 and 1984–85.

DEUTSCHE EISHOCKEY LIGA

Founded in 1994 to replace the ice hockey Bundesliga, the Deutsche Eishockey Liga has the highest number of Canadian and American ice hockey players outside North America and was ranked as the seventh strongest league in Europe by the IIHF in 2008. Two teams share the record for the most titles (five): Adler Mannheim (whose last title came in 2006–07) and Eisbären Berlin (who last won it in 2010–11).

SM-LIIGA

Ranked as the second strongest league in Europe by the IIHF in 2008, Finland's SM-liiga has been staged on an annual basis since 1975. The teams, of which there are currently 14, compete for the Kanada-malja, or Canada Cup, so named because it was donated to the league by Canada's Finnish community. HC TPS, a franchise based in Turku, have been the league's most successful team, winning the title on ten occasions – most recently in 2010.

Above: Janne Hauhtonen (15) scores for TPS Turku in 2010.

Women's Ice Hockey: Olympic Games

In July 1992, at the 99th session of the International Olympic Committee, approval was given for women's ice hockey's promotion to the programme of events at the 1998 Winter Games in Nagano – largely in order to increase the number of female athletes at the Games. The sport has been staged at the Games ever since, with Canada the dominant team, winning three of the four gold medals contested.

TWO CONSECUTIVE HAT-TRICKS

As the argument over a lack of competitiveness in the women's ice hockey competition at the 2010 Winter Games in Vancouver raged (12 of the 20 matches ended with one of the sides scoring five goals or more), the USA's Jenny Potter helped herself to a place in the record books: the Minnesota Whitecaps forward scored two hat-tricks in consecutive matches (against China and Russia). She is the only player in the tournament's history to achieve the feat.

Above: Jenny Potter of the United States made a record-breaking mark at the 2010 Winter Games in Vancouver.

MOST GOLD MEDALS

The record for the most gold medals won by a player in women's ice hockey at the Winter Games is three, held by Jennifer Botterill, Jayna Hefford, Becky Kellar and Hayley Wickenheiser. All four were part of Canada's title-winning teams in 2002, 2006 and 2010.

Right: Three-time Olympic champion Jennifer Botterill.

ALL-TIME GOAL-DIFFERENCE LEADERS: TOP TEN

Pos	Goal diff	Country (span)	GF	GA
1	+134	Canada (1998–2010)	158	24
2	+111	United States (1998–2010)	133	22
3	+4	Finland (1998–2010)	62	58
4	-6	Switzerland (2006–10)	28	34
5	-18	Russia (2002–10)	35	53
6	-22	Kazakhstan (2002)	2	24
7	-27	Germany (2002–06)	17	44
=	-27	Sweden (1998–2012)	54	81
9	-29	Slovakia (2010)	7	36
10	-42	China (1998–2010)	26	68

FIRST SUCCESS FOR CANADA

Despite the fact that Canada had bounced back from the disappointment of winning only a silver medal at Nagano 1998 by winning the IIHF Women's World Championships in 1999, 2000 and 2001, the United States were considered favourites to defend their title at Salt Lake City 2002 (going into the tournament, Team USA had put together a hugely impressive 31-game winning streak). But again a surprise lay in store after both Canada and the USA made it through to the final: this time Canada had the edge, winning a tight deciding match 3–2 to become Olympic women's ice hockey champions for the first time in their history.

YOUNGEST AND OLDEST

The youngest player to appear in the women's ice hockey competition at the Winter Games is Valentina Bettarini, who was 15 years 228 days old when she appeared for Italy at Turin 2006. The oldest is France St Louis, who was 39 years 115 days old when she played for Canada at Nagano 1998.

Above: The United States won gold at Nagano 1998.

UP AND RUNNING

Although the IOC had approved women's ice hockey's elevation to the programme of events for the 1998 Winter Games in July 1992, it was far from a done deal. The sport had not been on the programme when Nagano won the right to host the event, and the final decision to include women's ice hockey rested on the approval of the Nagano Winter Olympic Organizing Committee. In November 1992 (despite reservations), the NWOOC duly gave its approval. Canada, who had won every one of the IIHF Women's World Championships since the inaugural tournament was staged in 1987, were the firm favourites for gold, but it was the United States who took the honours, beating their North American rivals twice, 7–4 in the group matches and 3–1 in the final, to become the event's first-ever Olympic champions.

CANADA'S TRIUMPH IN TURIN

The third Olympic women's ice hockey tournament, at the 2006 Winter Games in Turin, also produced a surprise. Yet again Canada and the United States were heavy favourites to battle it out for gold, and although Canada eased through to the final (thanks to a comfortable 6–0 victory over Finland in the semi-finals), the United States came unstuck in dramatic fashion in the last four against Sweden. The US led 2–0 after two periods, but then the Swedes bounced back, levelling the game 2–2 and going on to win a shootout. Sweden could not repeat their heroics in the final, however, Canada winning 4–1 to become the event's first two-time champions.

GOALSCORING RECORDS

The record for the most goals in a single women's ice hockey tournament at the Winter Games is nine, set at Vancouver 2010 by Meghan Agosta (Canada) and Stefanie Marty (Switzerland). The record for the most goals in a single match at the Winter Games is four, set at Vancouver by Sweden's Pernilla Winberg (against Slovakia) and Switzerland's Stefanie Marty (against China).

Left: Meghan Agosta of Canada set a new scoring record at Vancouver 2010.

CANADA'S GOAL-SCORING BLITZ

The United States may have been the reigning world champions and the number one ranked team in the world going into the women's ice hockey tournament at the 2010 Winter Games in Vancouver, but defending champions Canada made a huge statement of intent in their opening game, beating Slovakia 18–0 (an Olympic record) and never looked back. The hosts kept up the pace, recording further wins over Switzerland (10–1) and Sweden (13–1) to win their group and then beating Finland (5–0) in the semi-finals to face, as expected, the United States in the gold-medal match. Two Marie-Philippe Poulin goals in the first period were enough to settle the match in Canada's favour, and as their players celebrated the country's third successive victory, they did so in the knowledge that they had achieved it in record-breaking fashion – their tally of 48 goals in the tournament is the highest of all time.

Below: Canada wins gold at home in 2010.

HOSTS ITALY IN RECORD-BREAKING TROUBLE

Like Japan at the 1998 Winter Games in Nagano, Italy faced the problem of having to field a team in the women's ice hockey event at the 2006 Winter Games in Turin without having a strong tradition in the game. And, as had been the case in Nagano eight years earlier, the hosts floundered, losing all five of their matches, scoring only three goals and conceding a colossal 48 – an all-time tournament record.

IIHF Women's World Championships

Considered the most prestigious event in women's ice hockey outside the Winter Games, the IIHF Women's World Championships were staged for the first time in 1990 in Ottawa, Canada, some 70 years after the inaugural men's competition had taken place. Every one of the event's gold medal matches has been between Canada and the United States, with Canada winning nine of them and the United States four.

ONLY OTHER CHAMPIONS

It was a case of close but not close enough for the United States in the early years of the IIHF World Championships: they reached every one of the tournament's first eight finals between 1990 and 2004, but lost every one of them to Canada. And then came 2005: the United States beat their North American neighbours to claim the title for the first time. They lost out to Canada in the 2007 final (5–1), but have added further titles in 2008, 2009 and 2011 and remain the only other country apart from Canada to have earned the world champions tag.

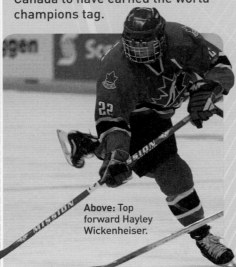

Above: Top forward Hayley Wickenheiser.

MOST AWARDS AS BEST FORWARD

Three women have collected the Directorate Award for the best forward at the IIHF Women's World Championships on two occasions: Finland's Rikka Niemenen (in 1990 and 1994); the United States' Jayna Hefford (in 2004 and 2005); and Canada's Hayley Wickenheiser (in 2007 and 2009).

REGAL RATY

Considered something of a childhood prodigy in her homeland (she made her debut for Finland's national team aged 15 and made her first appearance at the Winter Games, at Turin 2006, as a 16-year-old), Noora Raty is considered to be one of the leading goaltenders in the women's game. And she has shone at the IIHF Women's World Championships too, picking up three bronze medals (in 2008, 2009 and 2011), and is the only women in the tournament's history to have collected the Directorate Award for the competition's best goaltender on three occasions (in 2007, 2008 and 2011).

Right: Finland's Noora Raty has been the best goaltender at the IIHF Women's World Championships in recent years.

SHOOTOUT IN SWEDEN

It seemed as though the United States were set to be always the bridesmaids at the IIHF Women's World Championships. They had made it to every one of the first eight finals, only to lose to Canada on each occasion (in 1997 and 2000, agonizingly, they lost in overtime). But it was Canada's turn to suffer heartbreak at the 2005 Championships held in Sweden. After the gold medal match had ended in a 0–0 stalemate after overtime, the United States won the shootout to become world champions for the first time in their history. It is the only time in the tournament's history that a final has been settled by a shootout.

Above: Canada celebrate their 2007 Championship.

A CAREER TO SAVOUR

When Jennifer Botterill bowed out of international ice hockey following Canada's triumph at the 2010 Winter Games in Vancouver, she could look back on her hugely successful career with an enormous sense of satisfaction. She had won three Olympic gold medals (in 2002, 2006 and 2010), had been a world champion on five occasions (in 1999, 2000, 2001, 2004 and 2007), had set the all-time Harvard University scoring record in the NCAA (149 goals, 170 assists and 319 points) and is the only player in IIHF Women's World Championships' history to have won the tournament MVP award on two occasions (in 2001 and 2004).

DOMINANT CANADA

Canada found their stride in the first-ever IIHF Women's World Championships staged in Ottawa in 1990, comfortably winning all three of their group games (scoring 50 goals and conceding just one in the process), before beating Finland 6–5 in the semi-finals and the United States in the final (5–2). It was a sign of things to come: Canada have gone on to win the title on a further eight occasions (including the first seven in a row) and have featured in every one of the competition's 13 finals.

ALWAYS THE BRONZE

If the IIHF Women's World Championships final has been the exclusive preserve of Canada and the United States over the years (the two countries have contested every one of the 13 finals), the bronze medal match has virtually belonged to Finland. The Finns have played in all 13 third-fourth playoff matches, winning ten of them (a record) and losing three (to Russia in 2001 and to Sweden in 2005 and 2007).

OVERTIME JOY FOR CANADA

When Canada won their 1997 IIHF Women's World Championships gold medal match against the United States, the competition's most successful team had just come closer to defeat than they ever had before. Canada led 1–0 after the first period, the scores were locked at 2–2 after the second period and at 3–3 at the end of regulation time; it took an overtime goal (the first in a final in the tournament's history) before Canada could celebrate their fourth successive crown.

Right: Angela Ruggiero has won the Directorate Award four times as the best defenceman.

RECORD-BREAKING RUGGIERO

A four-time medallist at the Winter Games (one of them gold, at Nagano 1998), a three-time world champion (in 2005, 2008 and 2009) and the most capped United States player of all time, Angela Ruggiero's reputation as one of the best defencemen in women's ice hockey has been enhanced by her performances at the IIHF Women's World Championships. The Californian is the only player in the event's history to have collected the Directorate Award for the tournament's best defenceman on four occasions – in 2000, 2004, 2005 and 2008.

MEDALS WON (BY COUNTRY)

Pos	Medals	Country	G	S	B
1	13	Canada	9	4	0
=	13	United States	4	9	0
3	10	Finland	0	0	10
4	2	Sweden	0	0	2
5	1	Russia	0	0	1

Chapter 6
CURLING

Wherever snow has fallen or ice has formed, mankind has found a way to use Mother Nature's gifts as a platform upon which to compete. As a result, numerous less heralded sports are contested on these surfaces, among them: curling, which made its debut at the Winter Olympic Games in 1924 and which has a World Championship that dates back to 1959; ice stock (which originated in Germany); and broomball and ringette (which can trace their roots to North America).

Above: Kevin Martin of Canada shoots the stone, watched by Marc Kennedy in the Winter Games men's curling gold medal match against Norway at Vancouver 2010. The Canadians won the match and gold medal 6–3.

Men's Curling: Olympic Games

The ancient sport of curling was contested at the Winter Games for the first time in 1924 and, despite the fact that World Championships in the sport had been held on an annual basis since 1959, it had to wait until Nagano 1998 before it reappeared on the full-medal programme at the Games (although curling did appear as a demonstration sport on three occasions). Canada have been the event's most successful team, winning two gold medals.

Above: Norway's Torger Nergaard is a two-time curling medallist.

MOST MEDALS

The record for the most medals won in men's curling at the Winter Games is two, held by three men; Canada's Kevin Martin (gold at Vancouver 2010 and silver at Salt Lake City 2002); Norway's Torger Nergaard (gold at Salt Lake City 2002 and silver at Vancouver 2010); and Switzerland's Markus Eggler (bronze at Salt Lake City 2002 and at Vancouver 2010).

THE CLOSEST FINAL IN HISTORY

The men's curling final at the 2002 Winter Games in Salt Lake City was the closest in the event's history. The destination of the gold medal in the final between Norway and strong pre-tournament favourites Canada came down to the very last shot of the final end with the scores locked at 5–5. Norway held the winning lead, but Canada's Kevin Martin still had one stone to play: it took the right line but was fractionally too heavy, slipping past the required mark to hand Norway a surprise victory.

Left: Norway took gold in 2002.

AN UNUSUAL EVENT

The first men's curling competition at the Winter Games was full of anomalies: Sweden fielded two entirely different teams in their group matches against France (which they won 19–10) and Great Britain (which they lost 38–7), with their second team beating France for a second time in the silver-medal match (18–10). Unusually, both of Sweden's teams were then awarded a silver medal; even more unusually, Major D.G. Astley, who had played for Great Britain's victorious team, also played for Sweden in the playoff match, thus becoming the only person in history to have won both a gold and a silver medal in the same event at the Olympic Games.

OLDEST MALE MEDALLISTS

Carl August Verner Kronlund of Sweden holds the distinction of being the oldest male medallist in the history of the Winter Games. He was 58 years 157 days old when he picked up a silver medal in men's curling at the 1924 Winter Games in Chamonix. The oldest gold medallist in Winter Games history is Robin Welsh Sr, who was 54 years 101 days old when he won gold in men's curling for Great Britain at the 1924 Games.

SWISS SHOCK AT NAGANO

When men's curling made a welcome return to the full-medal programme at the 1998 Winter Games in Nagano, Sweden were the defending world champions (having surprisingly taken the title in Bern, Switzerland, the previous year). However, Canada were the firm favourites for gold – the country had won 24 of the 39 World Championships contested and, more tellingly, contained 90 per cent of the world's curlers. Canada duly made it to the final, but to general surprise found themselves 9–1 down to Switzerland after six of the ten ends and could not close the gap. Switzerland held on to win 9–3 and celebrated an unlikely gold medal.

Below: Switzerland upset Canada to win gold in the 1998 final.

Above: Canada won gold at Turin 2006.

BACK-TO-BACK JOY FOR CANADA

Canada had narrowly failed to strike gold in the men's curling competition at the previous two Winter Games in 1998 and 2002 when, despite starting as favourites, they had lost both finals, and that pattern of disappointment looked set to continue at Turin 2006 when they slipped to defeat against Sweden (8–7), Finland (8–7) and Italy (7–6) and had to win both of their remaining round-robin matches to qualify for the semi-finals. They did, then beat the United States in the last four (11–5) and Finland in the final (10–4) to win Olympic gold for the first time. The Canadians suffered no such anxiety in Vancouver four years later, winning all nine of their round-robin matches and beating Sweden in the semi-final (6–3) and Norway in the final (6–3) to become the first team in men's curling history to make a successful defence of its Olympic crown.

MOST MEDALS WON (BY COUNTRY)

Pos	Medals	Country	G	S	B
1	4	Canada	2	2	-
2	3	Switzerland	1	2	-
=	3	Norway	1	1	1
4	2	Sweden	-	2	-
5	1	Great Britain	1	-	-
=	1	Finland	-	1	-
=	1	France	-	-	1
=	1	United States	-	-	1

BRITAIN BREEZE TO INAUGURAL GOLD

The original entry list for the men's curling competition at the 1924 Winter Games in Chamonix (the first time the event had been staged at the Olympics) featured four teams: hosts France, Great Britain, Sweden and Switzerland. However, shortly before the event got underway, Switzerland withdrew its team (which was a shame because they were the only team expected to provide Great Britain with any real competition). As it was, the British team, made up entirely of Scots, romped to the gold medal, easing to lop-sided victories over both Sweden (38–7) and France (46–4) to become the sport's first-ever Olympic champions.

World Men's Curling Championships

Organized by the World Curling Federation and considered the sport's premier competition outside of the Winter Games, the World Men's Curling Championships were staged for the first time in 1959 in Scotland and have been staged on an annual basis ever since. Canada have enjoyed runaway success in the event, winning 33 of the 53 tournaments staged.

Right: Canada's skip Jeff Stoughton with the World Championship trophy in 2011.

MEDALS WON (BY COUNTRY)

Pos	Medals	Country	G	S	B
1	47	Canada	33	8	6
2	31	Scotland	5	19	7
3	21	United States	4	5	12
4	17	Sweden	5	6	6
5	16	Switzerland	3	6	7
=	16	Norway	3	4	9
7	10	Germany	-	5	5
8	2	Denmark	-	-	2
=	2	Finland	-	-	2
10	1	France	-	-	1

MOST CHAMPIONSHIPS WON AS A PLAYER

The record for the most gold medals won at the World Men's Curling Championships is four, set by four players: Ernie Richardson, Arnold Richardson and Garnet Richardson, who were all part of Canada's title-winning teams in 1959, 1960, 1962 and 1963; and another Canadian, Randy Ferbey, who equalled his compatriots' feat when he took gold in 1989, 2002, 2003 and 2005.

Left: Canada's four-time world champion Randy Ferbey (front).

CANADA RULE THE ICE

It was a family affair for Canada at the inaugural World Men's Curling Championships (known as the Scotch Cup until 1969) held in Scotland in 1959, and brothers Ernie and Garnet Richardson and their cousins Arnold and Wes Richardson did their country proud. They may have been favoured by the use of Canadian rules throughout the tournament – which allowed the delivery of the stone to the length of the near hogline – but they beat Scotland (the only other country to enter the event) in all five of the matches played to become the sport's first-ever world champions. It was the start of Canada's unprecedented run of success in the competition: they went on to win the first six tournaments (the event's longest winning streak); have won the title on 33 occasions; and have recorded more wins in the tournament (441 in 53 appearances in the competition) than any other country.

PISTOL PETE MAKES THE RECORD BOOKS

Nicknamed "Pistol Pete" for his notable accuracy, Scotland's Peter Smith has never appeared on the podium at the Winter Games, but he has left a considerable mark on the World Men's Curling Championships. He has played in eight finals – in 1986, 1990, 1991, 1993, 1996, 2006, 2008 and 2009 – the most by any player in the tournament's history.

Left: Scotland's eight-time finalist Pete Smith (centre) in action.

MOST MEDALS WON

The record for the most medals won at the World Men's Curling Championships is nine, held by two players: Norway's Eigil Ramsfjell (three gold – in 1979, 1984 and 1988; two silver – in 1978 and 1980; and four bronze – in 1983, 1987, 1989 and 1991); and Scotland's Peter Smith (three gold – in 1991, 2006 and 2009; five silver – 1986, 1990, 1993, 1996 and 2008; and one bronze – in 1988).

A YEAR OF FIRSTS

The 1967 World Men's Curling Championships marked a turning point in the history of the event. For the first time, Canada failed to finish in the top three – the defending champions' title defence came to an end when they lost to Scotland (8–5) in the semi-finals. Scotland's reward for beating Canada was a place in the final against Sweden, and the Scots won 8–5 to become the tournament's first-ever European champions.

NEAR MISSES FOR SCOTLAND

Although Scotland have won the title on five occasions (in 1967, 1991, 1999, 2006 and 2009), they have also had more than their fair share of tantalizing near misses. The Scots made six of the event's first eight finals and lost them all (every one of them to Canada) and amazingly have gone on to finish as runners-up a record 19 times.

MOST TOURNAMENTS AND MOST GAMES WON

Considered a pioneer of modern curling and a three-time world champion (in 1979, 1984 and 1988), Norway's Eigil Ramsfjell holds the all-time World Men's Curling Championships records for the most tournament appearances (15 between 1976 and 1996) and for the most games won by a player (103).

MOST LOSSES

The Germans may have enjoyed their fair of success at the World Men's Curling Championships, finishing as runners-up on five occasions (in 1983, 1987, 1997, 2004 and 2007), picking up the bronze medal on five occasions (in 1972, 1982, 1994, 1995 and 2005), and recording 177 wins, but no country has suffered more defeats in the tournament's history than Germany – 245 in 43 appearances between 1967 and 2011).

Below: Another near-miss for German skip Andy Kapp.

Women's Curling: Olympic Games

After two appearances as a demonstration sport (in 1988 and 1992), women's curling finally made its debut as a full-medal sport at the Winter Games at Nagano in 1998. In total, 12 countries have taken part in the competition, with Sweden enjoying the most success, winning back-to-back gold medals in 2006 and 2010.

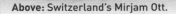

Above: Switzerland's Mirjam Ott.

MOST MEDALS WON (BY COUNTRY)

Pos	Medals	Country	G	S	B
1	4	Canada	1	1	2
2	3	Sweden	2	–	1
3	2	Switzerland	–	2	–
4	1	Great Britain	1	–	–
=	1	Denmark	–	1	–
=	1	China	–	–	1

MOST MEDALS WON

The record for the most gold medals won in the women's curling competition at the Winter Games is two, held by four players: Anette Norberg, Cathrine Lindahl, Eva Lund and Anna Le Moine were all part of Sweden's title-winning teams at Turin 2006 and Vancouver 2010. Along with Mirjam Ott of Switzerland, the Swedish quartet also hold the record for having appeared in the most finals (two).

MOST WINS/LOSSES

Although they have only won the gold medal on one occasion, Canada holds the record for the most games won in the women's curling competition at the Winter Games (33). The United States holds the unfortunate record of having suffered the most losses (24 in four tournament appearances between 1998 and 2010).

DEMONSTRATION PURPOSES ONLY

Women's curling made two appearances as a demonstration sport at the Winter Games: at Calgary 1988, when hosts Canada beat Sweden 7–5 in the final; and at Albertville 1992, when Germany finished with a resounding 9–2 victory over Norway.

Above: Canada won in 1998.

CANADA LIVE UP TO THEIR BILLING

As expected, given the country has more curlers than any other nation on the planet, Canada were the firm favourites to take gold at the Winter Games' inaugural women's curling competition at Nagano 1998. And the Canadians had an even greater reason to fancy their chances: they would be skippered by Sandra Schirmer, who had led them to gold in all three of the World Championships she had contested. And so it proved: Canada won six of their seven round-robin matches (losing only to Norway, 6–5), beat Great Britain in the semi-finals (6–5) and Denmark in the final (7–5) to become the event's first-ever Olympic champions.

MOST GAME WINS

As well as being one of only five players to have won two medals in women's curling at the Winter Games (she took silver medals at both Turin 2006 and Vancouver 2010), Switzerland's Mirjam Ott has won more matches in the competition that any other competitor in the tournament's history: 22 in three appearances in the competition.

YOUNGEST PARTICIPANT

Although her country only finished sixth out of the ten entrants in the women's curling competition at the 2010 Winter Games in Vancouver, Stella Heiss's appearance for Germany in the event earned her place in the record books: aged just 17 years 32 days at the time, she became the youngest person in history to compete in women's curling at the Olympics.

Above: Great Britain's Jackie Lockhart has made a record three appearances at the Winter Games.

MOST APPEARANCES

The record for the most appearances by a player in the women's curling competition at the Winter Games is three, held by six players: Russia's Nkeiruka Ezekh (in 2002, 2006 and 2010); Great Britain's Jackie Lockhart (in 1998, 2006 and 2010); Norway's Dordi Nordby and Marianne Haslum (in 1998, 2002 and 2006); the United States' Debbie McCormick (in 1998, 2002 and 2010); and Switzerland's Mirjam Ott (in 2002, 2006 and 2010).

Above: Sweden celebrate their last-gasp gold in 2006.

SWEDEN LEAVE IT LATE

The women's curling final at the 2006 Winter Games in Turin between Sweden and Switzerland was the closest in the event's history to date. At the end of the scheduled ten ends, the scores were locked at 6–6. But then Sweden's Anette Norberg took out two Swiss stones with her last stone of the first extra end to hand her country a first-ever gold medal in the event. At Vancouver four years later it was a case of déjà vu: this time, at the end of the ten scheduled ends in the final, Sweden were locked with Canada at 6–6; and once again Norberg was the heroine, scoring the only point in the first extra end to help her country become the only team in women's curling history to make a successful defence of its Olympic title.

THE BRITS CAUSE A SENSATION

Having dominated women's curling in the four years since their success in Nagano, Canada were widely expected to retain their Olympic title at Salt Lake City 2002, but their title defence came unstuck in dramatic fashion in the semi-finals against Great Britain (who had been forced to come through two tie-breakers just to be there). In the final shot of the fourth end, Canada's Kelly Law misjudged the line of her shot, pushed a British stone into the ring and surrendered two points. It was a crucial moment: a delighted Great Britain went on to win the match 6–5. They also came through a tense final against Switzerland (4–3, thanks to Rhona Martin's nerveless, game-clinching final stone) – in front of a British television audience of seven million – to become the first European country to take women's curling Olympic gold.

World Women's Curling Championships

The World Women's Curling Championships were staged for the first time in 1979 (some 20 years after the inaugural men's championships had taken place) in Perth, Scotland, and have been contested on an annual basis ever since. Canada has been the tournament's most successful team, winning gold on 15 occasions, most recently in 2008.

NOT THE BEST OF TIMES FOR UNCLE SAM

The performances of the United States have been one of the biggest disappointments at the World Women's Curling Championships. They have a poor record for a country with such a strong tradition in the sport, registering only one victory (in 2003), finishing runners-up on five occasions (in 1992, 1996, 1999, 2005 and 2006) and setting the unfortunate all-time competition record for having suffered defeat on more occasions than any other team, with 180 losses in 34 tournament appearances.

Right: Sweden's four-time world champion Louise Marmont barks out instructions.

MOST GOLD MEDALS WON BY A PLAYER

The record for the most gold medals won at the World Women's Curling Championships is four, held by four players: Louise Marmont, Elisabet Gustafson, Katarina Nyberg and Elisabeth Persson, who were all part of Sweden's title-winning teams in 1992, 1995, 1998 and 1999.

MOST CHAMPIONSHIP APPEARANCES

Two players hold the record for having made the most appearances at the World Women's Curling Championships (18): Norway's Dordi Nordby (between 1982 and 2006, winning two gold medals – in 1990 and 1991; three silver medals – in 1989, 1997 and 2002; and six bronze medals – in 1993, 1995, 1996, 2000, 2002 and 2005); and Germany's Andrea Schöpp (between 1985 and 2011, winning two gold medals – in 1988 and 2010; two silver medals – in 1986 and 1987; and one bronze medal – in 1989).

Above: No woman has been in as many World Championship finals as Anette Norberg.

MOST FINALS CONTESTED

Two players hold the competition's all-time record for having contested the most finals in World Women's Curling Championships (five): Norway's Dordi Nordby (in 1989, 1990, 1991, 1997 and 2004 – she won gold in 1990 and 1991); and Sweden's Anette Norberg (in 2001, 2005, 2006, 2009 and 2011 – she won gold in 2005, 2006 and 2011).

DEADLY DORDI'S ALL-TIME HIGHS

Dordi Nordby was the mainstay of Norway's women's curling team during an international career that spanned 26 years between 1981 and 2007, helping her country to back-to-back gold medals at the World Women's Curling Championships in 1990 and 1991 and setting numerous individual tournament records along the way. No woman has matched her 11 medals at the championships (two gold – in 1990 and 1991; three silver – in 1989, 1997 and 2004; and six bronze – in 1993, 1995, 1996, 2000, 2002 and 2005) or her 127 wins in 18 tournaments between 1982 and 2006.

Right: Dordi Nordby won 11 World Championship medals.

SENSATIONAL SWISS

The first-ever World Women's Curling Championships were staged in Perth, Scotland, between 17 and 23 March 1979 and featured 11 teams. Sweden led the standings after the round-robin phase (winning eight and losing two of their matches) and were joined in the semi-finals by Canada, Switzerland and hosts Scotland. And that is when the action hotted up: as expected, Sweden beat Scotland (7–5) in the first of the last-four matches; in the second, Switzerland produced a major shock when they beat pre-tournament favourites Canada (6–3). And the Swiss were in irrepressible form in the final too, crushing Sweden 13–5 to become the sport's first-ever world champions. They won again in 1983 (to become the event's first two-time winners) and claimed a third world crown in 2012.

CLASSY CANADA

No country has enjoyed more success at the World Women's Curling Championships than Canada. They took the title for the first time in 1980 (after picking up a bronze at the inaugural event in 1979), won again in 1984, defended the title in 1985 (to become the event's first three-time winners) and added further gold medals in 1986 and 1987 (their run of four straight wins is a tournament best). Their success did not end there: they have gone on to amass a record 15 tournament victories (most recently in 2008) and hold the record for the most game wins by a team in the tournament's history (294).

MOST MEDALS WON (BY COUNTRY)

Pos	Medals	Country	G	S	B
1	29	Canada	15	6	8
2	22	Sweden	8	7	7
3	13	Norway	2	4	7
4	10	Switzerland	3	2	5
=	10	Scotland	1	4	5
6	8	Germany	2	3	3
=	8	Denmark	1	2	5
8	6	United States	1	5	–
9	3	China	1	1	1

CHINA MAKE A BREAKTHROUGH

The 2009 World Women's Curling Championships held in Gangneung, South Korea, seemed to herald a new era in the sport. In 2008, China had caused a major surprise when they won a silver medal – after losing narrowly (7–4) to Canada in the final. The following year, the Chinese were sensational: they topped the standings after the round-robin phase (winning ten of 11 matches); beat Denmark 6–3 in the playoffs to qualify for the final; then they beat six-time winners Sweden (8–6) to become the first Asian world champions. Their best achievement since, however, is a bronze medal they won in 2011.

Left: China won a surprise gold medal at the 2009 World Championships.

Chapter 7
MISCELLANEOUS WINTER SPORTS

Several other winter sports are contested around the world, from the structured to the downright bizarre. Among the structured sports are: bandy, which has achieved enormous popularity in northern Europe; snowmobiling, which has a long-standing tradition in North America; ice swimming, which is gaining in popularity around the world; and ice fishing, where some competitions can attract thousands of contestants. Mass snowball fighting and snowman building are some of the "sports" grouped in the bizarre category.

Above: Action from Sweden's Bandy Premier League Elitserien in 2010 as Hammarby's Willie Johansson (left) shoots the ball into the goal past Sirius goalie Jakob Saleby.

Bandy

A cross between football and ice hockey, bandy sees two teams of 11 players on skates attempt to get a small ball into the other team's goal using sticks. There are currently three major international competitions for men: the Bandy World Championships (for countries), the Bandy World Cup and the Bandy Champions Cup (both for clubs) and numerous domestic leagues, most notably in Russia, Sweden and Finland. The Women's Bandy World Championships were staged for the first time in 2004.

FIRST BANDY WORLD CUP WINNERS

The Bandy World Cup is a tournament contested by the leading bandy club teams in the world, and has been held every year in Ljusdal, Sweden – except between 2009 and 2011 when it was staged in Sandviken while Ljusdal's indoor arena was being built. It was contested for the first time in 1974, and what a tournament it proved: two Swedish sides – Sandvikens AIK and Broberg/Söderhamn – made it through to the final, with Sandvikens AIK ultimately claiming the spoils 4–2 after the match had gone first to additional time and then to penalties.

Right: Hammarby's Patrik Nilsson (front) in Elitserien action.

MOST BANDY WORLD CUP TITLES

No club has won more Bandy World Cup titles than Sweden's IF Boltic. They took the title for the first time in 1980, retained it in 1981 (becoming only the second team in the competition's history to achieve the feat) and added further titles in 1985, 1986, 1995 and 1996. The Karlstad-based team, who merged with IF Karlstad-Göta to form the new club BS BolticGöta in 2000, are the only team in the tournament's history to have successfully defended their title on three occasions.

DEMONSTRATION SPORT AT THE WINTER GAMES

Bandy has made one appearance as a demonstration sport at the Winter Games, at Oslo in 1952. Three teams took part in the event (hosts Norway, Finland and Sweden), with Sweden proclaimed the winners (on goal difference) after all three teams had won one and lost one of their two games. The sport will reappear as a demonstration event at the 2014 Winter Games in Sochi, Russia, and hopes are high that it will be added to the full-medal programme for the 2018 Winter Games in Pyeongchang, South Korea.

MOST MEDALS WON

They may have been forced to play second fiddle to the Soviet Union in the early years of the Bandy World Championships (losing to them in seven finals between 1961 and 1979), but Sweden have gone on to win more medals in the championship than any other country with a total of 32 – ten gold, 15 silver and seven bronze.

DYNAMO MAKE AN IMPACT

Twenty-time Soviet/Russian champions and six-time European champions Dynamo Moscow chose not to take part in the Bandy Champions Cup in 2005, 2007 and 2009, but when they have played in the tournament they have made a considerable impact. In 2006, they beat compatriots Zorky in the final to win the event for the first time and, when they returned in 2008, they beat hosts Edsbyn to become the competition's first two-time winners.

MOST SUCCESSFUL COUNTRY

No country has enjoyed more title-winning success at the Bandy World Championships than the Soviet Union. The unchallenged kings of the competition in its early years, they won 11 straight titles between 1957 (the competition's inaugural year) and 1979. Their record-breaking run in the tournament finally came to an end in 1981, when Sweden took the title on goal difference. The Soviet Union went on to add further titles in 1985, 1989 and 1991 to take their record haul of gold medals to 14.

BROBERG/SÖDERHAMN BOUNCE BACK

Swedish club Broberg/Söderhamn may have suffered the bitter taste of defeat in the first-ever Bandy World Cup final in 1974, but they rebounded in spectacular fashion the following year, gaining revenge by beating Sandvikens AIK (their conquerors the previous year) 3–2 to win the trophy for the first time. The success did not end there: they beat fellow Swedish club IK Sirius 6–1 in the 1977 final (to become the event's first two-time winners) and Ljusdals BK (4–1) in the 1978 final (to become the first team in the event's history to make a successful defence of their title). A fourth title, the last in the club's history, was won in 1983.

Above: Sweden's Anna Jepson (centre) taking on Finland at the 2004 Bandy World Championships.

BANDY WORLD CHAMPIONSHIPS – MEDALS WON (BY COUNTRY)

Pos	Medals	Country	G	S	B
1	32	Sweden	11	15	7
2	27	Finland	1	7	19
3	17	Soviet Union	14	2	1
4	15	Russia	6	8	1
5	3	Kazakhstan	–	–	3
6	2	Norway	–	1	1

Above: Russia celebrate winning the 2008 Bandy World Championships.

MIXED FORTUNES FOR ZORKIY

Russian side Zorkiy's early experiences in the Bandy Champions Cup ended in disappointment. They lost the first three finals they contested (a tournament record): against Dynamo Moscow in 2006, against Edsbyn in 2007 and against Dynamo Kazan in 2008. Two years later, however, they were in the final again and beat Dynamo Moscow to win the title for the first time. They then beat Swedish outfit Bollnas in the 2011 final to become the first team in the tournament's history to make a successful title defence.

FIRST BANDY CHAMPIONS CUP WINNERS

A pre-season tournament held in Edsbyn, Sweden, the FIB Champions Cup was staged for the first time in 2004, with six clubs from Sweden and two from Russia competing for the trophy. Russian champions Vodnik (based in Arkhangelsk) emerged victorious, beating tournament hosts Edsbyn in the final to become the event's inaugural champions.

Other Men's Team Sports

Other winter games team sports played by men include: broomball, a variant of ice hockey in which players hit a ball (rather than a puck) with sticks called "brooms"; ice stock, also known as "Bavarian curling", which has made two appearances at the Winter Olympic Games and has its own World Championships; and snow rugby, which is increasing in popularity around the world.

Above: Broomball can trace its origins to Canada.

BROOMBALL

Similar to ice hockey, broomball is a team game that originated in Canada and which is contested on an ice rink between two teams of six players. Players hit a small ball around the ice towards a goal with a small stick, called a "broom". The sport is particularly popular in North America (especially in the Canadian province of Manitoba – where Glenella is considered the broomball capital of the world), but it has also reached other parts of the world, notably Australia and Japan.

SNOW RUGBY

Snow rugby is a form of rugby union that has been specially adapted to be played in winter conditions and is notably popular in, among other places, the Argentinian Ski Resort of Las Leñas, the Kashmir region in India (in 2009, Gulmarg hosted India's first-ever snow rugby tournament), Latvia, Canada and northern USA. During the 2011 Rugby World Cup, Mount Dobson, in New Zealand, hosted a specially created "20 Below Rugby in the Snow" seven-a-side tournament.

ICE STOCK WORLD CHAMPIONSHIPS: TEAM GAME

The team competition is one of three events staged at the Ice Stock World Championships, with Italy winning the inaugural event held in Frankfurt, Germany, in 1983. Germany has been the most successful team in the event, taking gold on a record six occasions – in 1990, 1998, 2002, 2004, 2008 and 2012.

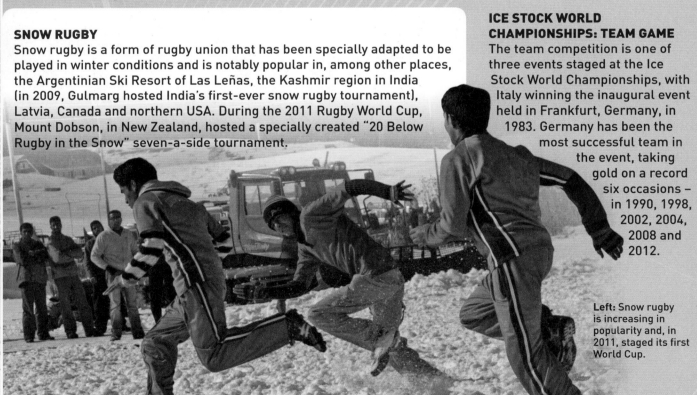

Left: Snow rugby is increasing in popularity and, in 2011, staged its first World Cup.

ICE STOCK WORLD CHAMPIONSHIPS: TARGET COMPETITION

The target competition, in which participants aim to deliver their stone as close to possible to a puck, is another event staged at the Ice Stock World Championships. Germany took the inaugural title at Frankfurt in 1983 and have gone on to enjoy the most success in the event, claiming a record five gold medals: in 1987, 1990, 1994 and 2002.

Left: An ice stock match on a frozen lake in Bavaria, Germany.

Right: Ice stock action at the 2008 Festival of Ice Sports.

ICE STOCK WORLD CHAMPIONSHIPS: WIDE COMPETITION

The wide competition, in which participants aim to propel their stone as far as possible along the ice, is another event staged at the Ice Stock World Championships. Germany took the inaugural title at Frankfurt in 1983, but Austria have since gone on to enjoy the most success in the event, claiming a record seven gold medals: in 1987, 1990, 1994, 2002, 2004, 2008 and 2012.

WORLD BROOMBALL CHAMPIONSHIPS

The first World Broomball Championships (known at the time as the Challenge Cup) were staged in Victoria, British Columbia, Canada, in 1991, and featured over 800 athletes representing 44 teams. The championships are currently held in even-numbered years. Canada's Embrun Plumbing took the first men's title, and another Canadian team has been the most successful in the competition's history: the Le Frost team is unique in having won three titles, emerging as victors in 2006, 2008 and 2010.

MEN'S ICE STOCK WORLD CHAMPIONSHIPS MEDALS WON (BY COUNTRY) – TEAM GAME COMPETITION

Pos	Medals	Country	G	S	B
1	9	Germany	6	2	1
2	8	Italy	2	2	4
3	7	Austria	1	4	2
4	1	Slovenia	-	1	-
=	1	Yugoslavia	-	-	1
=	1	Switzerland	-	-	1

MEN'S ICE STOCK WORLD CHAMPIONSHIPS MEDALS WON (BY COUNTRY) – TARGET COMPETITION

Pos	Medals	Country	G	S	B
1	9	Germany	5	3	1
2	8	Austria	2	2	4
3	6	Italy	1	3	2
4	2	Switzerland	-	1	1
5	1	Slovenia	1	-	-
=	1	Czech Republic	-	-	1

MEN'S ICE STOCK WORLD CHAMPIONSHIPS MEDALS WON (BY COUNTRY) – WIDE COMPETITION

Pos	Medals	Country	G	S	B
1	9	Austria	7	2	-
=	9	Germany	2	7	-
3	8	Italy	-	-	8
4	1	United States	-	-	1

ICE STOCK DEMONSTRATION SPORT AT THE WINTER GAMES

Ice stock, a sport similar to curling, has featured as a demonstration sport at the Winter Olympics on two occasions, not surprisingly when the Games were hosted by places where ice stock has traditionally been played – at Garmisch-Partenkirchen in 1936 and at Innsbruck in 1964. There has been talk of the sport making further appearances at the Games but, as yet, to no avail.

Other Women's Team Sports

Other winter games team sports contested by women include: ringette, a version of ice hockey developed in Canada in the 1960s specifically for women; broomball, another version of ice hockey in which players use sticks called "brooms" to propel the ball around the ice; and ice stock, a version of curling, which was developed in Germany and enjoys a large following in Europe's alpine countries.

WOMEN'S ICE STOCK WORLD CHAMPIONSHIPS
MEDALS WON (BY COUNTRY) – TEAM GAME COMPETITION

Pos	Medals	Country	G	S	B
1	8	Germany	5	3	-
2	7	Austria	3	2	2
=	7	Italy	1	-	6
4	4	Switzerland	-	3	1
5	1	Czech Republic	-	1	-

WORLD BROOMBALL CHAMPIONSHIPS

The women's World Broomball Championships were held for the first time in 2004 in Corner Brook, Newfoundland, and Labrador, Canada (some 13 years after the inaugural men's tournament had taken place), with home favourites Durham Angels picking up the gold medal. Every one of the competitions has seen a different winner, with Minnesota Selects winning in 2006, McMillan Sand and Gravel champions in 2008 and Italy Girls claiming a surprise title in 2012.

Left: The first women's World Broomball Championships were staged in 2004.

NATIONAL RINGETTE LEAGUE

Following the huge success of the 2002 World Ringette Championships in Edmonton, at which hosts Canada took gold, the National Ringette League (NRL) was founded and contested for the first time in 2004–05, with 13 teams taking part. The format of the competition was settled in the second season (2005–06), with teams split into two conferences to contest a regular season and then with the teams with the best record progressing into the playoffs to determine which two teams will contest a championship final. The all-time NRL record for the most championships won is three, and is shared by the Cambridge Turbos (winners in 2005–06, 2007–08 and 2008–09) and Edmonton Wow! (2006–07, 2009–10 and 2010–11).

Above: Ringette's popularity is spreading fast with the National Ringette League eight years old.

THE FIRST WORLD RINGETTE CHAMPIONSHIP

Initially staged every other year but now staged every three years, the World Ringette Championships (in which teams vie for the Sam Jacks Cup) were contested for the first time in Gloucester, Canada, in 1990, with teams from three countries (Canada, Finland and the United States) taking part. As expected, given they had created the sport, teams from Canada dominated the podium, with Alberta taking gold, Ontario silver and Quebec bronze.

WOMEN'S ICE STOCK WORLD CHAMPIONSHIPS MEDALS WON (BY COUNTRY) – TARGET COMPETITION

Pos	Medals	Country	G	S	B
1	9	Germany	4	5	-
=	9	Italy	1	2	6
3	7	Austria	4	2	1
4	1	Switzerland	-	-	1
=	1	Czech Republic	-	-	1

RINGETTE

First introduced in 1963 in North Bay, Ontario, Canada, ringette is a fast-paced team sport on ice (developed specifically for girls) in which players use a straight stick to pass, carry and shoot a rubber ring across the ice to score goals. Although predominantly a Canadian sport (the country has 50,000 registered players), ringette has enjoyed increasing popularity around the world, notably in the United States, Finland, Sweden, Russia and the Czech Republic.

FLYING FINNS

Finland ended the Canadian sides' domination of the World Ringette Championship by winning the title for the first time in 1994, the third edition of the event (held in Saint Paul, Minnesota, USA) and have gone on to enjoy unprecedented success in the competition, claiming further gold medals in 2000, 2004, 2007 and 2010. Their haul of five titles is an all-time competition record.

ICE STOCK WORLD CHAMPIONSHIPS: TARGET COMPETITION

The target competition was contested for the first time at the inaugural championships in 1983, with Italy taking a surprise gold. Germany (in 1987, 2002, 2008 and 2012) and Austria (in 19990, 1994, 1998 and 2004) have been the most successful countries in the event, winning four gold medals each.

ICE STOCK WORLD CHAMPIONSHIPS: TEAM GAME

The Ice Stock World Championships for women were held for the first time at Frankfurt, Germany, in 1983 (the same time as the inaugural men's tournament), with the hosts winning the first gold medal. It was a sign of things to come: the Germans have since gone to register a record five victories in the competition: in 1983, 1990, 1998, 2002 and 2004.

WORLD CHAMPIONSHIPS OF CLUBS

Ringette's World Championships of Clubs tournament, in which the six best teams from around the world played to determine the best club team on the planet, was contested for the first time in November 2008 at Sault Ste Marie in Canada. Ontario-based club Cambridge Turbos won the tournament after winning all five of their matches. The second championships were staged in Turku, Finland, between December 2011 and January 2012, with home favourites Lapinlahden Luistin-89 beating compatriots Raision Nuorisokiekko Ry 5–4 in the final to take the gold medal.

Snowmobiling

Ever since the birth of the modern snowmobile in the late 1950s, people have been finding ways to race them. There are several snowmobiling competitions: the World Championship Snowmobile Derby, the International 500, the World Championships Snowmobile Hill Climb and Iron Dog; and snowmobiling has featured at the Winter X Games for a number of years.

ANOTHER FAMOUS VILLENEUVE

The younger brother of Gilles Villeneuve and the uncle of Jacques (winner of the F1 World Championship with Williams), Jacques Villeneuve Sr may not have hit the heady heights of his more famous relatives in the world of Formula One (he tried to qualify for three races between 1981 and 1983 but failed to make it on to the starting grid on each occasion), but he did make considerable waves in the sport of snowmobiling. The Canadian, known as "Uncle Jacques" following the subsequent rise in fame of his nephew, won the World Championship Snowmobile Derby for the first time in 1980, collected a second title in 1982 and became the event's first three-time winner following his success in 1986. Two men (Dave Wahl and P.J. Wanderscheid) have gone on to equal his feat, but no one has bettered it.

Right: Jacques Villeneuve Sr made his name in the world of snowmobiling.

HUMBLE BEGINNINGS

Although the event now attracts over 1,400 entrants and in excess of 30,000 spectators, the World Championship Snowmobile Derby came from humble origins. Innkeeper John Alward, who had a couple of snowmobiles in his garage, decided to organize a rally event among his friends around Dollar Lake, Wisconsin, and the honour of winning the first-ever race in 1964 went to Stan Hayes, who was then an eighth-grade student. Within a few years the race, which is now held on the Eagle River Derby Track, had become one of the premier snowmobile events in the world.

TRAPP CAUSES A STIR

Wisconsin's Mike Trapp caused an enormous stir at the 1971 World Championship Snowmobile Derby when he rode his 440cc Yamaha vehicle to a surprise victory against several factory team 650cc snowmobiles. His feat earned him a factory ride on a Yamaha 650 the following year, when he won the Derby again to become the first rider in the event's history to make a successful defence of his title.

FIRST TWO-TIME INTERNATIONAL 500 WINNER

Grant Hawkins of Petoskey, Michigan, first tasted success in the International 500 when he partnered Mike Chisholm to victory on their Yamaha snowmobile in 1977. He won again in 1980 (partnered by Ed Goldsmith on this occasion) to become the event's first two-time winner.

ONE OF THE BEST IN THE BUSINESS

One of the most durable and successful snowmobile drivers in history, John Wicht III enjoyed 25-year career in the sport and achieved unparalleled success at the International 500. He won the event for the first time in 1988, claimed back-to-back triumphs in 1992 and 1993 (becoming only the second person in the event's history – after Brian Musselman in 1984 and 1985 – to achieve the feat) and took the crown for a record-breaking fourth time in 1995. His achievements in the sport led to his induction in the Snowmobile Hall of Fame in 2003.

Right: A crash between Brian Bewcyk (39) and Dustin Wahl (74).

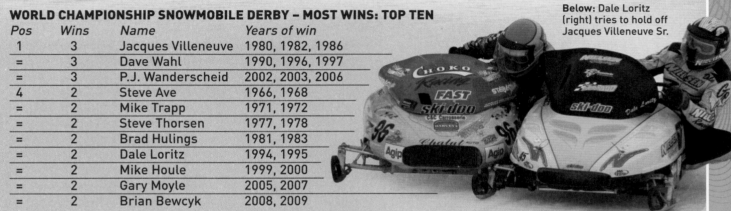

Below: Dale Loritz (right) tries to hold off Jacques Villeneuve Sr.

WORLD CHAMPIONSHIP SNOWMOBILE DERBY – MOST WINS: TOP TEN

Pos	Wins	Name	Years of win
1	3	Jacques Villeneuve	1980, 1982, 1986
=	3	Dave Wahl	1990, 1996, 1997
=	3	P.J. Wanderscheid	2002, 2003, 2006
4	2	Steve Ave	1966, 1968
=	2	Mike Trapp	1971, 1972
=	2	Steve Thorsen	1977, 1978
=	2	Brad Hulings	1981, 1983
=	2	Dale Loritz	1994, 1995
=	2	Mike Houle	1999, 2000
=	2	Gary Moyle	2005, 2007
=	2	Brian Bewcyk	2008, 2009

INTERNATIONAL 500 – FIRST WINNER

Born out of the question someone had posed, after watching motor-racing's Indianapolis 500 in 1968, as to whether anyone could race a snowmobile over 500 miles, the inaugural International 500 was staged in Sault Ste Marie, Michigan, in 1969. Forty-seven contestants qualified for the race, with Don Planck crossing the line in first place – some 13 hours and 42 minutes after he had started – to become the event's inaugural winner. The race has been staged on an annual basis ever since.

Left: The green flag signals the start of the International 500 Snowmobile Race in 2007.

MOST INTERNATIONAL 500 VICTORIES

During a racing career that started when he was 18 years old and that now spans 22 years, Corey Davidson has set a record-blazing trail at the International 500. He won the event in 1998, with the Polaris team for whom he has raced for 16 years, and went on to defend his title for the next two years to become the first racer in the event's history to win three titles in a row. His success at the event did not end there: further triumphs followed in 2003, 2006, 2008 and 2011, and his haul of seven International 500 victories is an all-time record.

LEGEND GILLES VILLENEUVE'S FIRST STAR TURN

Gilles Villeneuve went on to achieve legendary status in the world of Formula One, winning six races for Ferrari and finishing second in the 1979 World Championships before his untimely death in 1982, but the Canadian had already found fame in snowmobiling. Although he had always harboured a love for fast cars, his first professional racing career came on a snowmobile, and he achieved his first major result of any significance in the sport when he won the World Championship Snowmobile Derby in 1974.

WORLD CHAMPIONSHIPS SNOWMOBILE HILL CLIMB

Staged for the first time in 1975, the World Championships Snowmobile Hill Climb is an annual event held at Jackson Hole, Wyoming, in which competitors race to reach the top of the Snow Hill Resort in as fast a time as possible. The 37th edition of the event was staged in March 2012.

SNOCROSS PIONEER

A former Canadian national champion in motocross, Blair Morgan, who was born in Saskatchewan, Canada, on 9 October 1975, started racing in snocross full time in 1997 and, with his high-flying, aggressive approach to racing, helped to revolutionize the sport. A five-time gold medallist at the Winter X Games, he crashed while practising for a motocross event (which, ironically, was going to be his last before he made a permanent switch to snocross) and was left paralysed from the chest down.

Right: Blair Morgan won five snocross gold medals in at the Winter X Games.

PLENTY OF PLAUDITS BUT NO MEDAL

It may not have brought them any honours, but brothers Colton and Caleb Moore had the crowd on their feet during the best snowmobile competition at the 2011 Winter X Games in Aspen, Colorado. The brothers became the first pair in history to perform a two-man backflip during the event, but were later disqualified by the judges who ruled the event was an individual sport and awarded the gold medal to Sweden's Daniel Bodin.

FURTHEST DISTANCE COVERED IN 24 HOURS

When he discovered that his two-month-old daughter was suffering from a rare liver disease called biliary atresia, Illinois native Dustin Shoemaker decided to do something extraordinary to raise awareness of the condition. In February 2010, he went on an extraordinary journey, persevering through cold, hunger and pain to set a new world record for the most miles travelled in a snowmobile in 24 hours: 1,474 miles – to break the existing record by 67 miles.

SNOWMOBILE SPEED RECORD

The holy grail for speed snowmobilers is to break the 200mph barrier and, although no rider has yet reached that mark, plenty have come close: in 2009, in North Bay, Ontario, Canada, American Tom McKonkey rode his nitrous-enhanced vehicle to 190mph; a year later, in 2011, however, at the same venue, Dave Marshall went even better, reaching a speed of 191.8mph – the current world record.

IRON DOG LEGENDS

The record for the most wins in the legendary Iron Dog race is seven, and it is shared by two men, both of whom claimed a hat-trick of titles: John Faeo (who triumphed, with different partners, in 1984, 1986, 1987, 1988, 1990, 1991 and 1996); and his rival Scott Davis (who won it, again with different partners, in 1985, 1989, 1993, 1997, 1998, 1999 and 2007).

Left: Todd Palin (left) and Scott Davis before the 2009 Iron Dog race.

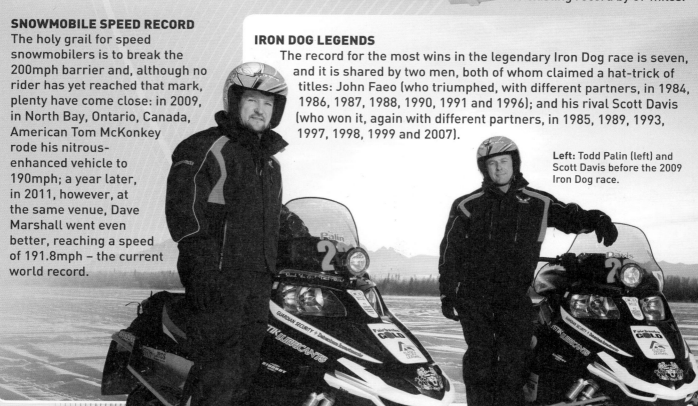

IRON DOG – ORIGINS AND FIRST CHAMPIONS

The longest snowmobile race in the world (it covers a course of 1,971 miles/3,172km), and the most challenging (contestants typically have to face temperatures approaching –20C), the Ice Dog event is staged in Alaska on an annual basis. The competition (contested by two-man teams for safety reasons as the course runs through some of the remotest parts of Alaska) was staged for the first time in 1984 and was won by John Faeo and Rod Frank.

FAMOUS IRON DOG COMPETITOR

He may be more famous for being the husband of former Alaska governor and the 2008 vice-presidential nominee for the Republican Party Sarah Palin, but John Palin has achieved notoriety in his own right for his performances at the Ice Dog race. He has competed at every race since 1993 and has won the event on four occasions, in 1995, 2000, 2002 and 2007 – only two men (John Faeo and Scott Davis) have more victories to their name.

MILEAGE MAN SETS NEW MARK

An avid snowmobiler known in his native Minnesota as "Mileage Man", Nick Keller lived up to his name between December 2010 and February 2011 when he tried to beat the record for the longest journey ever undertaken on a snowmobile that he had set the previous year (19,506 miles) as part of the Snowball Cancer Challenge. It was an astonishing success: on this occasion, he covered 22,150 miles in a 60-day period.

THE WORLD'S LONGEST SNOWMOBILE JUMP

In December 2011, Levi LaVallee, a four-time gold medallist at the Winter X Games, set out to beat the world record he had set the previous year for the longest jump ever recorded on a snowmobile (361 feet). And, undeterred by the fog that had started to settle over the course, he did it, improving his mark by 41 feet – the new world record now stood at 402 feet.

Left: Levi LaVallee leaps to a new world record distance at San Diego in December 2011.

Above: Heath Frisby pulls off his record-breaking front flip trick at the 2012 Winter X Games.

A FIRST FOR FRISBY

It was a move that not only earned him a gold medal in the Snowmobile Best Trick event at the 2012 Winter X Games at Aspen, Colorado, but also a place in the record books. During the competition, Idaho resident Heath Frisby, one of the best freestyle snowmobilers in the world, became the first person in history to land a front flip on a snowmobile – no mean feat on a machine that weighs more than 500lbs (226.8kg).

Recreational Winter Sports

There is a fine line between a recreational sport and a competitive one, and there is every chance that the sports featuring in the following pages will broaden their appeal and gain a wider following in the coming years. What is clear, however, is that human beings will endeavour to make the most out of any climate that confronts them: from ice swimming and ice sailing to mass snowball fights and snowman-making competitions, the spirit of adventure and competitiveness is very much alive even on the coldest of days.

BRAINERD ICE FISHING EXTRAVAGANZA

In the early 1990s, in an attempt to put Brainerd, Minnesota, on the map, locals came up with the idea for a project that would rally the community, raise money for local charities and attract tourists. As a result, in January 1991, the first Ice Fishing Extravaganza was staged. Over the years, the event has gone on to become the largest ice fishing competition in the world, with anglers competing for cash and prizes worth $150,000, and the tournament generating over $1 million in the area for local businesses and over $200,000 for local charities.

Left: Jerry Braumberger won at the 2008 Brainerd Jaycees Ice Fishing Extravaganza.

Right: Fishermen look through their ice holes for fish at the 2008 Brainerd Jaycees Ice Fishing Extravaganza.

THE ICE-SWIMMING MAIDEN

On 23 July 2011, Cecilia Schutte became the first woman (and the 18th person in history) to make it onto the International Ice Swimming Association's list of people who have swum at least one mile when the water temperature has been 5°C or less. The South African long-distance swimmer achieved the feat at Fraserburg's Nuwedam, in the northern Cape, swimming exactly one mile in 31 minutes 25 seconds in 5°C water.

FIRST REGISTERED ICE SWIM

According to the International Ice Swimming Association, the aim of ice swimming is to cover at least one mile when the water temperature is 5°C or less wearing nothing but a standard swimsuit. The first to achieve the feat was Ram Barkai, when he swam 1.37 miles in Lake Geneva on 31 January 2009 when the water was 4°C and the air temperature was −7.5°C. It took him 43 minutes to achieve the feat.

WORLD ICE AND SNOW SAILING CHAMPIONSHIP

The most prestigious winter sailing event in the world, the World Ice and Snow Sailing Championship was staged for the first time in 1980 in Helsinki, Finland, and is currently staged on an annual basis, with the host city alternating between Europe and North America. It is the only event in the world at which wings, kites and sails compete together on ice over various courses, from slalom to straight-line events.

WORLD ICE FISHING CHAMPIONSHIPS

The World Ice Fishing Championships, which typically feature competitors from between ten to 15 countries around the world, have been staged on an annual basis since the first event was contested in Latvia in 2004. Power augers for boring holes are not permitted at the event, nor are electronics of any kind; instead, anglers must carve a hole in the ice by hand and must rely on intuition, research, stamina, skill and experience to find and catch any fish during the two-day competition.

HWACHEON ICE FESTIVAL

Hwacheon, in Gangwon Province, is traditionally the first place in South Korea to freeze over (the river that runs through the county is soon covered with 16 inches of ice), and it celebrates the fact by hosting an annual Ice Festival, held throughout the month of January. The highlight of the event is a trout-grabbing competition: organizers carve in the region of 11,000 ice-fishing holes and invite competitors to grab as many trout as they can. It is estimated that as many as one million people travel to watch the event each year, making it the most watched ice-fishing event on the planet.

ICE SWIMMING PIONEER

A long-distance swimmer who found fame when she formed part of a team of teenagers who swam across California's Catalina Island Channel and subsequently twice broke the record for a woman for swimming across the English Channel in the fastest time, American Lynne Cox has been a true pioneer of ice swimming. In 1987, she swam across the Bering Strait (from Alaska to the then Soviet Union) in water that averaged 4°C, and she enhanced her reputation for fearlessness when, in 2003, she swam 1.22 miles in the icy waters of Antarctica. Her achievements have inspired a new generation of ice swimmers and, such is the esteem in which she is held, an asteroid has even been named after her.

Above: The United States' Lynne Cox set numerous benchmarks in ice swimming.

RAM SWAM IN THE COLDEST WATER

One of the most adventurous and famous open-water swimmers in the world (he has swum in both Antarctica and Alaska), South Africa-born Ram Barkai has set numerous ice swimming records. The first person to fulfil the International Ice Swimming Association's criteria of swimming a minimum of a mile in water with a temperature of five degrees Celsius or less, he has achieved the feat on four occasions (the only person in history to do so). The last time he achieved it, on 23 July 2011 at Loch Fiskaly in Scotland, the air temperature was a chilling −2.5°C and the water an icy 2°C. None of the 29 records set has been achieved in colder water.

INTERNATIONAL ICE SWIMMING ASSOCIATION COLDEST WATER TEMPERATURE SWIMS

Pos	Water temp	Name	Air temp	Location	Date
1	2°C	Ram Barkai	-2.5°C	Loch Fiskaly, Scotland	23 July 2011
2	3.3°C	Jason Malick	-10.5°C	Princeton Harbour, USA	15 Jan 2012
=	3.3°C	Lelané Roussow-Bancroft	-10.5°C	Princeton Harbour, USA	15 Jan 2012
4	4°C	Ram Barkai	-7.5°C	Lake Zurich, Switzerland	31 Jan 2009
5	4.4°C	Craig Lenning	4.4°C	Brainerd Lake, USA	10 July 2011
6	4.45°C	Karen Rogers	2.5°C	Lake Tahoe, USA	15 Jan 2012
=	4.45°C	Cathy Delneo	2.5°C	Lake Tahoe, USA	15 Jan 2012
8	4.5°C	Ram Barkai	5°C	Fraserburg, Nuwedam, SA	17 July 2010
=	4.5°C	Andrew Chin	5°C	Fraserburg, Nuwedam, SA	17 July 2010
=	4.5°C	Kieron Paltfarman	5°C	Fraserburg, Nuwedam, SA	17 July 2010
=	4.5°C	Rayn Stramrod	5°C	Fraserburg, Nuwedam, SA	17 July 2010
=	4.5°C	Toks Viviers	5°C	Fraserburg, Nuwedam, SA	17 July 2010
=	4.5°C	Theo Yach	5°C	Fraserburg, Nuwedam, SA	17 July 2010

Note: The International Ice Swimming Association stipulates that swimmers must swim at least one mile in a water temperature of 5°C or less

Above: The strange sight of the Belapl Hexe Festival takes place once a year in Valais, Switzerland.

BELALP HEXE

There can be no stranger downhill alpine skiing race in the world than that staged annually at the Belalp Hexe Festival held in the village of Belalp in Valais, Switzerland. To honour the local legend of a witch who was said to have been burned at the stake for the crime of murdering her husband, competitors take part in a race – known as the "Witches' Descent" – over a 7.5-mile course that drops 5,905 feet in altitude from start to finish. To make matters harder, participants undertake the challenge dressed in witches' costumes.

SHORTEST SNOWMAN

Measuring only 10 micrometres across, the world's smallest snowman was created by scientists at the National Physical Laboratory in Richmond upon Thames, London. It was made from two small balls normally used for calibrating electron microscopes. An ion beam was then used to etch the eyes, nose and even a smile on the little sculpture.

SHINNY

A hugely popular game for both men and women, the winter sport of shinny was developed by Native American tribes and, although various versions of the game exist, all of them are broadly similar to field hockey, with players using wooden sticks with a curved striking area to hit a ball (usually made of wood or stuffed animal skin) towards a goal (which could be marked by poles, mats or lines marked in the ground). However, teams can contain as many as a few hundred players for games played on a pitch that can vary in length from a few hundred yards to a mile.

Below: Shinny can trace its roots to Native American tribes.

FIRE AND ICE WINTER FEST

Every year in February, thousands of people descend on Lava Hot Springs in Idaho, USA, to take part in the Fire and Ice Winter Fest. The climax of the event sees participants competing in a tube race down the Portneuf River – the aim being either to set the fastest time or to complete the course wearing the most original costume.

WORLD'S LARGEST SNOWBALL FIGHT

The record for the largest number of participants in a single snowball fight is 5,837. The event was organized by Jong-Gi Park, the Mayor of Taebaek City, in Gangwondo province, South Korea, as a highlight for the 17th Mount Taebaek Snow Festival and took place at the Main Event Hall in Mount Taebaek on 22 January 2010. Given that the total population of Taebaek City is around 50,000, it means the record-setting event attracted roughly ten per cent of the city's population.

Right: Taking an icy plunge at the annual Slush Cup at Shanty Creek, Michigan.

MOST SNOWMEN BUILT IN ONE HOUR

The all-time record for the most snowmen built in one hour is 1,279, achieved by the American-based Clearlink group on the 18th fairway of the Mountain Dell Golf Course in Salt Lake City, Utah, USA, on 15 January 2011. Over 350 people took part in the record-setting exercise, building snowmen (who had to have two eyes and a carrot nose) for one hour between 12.45 pm until 1.45 pm.

SLUSH CUP AT SHANTY CREEK

Numerous strange winter festivals are staged around the world every year, but one of the strangest takes place at the Shanty Creek ski resort in northern Michigan, USA. For the past 30 years, contestants have taken part in the Slush Cup: a downhill competition for skiers or snowboarders, often clad in a variety of fancy-dress costumes, which culminates in a slide across a 40-foot icy pond. Other events at the festival include a frozen fish toss and a seal slide.

ICE CRICKET WORLD CUP

It could not be further removed from cricket in its traditional guise – with the comforting sound of leather striking willow on a beautiful summer's day – but ice cricket, a six-a-side version of the game played, naturally, on ice is increasing in popularity, and the Baltic country of Latvia has gained a reputation as the sport's spiritual home. In recent years, an Ice Cricket World Cup has been staged annually in the country's capital Tallinn, with past winners of the event hailing from Gibraltar, England, Australia and, most recently, the West Indies.

QUEBEC WINTER CARNIVAL

The Quebec Winter Carnival, in Quebec City, Canada, bills itself as the world's largest winter festival. It is best known for its life-sized ice palace, its snow sculptures, and its snowman mascot, but the Winter Carnival also has a wild streak. In the extreme canoe race, paddlers navigate the frozen St Lawrence River's snow and ice obstacles. For sports fans, there's a horse derby on snow and a hysterical giant table football game with human-sized players attached to long metal rods in rows of three.

TALLEST SNOWMAN

The record height for a snowman is 122 foot, set by a team of hundreds of local people (including busloads of schoolchildren) led by Robin Zinchuk, the executive director of the local chamber of commerce in the town of Bethel, Maine, USA, on 26 February 2008. Over 13 million pounds of snow was used to build it.

Right: Contestants prepare for the extreme canoe race at Quebec's Winter Carnival.

Iditarod Trail Sled Dog Race

Contested over an historic gold rush and mail route stretching some 1,150 miles through the heart of the Alaskan wilderness, the Iditarod Trail Sled Dog Race was staged for the first time in 1973 and has developed into the most revered and challenging dog sled race in the world; one that tests both man and dog to the absolute limit.

RIDDLES BREAKS THE MOULD

After finishing 18th and 20th in the 1980 and 1981 Iditarod races, Wisconsin-born Libby Riddles decided to move to Alaska and breed her own dogs in order to increase her chances of success in the race. The move paid dividends: in 1985, she was the only musher in the race to battle on through a treacherous blizzard and went on to cross the finishing line in first place (in a time of 18 days and 20 minutes) to become the Iditarod's first-ever female winner.

Left: Four-time Iditarod champion Lance Mackey.

BAKER SHAKES OFF NEARLY-MAN TAG

Between 1996 and 2006 Alaskan native John Baker had competed in the Iditarod Trail Dog Sled Race on 11 occasions and had finished in the top ten eight times (with a best placing of third in 2002) to earn the tag as the most successful top-ten musher never to win the race. He finally shook off that unwanted tag in 2011, beating off four-time champion Martin Buser's sustained challenge to cross the line in first place in a time of eight days 19 hours and 46 minutes – the fastest winning time in history.

FOUR IN A ROW FOR MAGICAL MACKEY

Lance Mackey had a lot to live up to when he entered the Iditarod race for the first time in 2001: both his father Dick (in 1977) and his half-brother Rick (in 1983) had been previous winners. Lance finished 36th that year, but his time in the spotlight would come: he won for the first time in 2007 – remarkably, both his father and half-brother had won the race for the first time at their sixth attempt (and all three had worn the number 13 bib) – and defended his title in 2008, 2009 and 2010 to become the only musher in history to win the race four years in a row.

Below: John Baker (back) set the Iditarod's fastest-ever time in 2011.

KING OF THE IDITAROD

A 26-time competitor in the Iditarod Trail Dog Sled Race and a 23-time top-ten finisher (both records), Rick Swenson is the most successful musher in the race's history – so much so he has earned the moniker "King of the Iditarod". He entered the race for the first time in 1976 (finishing 12th), won the following year, became the event's first two-time winner in 1979 and went on to enjoy further triumphs in 1981, 1982 and 1991. He is the Iditarod's only five-time winner, was the first musher to win successive races and is the only competitor in the event's distinguished history to have won the race in three separate decades.

WILMARTH WINS INAUGURAL RACE

Although two short races using a nine-mile stretch of the Iditarod Trail had been staged in 1967 and 1969, the Iditarod Trail Dog Sled Race as we know it today, from Anchorage to Nome, was held for the first time in 1973. Of the 35 mushers to start the race, 22 finished, with Alaska native Dick Wilmarth, who had only taken part to spend some time in the Alaskan wilderness, winning in a time of 20 days 49 minutes and 41 seconds to pocket the prize of US$12,000.

THE IDITAROD'S GREATEST FEMALE MUSHER

After recording six top-ten finishes in her first seven Iditarod races between 1978 and 1984 (with two runner-up finishes in 1982 and 1984), Susan Butcher's quest to become the first woman in history to win the race came to a disastrous end in 1985 when a pregnant moose killed two of her dogs and severely injured six others – forcing her to withdraw. But the Boston-born Alaskan resident bounced back in style, winning the race for the first time in 1986, retaining her title in 1987 and becoming the first musher in the race's history to win three successive titles when she won again in 1988. A further triumph followed in 1990. Tragically, Butcher died in August 2006, aged 51, following a lengthy battle with leukaemia.

FIRST NON-ALASKAN RESIDENT TO WIN THE RACE:

After finishing ninth, eighth and sixth in 1992, 1993 and 1994 respectively, Doug Swingley made history in 1995 when he finished ahead of defending champion Martin Buser to win the Iditarod race for the first time: the Montana-based musher had become the first non-Alaska resident in history to win the race. His success did not end there: further race wins followed in 1999, 2000 and 2001 and he is one of only six mushers in history to have won the Iditarod on four or more occasions.

FASTEST FINISHING TIMES: TOP TEN

Pos	Time	Name	Year
1	8 days, 19:46:39	John Baker	2011
2	8 days, 23:59:09	Lance Mackey	2010
3	8 days, 22:46:02	Martin Buser	2002
4	9 days, 00:58:06	Doug Swingley	2000
5	9 days, 04:29:26	Dallas Seavey	2012
6	9 days, 05:08:41	Lance Mackey	2007
7	9 days, 05:43:13	Jeff King	1996
8	9 days, 05:52:26	Jeff King	1998
9	9 days, 08:30:45	Martin Buser	1997
10	9 days, 11:11:36	Jeff King	2006

Above: Robert Sørlie won for a second time in 2005.

FIRST NON-US WINNER

As the legend of the Iditarod grew, so did the number of entrants: 35 mushers contested the inaugural event in 1973; a number that, by 2011, had grown to 62. But it still took some time before a non-United States resident won the race: that honour fell to Norway's Robert Sørlie, who won the race in 2003 (only the second time he had competed at the event) and again in 2005.

MACKEY BY A NOSE

The 1978 race was the closest, and most controversial, in history. With less than ten miles to go on the last leg, from Point Safety to Nome, Dick Mackey had established a two-mile lead over defending champion Rick Swenson, but by the time the pair reached the finishing straight they were neck and neck. And although Swenson (who had six dogs in harness) crossed the line first, Mackey (with eight dogs in harness) was awarded the victory (by one second), because his lead dog (rather than the sled) had crossed the finishing line first. It wasn't the last time a Mackey would stand on the top step of the Iditarod podium: Dick's son Rick won the race in 1983 and his other son Lance won four successive titles between 2007 and 2010.

Chapter 8
WINTER PARALYMPIC GAMES

Inspired by the success of the Summer Paralympic Games, which began in Rome, Italy, in 1960, the Winter Paralympic Games were staged for the first time in Örnsköldsvik, Sweden, in 1976 and are currently held every four years. Current sports on the programme of events are alpine skiing, biathlon and cross-country skiing (in which athletes compete in three categories – sitting, standing and visually impaired); and ice sledge hockey and wheelchair curling (for wheelchair-bound athletes).

Above: Japan's Takeshi Suzuki won a bronze medal in the men's slalom sitting event at the Vancouver Winter Paralympic Games 2010.

Alpine Skiing

Men and women have contested alpine skiing at every one of the Winter Paralympics since the inaugural Games were held at Örnsköldsvik, Sweden, in 1976. Since Turin 2006 three categories are used (sitting, standing and visually impaired) with various classes of competition in each category. Disciplines contested are combined, downhill, slalom, giant slalom and Super-G.

Above: Reinhild Möller has won 19 medals at the Winter Paralympics.

SUPERB SCHÖNFELDER

The low point in his life undoubtedly came when he lost his left arm following a car accident in 1989, but Germany's Gerd Schönfelder has put his disability to one side to produce some scintillating performances at the Winter Paralympics. He made his first appearance at the Games at Albertville 1992 and walked away with three gold medals – in the downhill, giant slalom and Super-G; it was the start of a gold medal blitz that would go on to earn him a place in the record books. He took two further gold medals at Lillehammer 1994; one at Nagano 1998; four at Salt Lake City 2002; two at Turin 2006; and four at Vancouver 2010 to end his career (he retired in January 2011) with an astonishing haul of 16 Paralympic gold medals. Coupled with the four silver and two bronze medals he won at the Games, his tally of 22 medals is an all-time record.

Right: Gerd Schönfelder of Germany is the best skier in the history of the Winter Paralympic Games, winning 22 medals – 16 gold – between 1992 and 2010.

MÖLLER'S INSPIRATIONAL GOLD-MEDAL-WINNING RUN

In spite of losing half of her left leg and some of her right arm in a farming accident aged only three, Reinhild Möller would go on to become one of the most inspirational figures in sport. And although she won a gold medal at the Summer Paralympic Games (in the women's 100m at Seoul 1988), it was through her performances at the Winter Paralympic Games that she made an indelible mark in the record books. In a career that spanned eight editions of the Games, she dominated alpine skiing, winning an incredible 16 gold medals, two silver medals and one bronze. Her individual haul of 19 medals is an all-time record for a female alpine skier at the Winter Paralympics.

MEDAL SWEEPS (MEN)

Austria achieved the first medal sweep in alpine skiing at the Paralympic Games in the men's combined event (in the IV B class) at the 1976 Games at Örnsköldsvik with Horst Morokutti winning the gold medal, Adolf Hagn the silver and Willi Berger the bronze. The feat has been achieved on four further occasions – by Austria in the men's slalom (2B class) at Geilo 1980; by Switzerland in the men's giant slalom (LW9 class) at Innsbruck 1984; by the United States in the men's giant slalom (LW2 class) at Nagano 1998; and by Austria in the men's giant slalom (LW11 class) at Salt Lake City 2002.

MOST MEDALS – WOMEN: TOP FIVE

Pos	Medals	Name (country, span)	G	S	B
1	19	Reinhild Möller (West Germany/Germany, 1980–2006)	16	2	1
2	13	Lana Spreeman (Canada, 1980–94)	1	6	6
=	13	Sarah Billmeier (USA, 1992–2002)	7	5	1
=	13	Sarah Will (USA, 1992–2002)	12	1	0
5	11	Pascale Casanova (France, 1998–2006)	3	6	2
6	10	Kuniko Obinata (Japan, 1998–2010)	2	2	5
=	10	Lauren Woolstencroft (Canada, 2002–10)	8	1	1

MOST MEDALS – MEN: TOP FIVE

Pos	Medals	Name (country, span)	G	S	B
1	22	Gerd Schönfelder (Germany, 1992–2010)	16	4	2
2	14	Rolf Heinzmann (Switzerland, 1980–2002)	12	2	-
=	14	Hans Burn (Switzerland, 1988–2002)	6	5	3
4	12	Martin Braxenthaler (Germany, 1998–2010)	10	1	1
=	12	Greg Mannino (United States, 1988–98)	6	4	2
=	12	Markus Pfefferle (West Germany/Germany, 1988–2002)	1	8	3

A GAMES TO REMEMBER FOR MOSER

Heinz Moser was the star of the show in the men's alpine skiing competition at the 1976 inaugural Winter Paralympic Games in Örnsköldsvik, Sweden. The Swiss star took gold in the men's combined, downhill and slalom events (the only races contested in class III – for standing competitors with a single-arm amputation) to become the first alpine skier in Winter Paralympics history to win three gold medals at a single edition of the Games.

MOST SUCCESSFUL NATION

No country has enjoyed more success in alpine skiing events at the Winter Paralympic Games than Austria. The country has picked up a staggering 253 medals in the discipline (88 gold, 82 silver and 83 bronze). In terms of gold medals won, however, the United States leads the way– with 89.

MEDAL SWEEPS (WOMEN)

Austria's women emulated the country's men by completing the first medal sweep in alpine skiing at the Winter Paralympics, in the women's downhill (B2 class) at Innsbruck 1988, with Elisabeth Kellner taking gold, Edith Hoelzl silver and Gabriele Berghoger bronze. The feat has been repeated on six further occasions: by Austria in the women's giant slalom (B2 class) at Innsbruck 1988; by the USA in the women's downhill (LW2 class) at Albertville 1992; and by the USA in the women's giant slalom (LW10-11 class), women's downhill (LW10-11 class) and women's Super-G (LW2 and LW10-11 classes) at Salt Lake City 2002.

WOOLSTENCROFT'S STAR TURN

Born missing her left arm below the elbow and both legs below the knee, Lauren Woolstencroft began skiing at the age of four and started to enter competitions by the age of 14. The Canadian made a successful debut at the Winter Paralympics at Salt Lake City in 2002, winning two gold medals (in the Super-G and slalom) and a bronze (in the giant slalom), and continued her medal-winning success at Turin 2006, picking up one gold (in the giant slalom) and one silver (in the Super-G). The best was yet to come: at Vancouver 2010, amazingly, she won every event she entered – the downhill, super combined, slalom, giant slalom and Super-G (all standing events) – to become the only female alpine skier in history to win five gold medals at a single edition of the Winter Paralympic Games.

Above: Lauren Woolstencroft had a Winter Paralympics to remember at Vancouver in 2010.

ONE GOLD, EIGHT SILVER FOR MARKUS

Markus Pfefferle achieved the ultimate success at his first-ever appearance at the Winter Paralympic Games, winning gold in the men's downhill in the LW6/8 class (for single-arm amputees), but it was the two silver medals he won at the same Games (in the slalom and giant slalom) that started a pattern that would guarantee the German an unique place in the record books. Although he failed to add to his gold medal collection at subsequent editions of the Games, he achieved six more second-place finishes (three at Albertville 1992 and three more at Nagano 1998) to notch up a record-breaking career haul of eight silver medals.

Biathlon

Biathlon was contested for the first time at the Winter Paralympic Games at Innsbruck in 1988, with men contesting a 7.5km race in three classes. Women's events were added to the programme at Lillehammer 1994, and by Vancouver 2010 there were seven events (three for men and four for women) in three different classes – standing, sitting and visually impaired.

MOST MEDALS – WOMEN: TOP FIVE

Pos	Medals	Name (country, span)	G	S	B
1	6	Verena Bentele (Germany, 1998–2010)	5	-	1
2	5	Olena Iurkovska (Ukraine, 2002–10)	3	2	-
3	4	Anne Floriet (France, 1998–2006)	1	2	1
4	3	Miyuki Kobayashi (Japan, 1998–2006)	2	1	0
=	3	Ragnhild Myklebust (Norway, 1994–2002)	2	-	1
=	3	Marjorie van de Bunt (Netherlands, 1994–2002)	2	-	1
=	3	Anna Burmistrova (Russia, 2006–10)	1	2	-
=	3	Lyudmyla Pavlenko (Ukraine, 2006–10)	-	1	2
=	3	Svitlana Tryfonova (Ukraine, 1998–2010)	-	1	2

FIRST ASIAN CHAMPION

Japan's Miyuki Kobayashi drove the home crowd wild at the 1998 Winter Paralympic Games in Nagano when she stormed to gold in the women's 7.5km Free Technique (B2-3 class) with a three-minute winning margin over Austria's Gabriele Berghofer, to become the first-ever female Asian Winter Paralympic champion. Her success did not end there: she won gold at Turin 2006 too, in the women's 12.5km event.

Above: Thomas Oelsner has won two Winter Paralympic biathlon golds.

BREM FINDS MEDAL-WINNING FORM

Although he also won three medals in cross-country skiing events at the Winter Paralympic Games (two silvers at Nagano 1998 and a bronze at Salt Lake City 2002), Wilhelm Brem has enjoyed his best moments in biathlon. The visually impaired German picked up his first medal (a silver) in the men's 7.5km Free Technique event (B1 class) at Lillehammer 1994. He struck gold for the first time (in the same event) at Nagano 1998 and successfully defended his title at Salt Lake City 2002. His medal-winning performances did not end there: he won bronze in the men's 12.5km at Turin 2006 and gold in the same event at Vancouver 2010 to take his career haul of biathlon Paralympic medals to five – an all-time record.

Left: Wilhelm Brem has won a record five medals in biathlon.

FURTHER SUCCESSFUL TITLE DEFENCES

Others, apart from Wilhelm Brem and Frank Höfle, who have retained a title in biathlon at the Winter Paralympic Games (or won back-to-back golds in the same events, but in a different class) are: Jouko Grip (Finland), who won back-to-back gold medals in the men's 7.5km (LW6/8 class) at Innsbruck 1988 and Tignes-Albertville 1992 (to become the first person in history to achieve the feat; and Thomas Oelsner (Germany), who took the men's 7.5km Free Technique event (in the LW5–8 class) at Innsbruck 1988 and won gold in the same event (in the LW6/8 class) at Tignes-Albertville 1992.

PARTICIPATION NUMBERS

The record for the lowest participation in the biathlon competition at the Winter Paralympic Games is 36 (men only), set at Innsbruck 1988. The record for the lowest number of competitors in biathlon with both men and women was 90 (58 men and 32 women), set at Turin 2006, and the record for the highest number of competitors was 126 (99 men and 27 women), set at Lillehammer 1994.

MOST MEDALS – MEN: TOP FIVE

Pos	Medals	Name (country, span)	G	S	B
1	5	Wilhelm Brem (Germany, 1994–2010)	3	1	1
2	4	Vitaliy Lukyanenko (Ukraine, 2002–10)	2	1	1
=	4	Frank Höfle (Germany, 1992–2010)	3	-	1
4	3	Vladimir Kiselev (Russia, 2006–10)	2	1	-
=	3	Josef Giesen (Germany, 1998–2010)	1	1	1
=	3	Udo Hirsch (Germany, 1992–8)	1	1	1
=	3	Kalervo Pieksaemaeki (Finland, 1998–2006)	1	1	1
=	3	Alexander Schwarz (Germany, 1992–2002)	1	1	1
=	3	Torbjørn Ek (Sweden, 1992–8)	-	2	1

MOST SUCCESSFUL NATION

Germany has been the most successful nation in biathlon at the Winter Paralympic Games, winning 40 medals (17 gold, nine silver and 14 bronze). Russia holds the record for the most records won at a single edition of the Games, with 16 at Vancouver 2010.

HÖFLE: A WINTER PARALYMPIC GAMES LEGEND

Frank Höfle will no doubt be remembered as being among the best cross-country skiers in Paralympic history (he has won an all-time record 17 medals in the event, ten of them gold, in eight hugely successful appearances at the Games), but the German has also made his mark in the biathlon competition. The Brackenheim-born star, who has also made two appearances at the Summer Paralympics (in 1992 and 1996), took gold for the first time in the men's 7.5km (B2-3 class) at Tignes-Albertville 1992; he took 7.5km Free Technique (B2 class) gold at Lillehammer two years later and defended his title at Nagano in 1998 to become men's biathlon's first three-time gold medallist at the Winter Paralympic Games – a record since equalled by Höfle's compatriot Wilhelm Brem.

Above: Olena Iurkovska is a triple biathlon gold medallist.

A NEW BIATHLON STAR

Olena Iurkovska made her Winter Paralympic Games debut as a 19-year-old at Salt Lake City 2002 and marked herself out as an athlete of serious potential when she won silver in the women's 7.5km sitski event. That potential was confirmed at Turin four years later when she won double gold in the women's 7.5km and 10km events. The Ukraine athlete went on to take women's 2.4km Pursuit (sitting) gold at Vancouver 2010, becoming only the second woman in history (after Verena Bentele) to win three biathlon gold medals at the Winter Paralympic Games.

Below: Verena Bentele is the only woman ever to win five medals in biathlon at the Winter Paralympics.

BRILLIANT BENTELE

Four-time world champion Verena Bentele had a dream Winter Paralympic Games debut at Nagano 1998, winning a gold medal in the women's 7.5km Free Technique (B1 class), and her subsequent performances at the Games have brought her further successes. The German retained her 7.5km Free Technique title at Salt Lake City 2002, won the 7.5km and 12.5km (blind) double at Turin 2006 and added two more gold medals – in the 3km Pursuit and 12.5km Individual (visually impaired) – at Vancouver 2010 (where, in addition, she took three cross-country skiing golds, to become only the second woman in history, alongside Canada's Lauren Woolstencroft, to have won five gold medals at a single edition of the Winter Paralympic Games). She is also the only woman in biathlon history to have won five gold medals at the Games.

Cross-Country Skiing

Cross-country skiing is one of only two sports (alpine skiing is the other) to have appeared at every one of the ten Winter Paralympic Games. Both men and women have contested the sport since the very beginning, and by Vancouver 2010 it consisted of ten events (five for men and five for women) in three classes – sitting, standing and visually impaired.

THE QUEEN OF CROSS-COUNTRY SKIING

One of the few people in Winter Paralympic Games history to have won gold medals in three different sports (biathlon, ice sledge speed racing and cross-country skiing), Norway's Ragnhild Myklebust will be principally remembered as the greatest female Paralympic cross-country skier of all time. She was untouchable: between Innsbruck 1988 and Salt Lake City 2002 she entered 16 cross-country skiing sitski events and took gold in every one of them – a feat that will surely never be bettered.

Right: Norway's 16-time gold medallist Ragnhild Myklebust.

MOST MEDALS – MEN: TOP FIVE

Pos	Medals	Name (country, span)	G	S	B
1	17	Frank Höfle (West Germany/Germany, 1984–2010)	10	5	2
2	13	Terje Loevaas (Norway, 1980–94)	10	3	-
=	13	Jouko Grip (Finland, 1980–2002)	8	5	-
4	11	Pertti Sankilampi (Finland, 1976–88)	6	4	1
=	11	Svein Lilleberg (Norway, 1984–2010)	4	7	-
=	11	Nikolai Ilioutchenko (EUN/Russia, 1992–2006)	4	2	5

Above: Russia's Tatiana Ilyuchenko (with flag) took her team to relay gold at the 2006 Winter Paralympic Games in Turin.

SUCCESSFUL TITLE DEFENCES (WOMEN)

Others, apart from the irrepressible Ragnhild Myklebust, who have retained a title in cross-country skiing at the Winter Paralympic Games (or won back-to-back golds in the same events, but in a different class) are: Liudmila Vauchok (Belarus) in the women's 10km sitski in 2006 and the women's 10km (sitting) in 2010; and Birgitta Sund (Sweden), who won the women's middle distance 10km (in the A class) in 1976 and the same event in the 5B class in 1980, as well as taking gold in the women's short distance 5km (A class) in 1976 and in the same event in the 5B class in 1980. Two teams have made successful defences of their Paralympic titles: Norway, in the 3x2.5km in 1994, 1998 and 2002; and Russia in the same event in 2006 and 2010.

SUCCESSFUL TITLE DEFENCES (MEN)

Others, apart from Frank Höfle, who have successfully defended a title in cross-country skiing at the Winter Paralympic Games (or won back-to-back golds in the same events, but in a different class) are: Brian McKeever (Canada), who won the men's 10km for the visually impaired in 2006 and 2010; Kirill Mikhaylov (Russia), who won the men's 20km (standing) in 2006 and 2010; Sergej Shilov (Russia), who won the men's 5km sitski (LW10 class) in 1998 and 2002; and Pierre Delaval (France) who won the men's short distance 5km (LW5-7 class) in 1984 and 1988. Norway's 4 x 5km relay team (LW2-9 class) is the only team to have retained a title, taking the gold medal in 1998 and 2002.

Below: Brian McKeever celebrates his win in the 10km for the visually impaired at Vancouver 2010.

PARTICIPATION NUMBERS

The record for the most participants in the cross-country skiing competition at a single Winter Paralympic Games is 213 (150 men and 63 women) at Nagano 1998. The record for the fewest is 125 (101 men and 24 women) at Ornskldsvik 1976, and the record for the fewest male competitors (88) was set at Turin 2006.

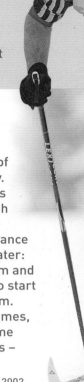

HISTORY-MAKING HÖFLE

Also a standout performer in biathlon at the Winter Paralympic Games, Germany Frank Höfle will ultimately be remembered as one of the greatest cross-country athletes in history. He made his first appearance at the Games as a 17-year-old at Innsbruck 1984 and, although he returned medal-less, gained invaluable experience. It showed during his next appearance at the Games, also at Innsbruck, four years later: he took gold in the men's Short Distance 15km and men's Long Distance 30km (B class) events to start a record-breaking association with the podium. By the last of his eight appearances at the Games, at Vancouver 2010, he had amassed an all-time record tally of 17 cross-country skiing medals – ten gold, five silver and two bronze.

Right: Frank Höfle wins the gold medal at Salt Lake City 2002.

BENTELE'S CROSS-COUNTRY SKIING SUCCESS

The leading female medal-winner in biathlon at the Winter Paralympic Games, Verena Bentele has also made a considerable impact in cross-country skiing events. She won three medals (two silver and one bronze) at her first appearance at the Games in Nagano in 1998, took three cross-country skiing gold medals at Salt Lake City 2002 (in the 10km Free Technique, 15km Free Technique and 5km Classical Technique events for the visually impaired) and continued her winning ways at Turin 2006, when she retained her 5km title. Three more gold medals at Vancouver 2010 (in the 1km sprint, 5km and 15km events) saw her become only the second woman in history, after Ragnhild Myklebust, to win more than five gold medals in cross-country skiing at the Winter Paralympic Games.

MOST MEDALS – WOMEN: TOP FIVE

Pos	Medals	Name (country, span)	G	S	B
1	16	Ragnhild Myklebust (Norway, 1988–2002)	16	–	–
2	10	Verena Bentele (Germany, 1998–2010)	7	2	1
=	10	Olena Iurkovska (Ukraine, 2002–10)	2	3	5
=	10	Siw Vestengen (Norway, 1992–2002)	2	2	6
5	8	Liudmila Vauchok (Belarus, 2006–10)	3	3	2

LUCKY THIRTEEN FOR LOEVAAS

A five-time medallist in six appearances at the Summer Paralympic Games (winning two silver and three bronze medals in athletics) between 1984 and 2000, Norway's Terje Loevaas entered 13 cross-country skiing events (in the visually impaired class) at the Winter Paralympics between Geilo 1980 and Lillehammer 1994 and, spectacularly, won medals in every one of them – ten gold (an all-time record shared with Germany's Frank Höfle) and three silver.

Ice Sledge Hockey

Ice sledge hockey, which is open to male competitors with a physical disability in the lower half of their body, is played to modified international ice hockey rules. Players sit on sledges with two blades that allow the puck to pass underneath them and use two sticks, one for propelling themselves across the ice and the other for striking the puck. The sport has been part of the Winter Paralympic Games programme of events since Lillehammer 1994.

Above: Team USA cruised to the gold medal at Vancouver 2010 to become Winter Paralympic ice sledge hockey's first two-time champions.

CLASSY USA EASE TO GOLD

The United States were the class act of the eight-team field in the ice sledge hockey competition at the 2010 Winter Paralympic Games in Vancouver. They beat Japan (6–0), the Czech Republic (3–0) and South Korea (5–0) to ease to the top of their qualifying group, and cruised past Norway in the semi-finals (3–0) to face Japan again in the final. The Japanese had shocked defending champions Canada in the semi-final, but the USA won again (2–0) to become the competition's first two-time winners.

NORWAY MAKE AMENDS

As seven countries entered the ice sledge hockey competition at the 1998 Winter Paralympic Games at Nagano, the event saw a change in format, with two groups created and the top two from each group progressing to the semi-finals. Defending champions Sweden topped Group A, ahead of Estonia, while 1994 silver medallists Norway headed Group B ahead of Canada. Sweden's title defence came to an abrupt end following a 2–1 defeat by Canada in the first semi-final, and Norway eased past Estonia (4–1) to reach the final again. And the Norwegians made up for their Lillehammer disappointment when they beat Canada 2–0 to win the gold medal for the first time. It is the only time in the event's history that a runner-up has gone on to win gold at the next edition of the Games.

FULL MEDAL SET

The first players (of five) to complete a full set of medals (gold, silver and bronze) in the ice sledge hockey at the Winter Paralympic Games were Herve Lord, Todd Nicholson and Shawn Matheson. The trio all played for Canada in the teams that won bronze at Lillehammer 1994, silver at Nagano 1998 and gold at Turin 2006. Norway's Helge Bjornstad and Eskil Hagan are the two other players to have achieved the feat.

Above: Norway's Helge Bjornstad has won five medals in ice sledge hockey.

MOST MEDALS

Two players, Helge Bjornstad and Eskil Hagan, share the record for the most medals won by a player in ice sledge hockey at the Winter Paralympic Games. The pair, who have been part of the Norway team at every one of the five competitions played to date, have won five medals – one gold (in 1998), three silver (in 1992, 2002 and 2006) and one bronze (in 2010).

CANADA BREAK THEIR DUCK

Given their long-standing tradition in ice hockey, Canada would have been disappointed with their performances in the first three editions of the ice sledge hockey competition at the Winter Paralympic Games: they had twice won medals (bronze at Lillehammer 1994 and silver at Nagano 1998), but as yet no gold medal. And then came Turin 2006: after losing their opening match to Norway (4–1), they rallied in style, winning their final two group games to qualify for the semi-final, crushed Germany (5–0) in the last four, and then exacted revenge over Norway in the final, winning the match 3–0 to become Paralympic champions for the first time. In doing so, they had become the first country in the event's history to complete the full set of gold, silver and bronze medals.

Right: Raymond Grassi celebrates after scoring Canada's third goal in the 2006 ice sledge hockey final against Norway.

MOST MEDALS WON (BY COUNTRY)

Pos	Medals	Country	G	S	B
1	5	Norway	1	3	1
2	3	United States	2	-	1
=	3	Canada	1	1	1
=	3	Sweden	1	-	2
5	1	Japan	-	1	-

HOWARD STRIKES DOUBLE GOLD

Joe Howard's dreams of playing in the NHL were shattered when, at the age of 15, he lost both of his legs after being hit by a train. But the ice would go on to tempt him again: in 1996, when he was 20, someone introduced him to ice sledge hockey and he never looked back; within two years he had made it on to the US team for the 1998 Winter Paralympic Games. It may have been a tournament to forget for his countrymen (the United States finished sixth out of seven teams), but Howard showed his immense talent, scoring six of his team's goals – an all-time competition record – in a 7–0 win over Great Britain. He was at the forefront of the United States team that took gold at Salt Lake City 2002 and was the only member of that victorious team to play at Vancouver 2010. There the US struck gold again, and Howard remains the only person in ice sledge hockey history to have won two gold medals at the Winter Paralympic Games.

Below: Joe Howard of the Unied States enjoyed gold-medal-winning success at Salt Lake City 2002 and Vancouver 2010.

PARTICIPATION NUMBERS

The lowest number of competitors to take part in the Ice Sledge Hockey competition at the Winter Paralympic Games is 57, at the inaugural competition at which only five teams took part. The highest number of competitors to take part is 117, at Vancouver 2010, a competition that saw eight teams vying for the gold medal.

UP AND RUNNING

The first ice sledge hockey competition in Winter Paralympic Games history took place at Lillehammer 1994, with five countries – Canada, Estonia, Great Britain, Norway and Sweden – taking part. At the end of the round-robin phase of matches, hosts Norway (with two wins and two draws) and Sweden (with three wins and one defeat) headed the table with six points apiece and went through to the final. The gold medal match was a nail-biting affair, with the two teams locked at 0–0 after regular time, but a solitary Swedish goal in extra time was enough to settle the outcome of the match and Sweden had earned the right to be called the sport's first Paralympic champions.

Other Paralympic Sports

Two other sports have appeared on the programme of events at the Winter Paralympic Games: ice sled speed racing, in which competitors propel themselves around an ice rink by jabbing sharp-ended sticks into the ice in races of various distances (from 100m to 1500m), which appeared at five Winter Paralympic Games between 1980 and 1998; and wheelchair curling (open to men and women), a variant of the traditional game of curling, which made its first of two appearances at the Games at Turin 2006.

MOST MEDALS IN CURLING

Four people hold the record for the most medals in wheelchair curling at the Winter Paralympic Games (two): Sonja Gaudet, who was part of the Canada teams that won gold at Turin 2006 and Vancouver 2010; and Glenn Ilkonen, Jalle Jungnell and Anette Wilhelm, who all belonged to the Sweden teams that won bronze at the same two Winter Paralympic Games.

Right: Glenn Ilkonen (left) is one of four two-time medallists in wheelchair curling at the Winter Paralympic Games.

NORWAY'S FINEST

Norwegian ice sled speed racer Brit Mjaasund Oejen was one of the undoubted stars of the 1980 Winter Paralympic Games at Geilo, winning all three competitions she entered in her class (in the 100m, 500m and 800m). She was the woman to beat at Innsbruck 1984 too, and left the Games with four medals to add to her growing collection – three gold (in the 100m, 500m and 700m) and one silver (in the 1000m). Her third and final appearance at the Winter Paralympic Games came at Lillehammer in 1994 and once again she excelled, taking gold in the 100m and 500m events, silver in the 1000m and bronze in the 700m. Her career haul of 11 medals is an all-time record for a female ice sled speed racer at the Winter Paralympic Games (shared with her compatriot Sylva Olsen), as is her collection of eight gold medals.

CANADA TAKE FIRST PRIZE

The inaugural wheelchair curling event at the Winter Paralympic Games took place at Turin in 2006, with eight countries vying for the gold medal. In the first phase of the competition, all the teams played each other once, with the top three teams automatically progressing to the semi-finals and the teams in fourth and fifth places contesting a playoff for the right to join them. Canada topped the group (with five wins and two losses) and maintained their league-topping form in the knockout stages of the competition, beating Norway in the semi-final (5–4) and Great Britain in the final (7–4) to become the event's first-ever Paralympic champions.

Left: Canada beat Norway in the semi-final and Great Britain in the final to become the first Winter Paralympic Games wheelchair curling champions at Turin 2006.

MOST SUCCESSFUL NATION

Norway dominated the ice sledge speed racing event, winning 128 of the 232 medals contested (a staggering 55.17 percent of them), with 44 gold, 46 silver and 38 bronze. This makes it surprising that the country only shares the record for the highest number of medals won at a single edition of the Winter Paralympic Games: Norway's haul of 32 medals at Geilo 1980 was equalled by Japan at Nagano 1998, the last time the event featured at the Games.

Right: Miki Matsue won gold at Nagano 1998.

LUNDSTROEM CREATES HIS LEGEND

Although he lost both legs in a shipyard accident in August 1978 when he was 27, Norway's Knut Lundstroem rebuilt his life and went on to become one of the great Paralympians in history. He made his debut at the 1988 Winter Paralympic Games in Innsbruck and had a week to remember, taking ice sled speed racing gold medals in the 100m, 500m, 1000m and 1500m (in the grade II class). The sport was not contested at Tignes-Albertville 1992, and Lundstroem wasn't at his best at Lillehammer two years later, picking up four medals yet again, but none of them gold. He put that right at Nagano 1998 (the last time the sport was contested at the Games) by repeating his feat of a decade earlier, winning all the events he entered – the 100m, 500m, 1000m and 1500m. His career haul of 12 medals (eight of them gold) is an all-time record for an ice sled speed racer at the Winter Paralympic Games.

ICE SLED SPEED RACING – MOST MEDALS (WOMEN): TOP FIVE

Pos	Medals	Name (country, span)	G	S	B
1	11	Brit Mjaasund Oejen (Norway, 1980–94)	8	2	1
=	11	Sylva Olsen (Norway, 1980–88)	1	6	4
3	8	Ragnhild Myklebust (Norway, 1988–94)	4	3	1
4	7	Lahja Haemaelaeinen (Finland, 1980–84)	4	–	3
=	7	Kirsti Hooeen (Norway, 1988–94)	1	1	5

ICE SLED SPEED RACING – MOST MEDALS (MEN): TOP FIVE

Pos	Medals	Name (country, span)	G	S	B
1	12	Knut Lundstroem (Norway, 1988–98)	8	3	1
2	11	Erik Sandbraaten (Norway, 1980–88)	3	4	4
3	7	Rolf Oejen (Norway, 1980–84)	2	3	2
4	6	Atle Haglund (Norway, 1984–94)	3	2	1
5	5	Veikko Paputti (Finland, 1980–98)	5	–	–
=	5	Felix Karl (Austria, 1988–94)	4	–	1
=	5	Lars Andresen (Norway, 1994–98)	2	–	3

IF ONLY FOR OLSEN

By the time Sylva Olsen arrived at her third and final Winter Paralympic Games at Innsbruck in 1988, her previous results in ice sled speed racing read like a catalogue of near misses. The Norwegian had picked up an impressive seven medals – three silver and four bronze. While she did finally pick up a gold medal at Innsbruck (in the 500m grade II class), she also added to her haul of silver medals, finishing runner-up in the 100m, 700m and 1000m. No woman has picked up more medals in ice sled speed racing at the Winter Paralympic Games (11 – a record she shares with her compatriot Brit Mjaasund Oejen); nor has any woman finished runner-up on more occasions (six).

FIVE MEDALS – ALL OF THEM GOLD

One of the great pioneers of disabled sport in Finland, Veikko Paputti competed at the Summer Paralympic Games on four occasions between 1968 and 1980 (winning a silver medal in the archery in 1976) and then switched his attentions to the Winter Paralympic Games and ice sled speed racing. Although he could not match the quantity of medals won by Knut Lundstroem, he left his own indelible mark on the sport: he won five medals in the event between 1980 and 1988 – and all of them were gold.

TWO OUT OF TWO FOR CANADA

The number of entrants may have increased for the wheelchair curling competition at the 2010 Winter Paralympic Games in Vancouver (from eight to ten), but other than that it was business as usual. Defending champions Canada and the United States posted the best records in the round-robin phase (with seven wins and two losses) and, for the second tournament in a row, Canada were the kings of the knockout phase of the competition, beating Sweden in the semi-finals (10–5) and South Korea in a nervy final (8–7) to complete a successful defence of their title.

Below: Canada won another wheelchair curling gold at Vancouver 2010.

The publishers would like to thank the following sources for their kind permission to reproduce the pictures in this book. The page numbers for each of the photographs are listed below, giving the page on which they appear in the book.

Location indicator: (T-top, B-bottom, C-centre, L-left, R-right)

Action Images: /Reuters: 65TR
Alamy: /Stefan Kiefer/Vario Images: 195TR
Corbis: /Bettmann: 22BL, 54L; /Juergen Feichter/NewSport: 175BR; /Dimitri Lundt/TempSport: 36BR; /Jerome Prevost/ TempSport: 63TL; /Jean-Yves Ruszniewski/TempSport: 25B; / Leon Switzer/Zuma Press: 198, 199T; /Universal/TempSport: 82L
Getty Images: 166TR; /AFP: 12BR, 13T, 13R, 14L, 15TR, 16BL, 16TR, 28B, 50BL, 54R, 68BR, 79BL, 84BL, 84TR, 85TL, 90B, 95BL, 106R, 109TR, 116BR, 157T, 157B, 184TR, 193T, 193R; / Luis Acosta/AFP: 152-153, 177R, 178R; /Agence Zoom: 8-9, 18R, 24BL, 28C, 32R, 33BL, 45L, 45TR, 48BR, 49TR, 53B, 61TL, 61R, 140L, 141TL, 148TR, 149T; /Alinari Archives: 78B; /Carlo Allegri/AFP: 86BL, 93TR; /Allsport: 37BL; /Vincent Amalvy/ AFP: 69BL; /Henning Angerer/Bongarts: 195TL; /Brian Bahr: 44BL, 102B; /Lars Baron/Bongarts: 22TR, 218TR; /Nancie Battaglia/Sports Illustrated: 125B; /Sandra Behne/Bongarts: 174BL; /Al Bello: 106B, 169TL, 200T; /Doug Benc: 178L; / Terje Bendiksby/AFP: 56BR; /Bruce Bennett: 160BL, 160R, 162TR, 164TL, 165B, 166BL, 167L, 167TR, 177TL; /Clemens Bilen/AFP: 185TL; /Nathan Bilow: 23TR; /Matti Bjorkman/ AFP: 58BR; /Torsten Blackwood/AFP: 146B; /David Boily/AFP: 103T; /Bongarts: 62B; /Lutz Bongarts/Bongarts: 34R; /Shaun Botterill: 21BR, 40TR, 57BL, 58TR, 100L, 122TR, 128BR, 132C, 147B, 183BL, 186L; /Clive Brunskill: 51L, 72L, 140BR; /Simon Bruty: 25TL, 33TL, 91TL; /Simon Bruty/Sports Illustrated: 200B; /Central Press: 107BL, 119, 137; /ChinaFotoPress: 99B; /Jean-Pierre Clatot/AFP: 29T, 129TR; /Fabrice Coffrini/ AFP: 55BL, 150R; /Chris Cole: 44R, 155B; /Phil Cole: 131TR; / Laurence Coustal/AFP: 154B; /Harold Cunningham: 204TL; / DK Photo: 171BR; /Adrian Dennis/AFP: 42L, 42BR, 47B; / Melchior DiGiacomo: 161T, 169BR; /Dimitar Dilkoff/AFP: 17BR; /Kevork Djansezian: 85BR, 91R; /Tony Duffy: 69TR; / Emmanuel Dunand/AFP: 99R; /Don Emmert/AFP: 15B; / FPG: 37TR; /Dominique Faget/AFP: 30BL; /Dominic Favre/ AFP: 62R, 63BR, 64BR; /Alexander Fedorov/AFP: 87T; /Eric Feferberg/AFP: 117TL; /Jonathan Ferrey: 102TR; /Ruediger Fessel/Bongarts: 46TR, 55TR; /Franck Fife/AFP: 10-11, 50TR, 101BL; /Stuart Franklin/Bongarts: 173BR; /George Frey/ AFP: 88B, 92BL; /Gamma-Keystone: 18BR, 108TR; /General Photographic Agency: 86TL; /John Gichigi: 35BR; /Georges Gobet/AFP: 39T; /Jeff Gross: 118L, 124BL; /Sergei Guneyev/ Time & Life: 38R; /Scott Halleran/Podium AAO: 97TR; / Alexander Hassenstein/Bongarts: 20BR, 52C, 90L, 134B; / Jeff Haynes/AFP: 130B; /Richard Heathcote: 60TR, 114L; / Harry How: 177BL; /Hulton Archive: 19TR, 34BR, 68TR, 80BL, 111B; /IOC Olympic Museum: 21T, 72B, 76BL, 129BR; / Imagno: 26BR; /Jed Jacobsohn: 29B, 39BR, 149BR, 150BL; / Daniel Janin/AFP: 73TR; /Ron Jenkins/MCT: 12L; /Hannah Johnston: 208-209; /Jasper Juinen: 95TR, 103BR; /KHL Photo Agency: 172B, 173TR; /Yuri Kadobnov/AFP: 66-67; /Menahem Kahana/AFP: 133C; /Koichi Kamoshida: 59TL; /Michael Kappeler/AFP: 32BL; /Mark Kauffman/Time & Life: 78TR; / Allen Kee/WireImage: 2; /John Kelly: 17TL, 36L; /Michael Kienzler/Bongarts: 20TR; /Toshifumi Kitamura/AFP: 182TR; / Joe Klamar/AFP: 43BR, 146TR, 151T; /Heinz Kluetmeier/ Sports Illustrated: 75BL; /David E Klutho/Sports Illustrated: 164BR; /Christof Koepsel/Bongarts: 60C; /Jens-Ulrich Koch/ AFP: 31BR, 126BR; /Joerg Koch/AFP: 127L; /Dima Korotayev/ Bongarts: 158BR; /Robert Laberge: 51TR, 117BR, 205BR; /

Nick Laham: 210TR, 217TL, 218BL; /Oliver Lang/AFP: 115TL, 115BR; /Streeter Lecka: 138-139; /Bryn Lennon: 188BL; /Alex Livesey: 187T; /MCT: 176BL, 206BL, 206R; /John G Mabanglo/ AFP: 212TR, 215TR; /John MacDougall/AFP: 100R, 187L; / Francois Marit/AFP: 35T; /Bob Martin: 94BL, 121BL; /Clive Mason: 38BL, 97B, 132TR, 188TR; /Jamie McDonald: 210BL, 212BL, 213TR, 215BL; /John D McHugh/AFP: 133BL; /Jim McIsaac: 165TL; /Jack Mikrut/AFP: 189TR; /Manny Millan/ Sports Illustrated: 79TR; /Norbert Millauer/AFP: 111TR; / Donald Miralle: 136L, 147T, 151BR; /Filippo Monteforte/ AFP: 98R; /Olivier Morin/AFP: 43R; /Ralph Morse/Time & Life: 14TR; /Gray Mortimore: 130R; /Sven Nackstrand/AFP: 27BR; /Mike Nelson/AFP: 113TR; /Alexander Nemenov/ AFP: 30R, 175TR; /New York Times Co: 108B; /Oleg Nikishin/ Epilson: 83TL; /Kazuhiro Nogi/AFP: 94TR, 128L; /Scott Olson: 202L, 202R; /Valero Pennicino: 71R; /Doug Pensinger: 47T, 74R, 77TR, 83BR, 143BL, 145T, 145BR, 154L, 201T; /Frank Peters/Bongarts: 27L, 53TR; /Christopher Pike: 179TL; / Alberto Pizzoli/AFP: 6-7, 144L; /Joern Pollex/Bongarts: 93B; / Christian Pondella: 201R; /Mike Powell: 41TR, 48C, 87BL, 109B, 110BL, 114TR; /Lennart Preiss/AFP: 89TR; /Gary M Prior: 101TR, 182BL; /Dave Reginek/NHLI: 170TR; /Chris Relke: 172TR; /Robert Riger: 24TR, 26BL, 155TL; /Pascal Rondeau: 40B, 107TR, 116L; /Quinn Rooney: 211; /Clive Rose: 183TR, 186TR; /Martin Rose/Bongarts: 213B, 216L, 216B, 217R, 219BR; /Toshio Sakai/AFP: 89L; /Dave Sandford: 168TR; /Sankei Archive: 46BR; /Daniel Sannum Lauten/ AFP: 56R; /Timm Schamberger/AFP: 88T; /Gerd Scheewel/ Bongarts: 19BR, 118BR; /Eric Schweikardt/Sports Illustrated: 76R, 203; /Ezra Shaw: 4-5, 120TR, 135BL; /Johannes Simon/ AFP: 112; /Janek Skarzynski/AFP: 59BR; /Javier Soriano/AFP: 142BL, 142TR, 143TR, 144TR, 148BL; /Cameron Spencer: 77BL, 141BR, 180-181; /Jamie Squire: 199R; /Christof Stache/ AFP: 113B, 135TR; /Melanie Stetson Freeman/Christian Science Monitor: 194L; /Rick Stewart: 163T; /Matthew Stockman: 96BL, 131B, 214TR; /Damian Strohmeyer/ Sports Illustrated: 176TR, 179R; /Robert Sullivan/AFP: 156; /Bob Thomas: 31TL, 73BL, 80TR, 81L, 81R, 96TR, 122B; / Topical Press Agency/Hulton Archive: 74B; /Tony Triolo/ Sports Illustrated: 163B; /Markku Ulander/AFP: 159BR; /Jeff Vinnick/NHLI: 170BL; /Anton Want: 75TR; /Jim Watson/AFP: 207; /Richard Wolowicz: 171TL; /Ilmars Znotins/AFP: 104-105, 121TR, 126TR
iStockphoto: 197
Press Association Images: 71BL; /AP: 41BR, 98BL, 110TR, 124TR, 159TL, 161B, 205TL; /Ed Andrieski/AP: 123B; / Giovanni Auletta/AP: 214BL; /Nathan Denette/The Canadian Press: 184BL; /Patrick Gardin/AP: 49BR; /Tony Gilbert/ AP: 199L; /Mike Groll/AP: 134TL; /Tom Hanson/AP: 204B; /Johnathan Hayward/AP: 185BR; /Michele Limina/AP: 174TR; /Pontus Lundahl/AP: 192; /Olivier Maire/AP: 64T; / Tony Marshall: 99TL; /Tsugufumi Matsumoto/AP: 219T; / Henrik Montgomery/AP: 190-191; /Tom Pidgeon/AP: 162BL; /Gene J Puskar/AP: 196BL; /Eric Risberg/AP: 120BL; /S&G and Barratts: 70BL, 70TR; /Eckehard Schultz/AP: 125TR; /A Steiner/AP: 136BR; /Armando Trovati/AP: 65BR; /Dar Yasin/ AP: 194B; /Ahn Young-Joon/AP: 189BL
Private Collection: 168B, 196TR
Topfoto: 23L, 52BL; /RIA Novosti: 82BR, 92TR, 127BR, 158TR; /
Ullsteinbild: 57TR, 123TL

Every effort has been made to acknowledge correctly and contact the source and/copyright holder of each picture, and Carlton Books Limited apologises for any unintentional errors or omissions, which will be corrected in further editions of this book.